PROJECT
MANAGEMENT
IN
ELECTRONIC
DISCOVERY

PROJECT MANAGEMENT IN ELECTRONIC DISCOVERY

An Introduction to Core Principles of Legal Project Management and Leadership in eDiscovery

MICHAEL I. QUARTARARO

PROJECT MANAGEMENT IN ELECTRONIC DISCOVERY:

An Introduction to Core Principles of Legal Project Management and Leadership in eDiscovery

ISBN: 978-0-9970737-0-6
ISBN: 978-0-9970737-1-3 (eBook)
LCCN: 2016907721

Printed in the United States of America

Learn more at: www.ediscoverypm.com

This cuneiform is the earliest known written form of the words "liberty" or "freedom." Found inscribed in clay in the Sumerian city of Lagash circa 2300 B.C., it represents here the author and publisher's strong personal belief in the fundamental human right of freedom of expression.

CONTENTS

FOREWORD   xi

ACKNOWLEDGMENTS   xiii

PREFACE   xvii

INTRODUCTION   xxv

CHAPTER ONE
The Legal Process: Understanding the Body of Work in the Legal Industry   1

Figure 1: Phases of the Litigation Process   4

Understanding the Phases of the Legal Process   4

Law Firm and Legal Department Structure   6

Challenge to the Law Firm Business Model   9

Conclusion   11

CHAPTER TWO
The Discovery Process: Narrowing the Issues, Avoiding Surprise and Uncovering the Truth   13

What Is Discovery?   13

Technology Transforms Discovery   14

The Electronic Discovery Reference Model   17

Figure 2: The Electronic Discovery Reference Model   18

Conclusion   23

CHAPTER THREE
The Fundamentals of Traditional Project Management   25

What is Project Management?   27

Who is a Project Manager?   29

Project Management Roles and Responsibilities   33

Organizational and Environmental Factors 34

Conclusion 36

CHAPTER FOUR

The Project Management Lifecycle 39

Project Management Process Groups 39

Figure 3: Five Project Management Process Groups 39

Project Management Knowledge Areas 41

Table 1: Project Management Process Groups and Knowledge Areas 43

Initiating: The Project Charter and Stakeholder Identification 44

Planning: The Project Management Plan 48

Figure 4: The Project Management Triple Constraint 50

Executing: Directing and Managing Project Work 60

Monitoring & Controlling: Analysis and Verification of Project Work 64

Closing: Documenting and Learning from a Project 69

Conclusion 70

CHAPTER FIVE

Preparing for the Discovery Process 75

Applicable Federal, State, and Local Rules 75

The Scope and Limits of Discovery 77

Planning for the Discovery Meet and Confer 79

Certification of Discovery Requests and Responses 82

Rule 37 and Discovery Sanctions 83

Forms of Production 85

Inadvertent Production, Waiver and Claw-back Provisions 89

Cost Expectations in Electronic Discovery 90

Conclusion 93

CHAPTER SIX

**Information Governance: The Foundation
of Legal Discovery Projects**   97

Information Governance Meets eDiscovery   99

Understanding Records and Information Management   100

Components of an Information Management Policy   101

Understanding a Client's RIM Policies
and Technology Infrastructure   103

Figure 5: Simple Network Topology   106

Conclusion   108

CHAPTER SEVEN

**Identification and Preservation
of Electronically Stored Information**   111

Project Planning in the Identification and Preservation Stage   112

Identifying Documents and ESI   113

Implementing a Litigation Hold   115

Preserving Documents and ESI   118

Interviewing Potential Custodians   121

Reasonably Accessible Data   122

Documenting and Monitoring the Litigation Hold   124

Conclusion   125

CHAPTER EIGHT

Collection of Electronically Stored Information   129

Planning the Collection   130

Collecting ESI   134

Documenting the Collection of ESI   140

Conclusion   140

CHAPTER NINE

Processing Electronically Stored Information   145

Processing to Reduce the Volume of Documents   147

Processing to Facilitate Efficient Document Review   151

Developing an ESI Processing Plan   153

Format of the Deliverable   154

   Figure 6: Sample Image Load File   158

   Table 2: Metadata Fields Extracted During Processing   159

   Table 3: Other Data Fields   160

Analysis and Reporting   163

Creating and Maintaining a Document Review Database   164

Conclusion   167

CHAPTER TEN

Document Review

  171

Roles and Responsibilities   172

Defining the Scope of the Review   174

The Mechanics of Document Review   175

Technology-Assisted Review   181

Contract Attorneys and Document Review   184

Review of Privileged and Work-Product Documents   185

Conclusion   189

CHAPTER ELEVEN

Document Production

  193

Planning a Document Production   194

Forms of Production   195

Producing Metadata and Searchable Text   198

   Figure 7: Excerpt from a DAT File   199

   Figure 8: Standardized Production Directories   200

Quality Checking a Document Production   201

Maintaining a Production Log   203

Productions from Other Parties   203

Conclusion   204

CHAPTER TWELVE

Presentation of Electronic Documents 209

  A Brief History of the Use of Technology in Trials 210

  Modern Trial Preparation 212

  Trial Presentation Applications 217

  Trial Equipment 217

  Conclusion 219

CONCLUSION 221

APPENDIX A

**Project Management Process Groups
and Sample Project Management Forms** 225

  A.1 Project Management Process Groups
  and Knowledge Areas 225

  A.2 Sample Project Charter 235

  A.3 Sample Project Management Plan 236

APPENDIX B

**Federal Rules of Civil Procedure and Rule 502
of the Federal Rules of Evidence** 239

  B.1 Federal Rules of Civil Procedure, Rule 1, 16, 26, 30-31, 33-
  34,-36-37 239

  B.2 Federal Rules of Evidence Rule 502 (as amended in 2008) 270

APPENDIX C

Sample E-Discovery Forms 273

  C.1 Sample Proposed Discovery Plan 273

  C.2 Sample IT Infrastructure Questionnaire 284

  C.3 Sample Custodian Interview Form 288

  C.4 Sample Collection Specification 291

  C.5 Sample Collection Log 293

  C.6 Sample Chain of Custody Form 294

C.7 Sample Processing Specification   295

C.8 Sample Document Review Protocol   298

C.9 Sample Production Specification   302

GLOSSARY
305

ABOUT THE AUTHOR
325

Foreword

Project Management in Electronic Discovery is a prescription and cure for our fragmented and often dysfunctional electronic discovery industry and practice. E-discovery practices are dominated by roles and paradigms inherited from over 75 years of earlier paper-based document discovery. Electronic discovery arrived in 2000, but without a concomitant fundamental practice change at law firms. Attorneys continued to use the same forms, review paper documents, and engage in "take-no-prisoners" combative behavior. Paralegals continued to organize paper documents to prepare attorneys for hearings, depositions, and trial. Litigation support professionals continued to prepare paper exhibits and trial boards. The habitual law firm roles persisted. The result was nearly catastrophic. The number of e-discovery sanctions cases rose in tandem with escalating costs and inefficiencies while the cause of justice suffered.

Project Management in Electronic Discovery offers an obvious but revolutionary cure: Integrate the roles of the various professionals in law firms and legal departments. *Project Management in Electronic Discovery* blends the distinct, and traditionally separate, domains within law firms and legal departments into a seamless web that transforms electronic discovery into a collaborative activity of mutually supporting skills based on a shared mission. *Project Management in Electronic Discovery* applies the established principles of project management to each phase of e-discovery, blending the roles of attorney, paralegal, and project manager into a complementary collaboration. Each professional has a role, but these roles must function together. *Project Management in Electronic*

Discovery shows us how. It is a critically important book for attorneys, paralegals, litigation support technicians, and their project managers.

Project Management in Electronic Discovery is not an abstract study about stakeholders, dependencies, planning, and verifying. Rather, it is a practice manual that concretely applies project management principles to each phase illustrated in the Electronic Discovery Reference Model. The book does not pull any punches nor conceal any secrets. It simply clearly and concisely shows how we can competently practice e-discovery *together*.

Project Management in Electronic Discovery is optimally organized. The initial chapters articulate the foundations of the modern law firm, the basic principles of project management, and the litigation process with ease and insight. The following chapters then address in turn each phase of an e-discovery project. *Project Management in Electronic Discovery* is best read in sequence, but each chapter can be read when needed. It is a book not to be read and then put aside; it is an everyday –indeed every hour—practice companion. As a special bonus, each chapter ends with a chart and checklist distilling the chapter's e-discovery project management issues, options, decisions and best practices.

Project Management in Electronic Discovery will change the practice of electronic discovery. It contains a flowing abundance of wisdom, excitement, and a love of electronic discovery. If we do it right, electronic discovery will become the real locus and focus of truth seeking in the litigation process. *Project Management in Electronic Discovery* teaches us how.

William F. Hamilton, Executive Director
International Center for Automated Information Retrieval
UF E-Discovery Project
University of Florida Levin College of Law
Gainesville, Florida

Vice Chancellor, Bryan University
Tempe, Arizona

January 2016

Acknowledgments

A book does not get written without the help of many people, each to whom I owe a debt of gratitude. First and foremost, to Patricia, my wife of 25 years, for her unwavering support, love, patience and understanding. I work in an industry that almost requires successful people to be "on" at all times and this has resulted in long hours at work, significant time away from home, and a good degree of emotional absenteeism. But through it all, and despite my many personal flaws, Pat has stood by me with grace and poise where a lesser person may have walked away years ago. She is my biggest fan and chief defender and she keeps me grounded. I only wish I could be as devoted as her. I am eternally thankful for her presence in my life, her continued support and unrelenting love.

Many people in the legal business have impacted my life and career in ways they likely underestimate. Professors James Cohen and Beth Schwartz, thank you for everything. Period. You taught me so much about the law and legal process and I feel that I may owe you six figures for a first-rate education. Thanks also to Henriette Hoffman, whose unvarnished view of and passion for the law simply amazed me. I try to take the same approach in my work today.

When I first joined Stroock & Stroock & Lavan LLP, I would not have predicted it would be the most rewarding and fulfilling job I have had. Thanks to managing partners, Alan Klinger and Stuart Coleman, for their leadership during a changing and tumultuous time in the legal business. Thank you Harvey Brown, for supporting my work, my ideas, and new technologies and initiatives, all of which I believe better serve clients and the Firm. Thanks to Kermit Wallace for backing me up when needed and calling BS when necessary. Thanks to both of you for your trust, the freedom to make hopefully smart decisions, and for allowing me to be myself. Thanks to Curt Mechling, a supporter and advocate of technology. Everyone who works in my position needs a hero, and you have been mine. To Royce Cohen, thanks for being authentic, for letting me speak my mind, and for reminding me that it is always better to build a fence at the top of the cliff than to position an ambulance at the bottom. And thank you Bruce, Steve, and Richard for reviewing the manuscript. Carole, you're simply invaluable. Thank you. I am thankful to many others at Stroock who help make my life easier. Having the opportunity to build and grow something of value, something that positively impacts the business operations of clients, the Firm, and people's lives, is a rewarding challenge. I am proud and happy to have the chance to do it at Stroock.

Kimberlee Keller, Shira Tannor and Gregg Scaglione are people without whose support and kindness I would likely not be where I am today. They gave me opportunities others might not have, and from them I learned a great deal about law firm operations, leadership and management. Gregg, thank you for being a friend and a great manager. I am grateful also to Steve Shankroff and Mik Wenczl, to their staff, and to many others at Skadden for their support and friendship. Skadden Arps was a great place to work and a fantastic place to learn. I owe a good deal of my success to the nearly ten years I worked there.

To my good friend, Bill Hamilton, an educator, a lawyer, a fan of technology, a confidant, and a person I trust and admire personally, I am thankful for your support and the opportunities and challenges you have put before me and for your belief and confidence that I could handle them. Thanks also to Don Gull, who had he not walked up to me several years ago and seemingly randomly introduced himself, I would not be doing something I love today—teaching. Thank you Chad, Don and Eric for your leadership and vision, for inspiring trust, and for believing in me. To the advisory board, faculty and staff at

Bryan University, thank you for being the kindest, most professional group of people I have ever met and had the pleasure of working with.

There are many others —friends, colleagues, mentors and students—who have influenced my life and inspired this book. Far too many to mention here. Jesse, what can I say? Keep doing what you do. Simon, the work you do is awe-inspiring. Gary, Ron, Les, Father Jim, you made it make sense and made the unbearable tolerable. Many others who know who they are —I am grateful for the encouragement and inspiration that has led to the modicum of success I have had in my work.

It is appropriate to pay tribute and to thank the many men and women who work in support roles throughout the legal industry, dozens of whom have worked with or for me directly, and many more who are friends, colleagues or acquaintances. The goal of course has always been to implement more efficient and effective ways of using technology in the practice of law. These folks are responsible for massive amounts of data, and they manage some of the most unwieldy projects, often for long hours, on little sleep, and for demanding stakeholders. They help manage risk, they impact strategic decisions about the course and conduct of a case, and they directly affect the timing and delivery of discovery and trial-related processes. They work on tight deadlines and use technology to often accomplish nothing short of miracles and produce results that a few years ago would not have been possible. Some are technologists, some have a legal background, and some were just stopping over on their way to greater things. Together they fuel the engine that drives successful outcomes in a legal support environment. This book is as much a tribute to the work of the dedicated people with whom I have had the pleasure of working, as it is inspired by their work and accomplishments. The practice of law will likely never be the same —such is the impact these individuals have had on the honored profession. Thank you to each and every one of you. And thank you especially to the Litigation Support personnel at Stroock, who on more occasions that I care to recount have consistently pulled through complicated projects and made me look good.

Thank you to Damian, Wendy, Brad, George, Scott, Bill, Mike, Jason, Tom, Robin and others I'm sure I am forgetting, for reading and/or commenting on early drafts, for enduring my questions, and for encouraging me to continue writing. Thank you Maribel for your continuous support and promotional efforts. And last, but not least, thank you Tiffany, for your work on the manuscript.

This is for you mom and dad. Dad, I miss our talks —scotch will never be the same.

"The best revenge is massive success"
F. A. Sinatra

Preface

There has been considerable discussion regarding the applicability of project management in a legal setting. Driving the debate in part is the need of law firms and corporate legal departments to find efficiencies and reduce legal expenses. Law firms, which rely upon corporations for a slice of the $300 billion legal services market, have begun to listen. Most firms are adjusting hourly rates, staffing cases leanly, or have entered into unique and tailored billing agreements. Fewer firms, however, have dramatically altered the ways in which lawyers work and fewer still have adopted project management principles into their business model. This book addresses how project management may be used in a legal setting to make one aspect of legal work more efficient—the discovery process.

A distinction needs to be made at the outset between applying project management principles to the entire operation of a law firm and the application of project management to discreet aspects of legal practice. It is of course possible to apply project management methodologies to the operation of a law firm, from business development to matter management and throughout the individual cases, transactions, and subordinate tasks that make up the core of attorney practice. Indeed, a few firms focus on just that. The emphasis in this book, though, is on the application of project management principles in the context of providing litigation support services and the integration of project-oriented processes into managing legal discovery projects and, more specifically, electronic discovery projects.

There is much work to do in this area. In the United States, which is 80% of the global market, the electronic discovery market is growing incredibly fast. The market worth of the global electronic discovery industry has doubled since 2010 and is projected to quadruple by 2020. Driven by the massive growth of electronically stored information and the need to manage that information for civil litigation, the e-discovery market, including services and software, grew to over $7 billion in 2015.[1] A recent report by Transparency Market Research projects 16% compound annual growth rate for services and software through 2022, increasing the market to more than $21 billion.[2] A 2015 report by Gartner similarly projects double-digit year-over-year U.S. growth in e-discovery software.[3]

However, due in part to the recession and the slower than expected economic recovery, the legal services industry is undergoing considerable change. Law firms have folded, others have merged, and even the best firms have reduced personnel by 10% to 30% in the past six years. Corporate legal department budgets are shrinking, and they face pressure to reduce legal expenses. One need not have an MBA or a law degree to conclude that the current business model at many law firms may not be sustainable in the long term. To survive, lawyers and

---

1   Research and Markets, *E-Discovery Market by Solution, Service, Deployment, Industry, & Region - Global Forecast to 2020* (July 2015), see http://www.researchandmarkets.com/ research/zhg5cn/ediscovery (noting that the global e-discovery market, comprised of software and services, is expected to grow from $7.01 billion in 2015 to $14.2 billion in 2020, a compound annual growth rate of 15.3%). See also, International Data Corporation, *Worldwide eDiscovery Services Forecast 2014–2019* (study announcing the global e-discovery market surpassed $10 billion in 2015 and will total $14.7 billion by 2019).

2   Transparency Market Research, *eDiscovery Market – Global Industry Analysis, Size, Share, Growth, Trends and Forecast 2014-2022*, see http://www.transparencymarket research.com/ediscovery-market.html, (last accessed via Business Wire on 10/1/2015, http://www.businesswire.com/news/home/2015100 1006057/en/).

3   Zhang & Landers, *Magic Quadrant for E-Discovery Software, Market Overview* (May 18, 2015) http://www.gartner.com/technology/reprints.do?id=1-2G57ESF&ct=150519&st=sb (e-discovery software market grew to $1.8 billion in 2014 and estimating five year CAGR of 12% with software market growth to more than $3 billion by 2019).

legal support staff in the U.S. and abroad—those at larger law firms in particular—need to change the way they practice and deliver legal services. Applying project management methodologies to the practice of law is one tool that will differentiate great firms from good firms and provide the efficiency and sustainability needed in a legal market that is very different today from just a few years ago. Additionally, project management brings structure and common business sense to law firms, which traditionally are not run like a business.

By far, the most costly and time consuming aspect of litigation is the discovery process. "Demands for data and documents in electronic form are now the prime suspect in what is characterized as a disproportionate increase in discovery costs compared with the overall expense of litigation."[4] It used to be that junior lawyers gathered in rooms filled with boxes to review documents. Technology has changed this. Discovery is no longer about boxes of paper; instead, it is about terabytes of data. A single terabyte of electronic documents could equal as many as 25 million documents. That is more than 8,000 boxes of printed paper. Information is now everywhere. Email and text messaging are ubiquitous, and social media, smart phones, and the Internet have invaded our lives.[5] All this data is discoverable in litigation. Discovery is not more costly because of inflation or because attorney hourly rates have risen. In fact, the costs associated with discovery, particularly with electronic discovery, have gone down considerably. Discovery costs more today because there is so much more information and costs are driven almost entirely by the volume of data. These things—the volume

---

4   See, *Where the Money Goes: Understanding Litigant Expenditures for Producing Electronic Discovery*, p. 1 (Rand Corporation, Institute for Civil Justice 2014) (including case studies illustrating that nearly 75% of expenditures in litigation result from discovery).

5   According to one research firm, the business world accounts for more than 108 billion emails sent and received per day, and that number is expected to grow to 140 billion by 2018. The Radicati Group, *Email Statistics Report 2014-2018* (Apr. 2014). In addition, Gartner projects that by 2020 more than 25 million devices will be connected to the Internet. See *Forecast: Internet of Things, Endpoints and Associated Services, Worldwide* (2014).

of data, the time and cost it takes to manage this information—understandably have corporations, law firms, and the government concerned. In a world overrun by electronically stored information, it should not surprise anyone that new processes, new technologies, and a new breed of legal support personnel have emerged.

In the mid-1990s, as computers began to arrive at every employees' desk, it became abundantly clear that email and electronic documents were a new source of discovery material. Still, it took years before the legal community prepared rules that even acknowledged the discovery of electronic documents. Today, almost all documents are created on computers and they are stored not in file cabinets or boxes, but on optical disk and in databases. Analytics software, long used in other industries, is now used to parse through vast amounts of data and to find documents that make or break a case. The litigation support industry and the process of electronic discovery were born out of the need to integrate technology into the legal process. People who work in the industry provide technical support, software, project management, and consulting services to law firms, corporate legal departments, and the government. A completely new body of case law and rules governing the proper preservation, collection, review, and production of electronic documents has also emerged.[6] This once nascent industry is beginning to mature and stabilize, and it seeks standardization and increased efficiency.

This is the backdrop for a book that introduces new and better ways to manage electronic discovery projects.

---

6   The Federal Rules of Civil Procedure governing discovery were amended in 2006 to specifically include "electronically stored information" among the sources of discoverable information. The Federal Rules were amended again in 2015. See Appendix B.1, *infra*. At the same time, the number of reported cases involving e-discovery –particularly cases involving discovery sanctions—has increased dramatically since 2006. See, Willoughby, *Sanctions for E-Discovery Violations: By The Numbers*, 60 Duke Law Journal 789, 828 (2010) ("Sanction motions and sanction awards for e-discovery violations have been trending ever-upward for the last ten years and have now reached historic highs. At the same time, the frequency of sanctions against counsel for e-discovery violations, though small in number, is also increasing.").

This book is written about the work that a project leader may undertake but, more importantly, it is written for lawyers, paralegals, students, and support staff at law firms and in corporate and government legal departments or at service providers. It captures the principles of project management and the best practices of discovery in litigation, particularly as they relate to the management of large volumes of electronically stored information. At the same time, it serves as a guide and reference for students of the law, paralegals, and attorneys, and illustrates how project management processes and technology may be used to provide efficient, client-oriented services and high-quality deliverables in a litigation support environment—at scope, on time, and within budget. While much of the focus is on providing these services in the context of discovery projects within a law firm or legal department, the concepts and principles covered in this book could just as easily apply in a service provider setting or a consulting firm.

I am inspired here as much by the need for proper discourse on the use of project management in legal discovery projects as by the growing insistence that legal teams function more efficiently and cost effectively. That and the realization I came to recently when I was asked to help design and teach a project management class for students eager to break into the litigation support field. Try as we might, neither the university nor I could find an appropriate text for an electronic discovery project management class. An article I authored a few years ago that outlined some of the material presented here for a trade magazine served as a jumping off point for this book.

Another contributing factor has been my more than 20 years of working with lawyers and in law firms, most recently as the Director of Litigation Support Services at Stroock & Stroock & Lavan LLP. Putting in countless hours, making I imagine nearly every mistake possible, and observing a good deal of inefficiency, and now having designed and implemented litigation support and electronic discovery work-flows, I have some sense of what does and does not work. To be sure, not all project management principles strictly apply in the context of every legal discovery project. But many of the core principles can be applied and, in my experience working in the legal business, it has now become abundantly clear to me at least that using project management principles can and will serve law firms and their clients well.

Some useful tips on how to use this book:

- Each chapter contains a brief summary of the key points raised in the chapter. Read each chapter in full, and then review the summary of key points. The summaries are a synopsis of the chapter and important concepts, terms, and phrases, and are useful for future reference.

- The summaries for each of the discovery project phases in chapters 6 through 12 also contain a useful list of suggested project management-related tasks and corresponding documentation intended to help plan and execute a defensible discovery process.

- The forms in the appendix have been simplified and cleansed of any reference related to their prior use and may be used as examples of the types of documentation that should generally be created and retained on each discovery project.

- Italicized terms and phrases throughout the text are the frequently used and most essential terms in the lexicon of electronic discovery, litigation support, and project management. They are either defined in the text or have definitions in the glossary at the end of the book.

- The glossary is developed from dozens of sources throughout the legal, litigation support and project management industries, with added commentary to explain or clarify definitions.

- Reproduced in the appendix are excerpts from the Federal Rules of Civil Procedure that are most commonly referred to during discovery projects. The 2015 revisions are included as are brief author commentaries at the end of each rule explaining recent amendments.

- Project management is a gender-neutral profession (as all occupations should be), and therefore interspersed throughout the text is the intentional alternating use of *he* or *she* when referring to project managers.

- The chapters are organized to hopefully make use of the book more efficient, depending upon the reader's level of knowledge and skill. Lawyers and paralegals may choose to skip or breeze through chapters 1 and 2, since they typically would already understand the legal process and discovery. Formally trained project managers may not need to read chapters 3 and 4 (though I recommend that they do). Chapters 5 through 12, however, deal explicitly with electronic discovery and will be of benefit to everyone.

Much has been written recently about the changing legal landscape and the future of legal practice in a post-recession world. However, while authors and commentators discuss the need for change, many stop short of providing a solution; that is, a detailed and actionable plan on how project management, new strategic practices, and improved technologies might enhance the practice of law. This book fills a void and provides insight from a perspective the reader does not typically see in books about the legal industry. There are many books about project management, and even more have been written about the legal discovery process. This book is unique in that it marries these two subjects in a way that fits the new and emerging legal technology market and the contemporary practice of law.

My hope, of course, is that readers will find this book to be useful and a better-than-average teaching tool. Any misstatements in the text are entirely mine, and the views, opinions and suggestions made here are mine alone and do not reflect the views of my current firm, its clients or affiliated parties. Nor do the principles and practices recommended or suggested in this book constitute legal advice. This is a practical guide designed and written with the practicing project manager in mind. There really is no secret sauce in this book; rather, I have attempted to aggregate the knowledge, skills, and experience I have gained over the years and combine it with some personal commentary to make the material presentable.

Introduction

This book focuses on project management and the person who carries out project management methodologies in the context of legal discovery projects. This could be a project manager in a litigation support role, either at a law firm, in-house at a corporation, or at a service provider. It could also be an attorney, a paralegal, or a specialist or generalist working in the litigation support field. In many ways, everyone in every area of business is a project manager. Lawyers, bankers, journalists, doctors, consultants, retailers—anywhere there is a leadership or hierarchical structure and there is work being performed, someone is functioning as a project manager, even if they do not realize it. They are all just solving problems unique to their industries.

The book begins with an introduction to the legal services industry, the phases of the legal process, and a framework for how discovery projects in general are handled. In chapters 1 and 2, the reader will gain an understanding of the context in which a project manager works and weaves her way through the legal discovery process. This context is critical to the effective use of project management principles in a legal environment. The reader will gain insight into some of the organizational challenges that apply in a legal setting, and then delve into the nature and mechanics of the legal discovery process. Unlike industries where project management is more prevalent, the legal business does not produce a product. Instead, it is service oriented, with little incentive among mostly adversarial parties to cooperate and be more efficient. Additionally, every law firm and corporation is different and has its own culture and values. Understanding the nuances of working in a legal environment is essential to succeeding as a project manager. Perhaps more important, though, is understanding the discovery process itself and the rules that govern the process.

Chapters 3 and 4 introduce the reader to the principles of project management. The focus is on making project management more understandable, clearly defining important terms, and introducing the reader to the basic tenets of project management. It is first through an understanding of the core principles of project management that individuals can start to appreciate and think in a process-oriented manner about applying project management principles in the context of a discovery project, either at a law firm, in a corporate legal department, or within a government entity. Readers are exposed to the five process groups that form the pillars of traditional project management: Initiating, Planning, Executing, Monitoring & Controlling, and Closing. The book explores the core knowledge areas that every project leader must know and understand, such as the management of scope, cost, time, and quality. The reader will examine the inputs, tools and techniques, and outputs of each knowledge area, and begin to understand how project management methodologies may be put into action. Along the way, examination of some of the characteristics of good project leaders are undertaken.

Chapter 5 returns to the world of legal discovery and provides an examination of the federal and state civil discovery rules. These rules govern legal discovery and provide a procedural foundation for practitioners. They are explored here in a way that project managers —whether they have legal training or not—may understand.

In chapters 6 through 12, this book outlines how to provide best-in-class litigation support and electronic discovery services. The book discusses best practices for delivering sound, defensible discovery services in a litigation support environment that are both efficient and valuable to clients. Systematically, the reader will walk through exactly what he or she needs to do to perform and deliver as a project leader, focusing on the tasks and responsibilities of a project manager. The discovery process is dissected and the workflows, tasks, and responsibilities that make a project manager successful are identified. In the end, the reader will come away with practical knowledge and actionable plans on how to approach electronic discovery projects.

It should come as no surprise to practitioners that this book explores project management and the discovery process in particular in the context of the Electronic Discovery Reference Model (EDRM). The EDRM was envisioned and created to address the lack of standardization in the industry. This framework has become the accepted standard for workflow management in the litigation support industry, and it provides an established, commonly understood, and easy-to-follow guide for service delivery and product development in the litigation support and electronic discovery industry.

If the focus of your work or a goal in your career is learning the principles of project management, how they apply in a legal support setting, and how to use these principles to improve litigation support and electronic discovery deliverables in the legal industry, this book is the most comprehensive exposition on these subjects to date. Not only will it provide an understanding of the basic principles of traditional project management, this book also outlines the best practices in a relatively young industry in search of standardization. These two things make this book incredibly valuable to the novice. In addition, for the experienced practitioner and the journeymen in the industry, this book will provide a useful reference for years to come.

The Legal Process: Understanding the Body of Work in the Legal Industry

One of the most important things any project manager in any industry must understand is the body of work within their industry. That is, the nature of the work performed by project teams and stakeholders and the outcomes, services or results of that work – known as "deliverables." In the legal business, this means having more than just passing knowledge of the legal process. A project manager in the legal business needs to understand the work of lawyers and paralegals, how the courts and government work, and the necessary phases or parts of a litigation. Does this mean one must be a lawyer or paralegal or have a legal education to succeed as a project manager in a legal environment? Not necessarily. Very few, if any, project managers are constitutional scholars. However, comprehension of the legal framework, how legal disputes arise and are settled, and the organizational and environmental factors present within a legal setting are critical to the success of the project manager in a litigation support role. The chapter examines some of the factors.

Several aspects of project management in a legal setting are unique, and tend to differentiate it from project management as applied to, say, manufacturing turbines or designing and building a new automobile. It is important to understand the differentiators. First, work performed in the legal industry is less predictable and less precise. In a legal setting, many stakeholders with different influences and people outside the project organization sometimes dictate the nature and course of a project. Judges, for example, are outside of law firms and they may not be viewed as traditional stakeholders, but the fact is that they have a stake in the course and conduct of a litigation. Likewise, opposing parties—or even third parties—each have their own concerns and may have individual interests that could influence the outcome of a project. In the end, human beings are involved in legal disputes, together with their various personalities, agendas, and perspectives. Of course, there are rules, and they must be followed, but even the rules can become the subject of debate in a legal dispute. Deadlines are often set, then renegotiated or seemingly arbitrarily moved up or back. The measurements and precision required in, for example, manufacturing, are simply not present in litigation.

Second, the work of lawyers typically takes place amidst an adversarial process that does not always lend itself well to measured and standardized methodologies. Unlike other industries where cooperation seems to be the norm, in litigation, two or more parties are frequently at odds over a real or perceived wrongdoing or have interests in a transaction that are diametrically opposed to one another.

Third, the individuals at the top of the food chain in the legal industry—usually a partner at a law firm, the general counsel within a corporation, or a judge—are generally not overly interested in being project managers themselves, although their positions would seem to make them the most logical choice to lead a legal project. The result is that project management responsibilities typically fall on middle managers or other talented individuals who do not have full authority to make final decisions, thus adding a layer of bureaucracy and, at times, indecisiveness that may not exist in other industries.

Fourth, the legal business is a service industry, and those who work in law firms, corporate legal departments, the courts, and government will attest that the deliverables in a legal environment are quite different from deliverables in a manufacturing process that produces a physical product. Deadlines, for example, can be a moving target. They are often set by judges with little or no regard for the actual project work. A judge may not have practiced in many years, may have a busy caseload, or lack appreciation for the volume of work to be performed on a given case. The outcome of legal disputes hinge on the complexity of the legal issues, the knowledge and skill of the lawyers involved and the resources available to them, and the thought processes, judgment, and reasoning of not just the lawyers, but also of judges and existing judicial precedents. Sometimes the deliverable is just legal advice, rather than a physical deliverable. The end objective may be a conversation indicating whether or not a particular action is prudent or advisable.

Lastly, the notion of efficiency has not always been the cornerstone of legal practice. Law firms are not the only ones to blame for this. True, law firms are not typically run like a business. But the legal marketplace has changed in recent years. Clients—including large financial institutions that, at one time, did not bat an eye upon receiving a law firm bill—are now scrutinizing every billable hour, disbursement, and expense. Organizations are under pressure to reduce legal expenses, particularly in the litigation arena. Lawyers and law firm management are under the same pressure to reduce rates, offer discounts, and perform more efficiently, sometimes within the parameters of alternative fee arrangements that yield margins lower than the traditional billable hour.

In addition, the legal industry, in general, has been besieged in recent years by what author and Professor Richard Susskind characterizes as "disruptive technologies"[7] that are changing the way we think about the practice of law and delivery of legal services, particularly in the area of electronic discovery and litigation support. Although not all legal services are capable of being packaged, the fact is that some aspects of legal practice could be commoditized and technology may certainly be used to make legal practice more efficient. New economic realities and the advent and adoption of more sophisticated technologies has made it difficult to convince law firm and corporate leaders who have not kept pace with emerging technology that they need to rethink their methods and make the

---

7   Richard Susskind, *The End of Lawyers? Rethinking the Nature of Legal Services* (New York: Oxford University Press 2010).

investment in technology—not for the sake of technology, but to stay competitive and provide efficient client services.

Although project management may not benefit all aspects of legal work, there are some areas in which it could be most beneficial. But first, it is critically important that the project manager working in the legal industry understand the legal process. This is consistent with the notion that a successful project manager will have broad knowledge of the body of work within the industry in which they are employed.

Understanding the Phases of the Legal Process

Leading a project in the legal business—particularly a large document or data-intensive project—can be a complex undertaking and, quite apart from one's ability to manage people or other resources, a project manager must be able to navigate the complex web of relationships among people, process, and technology throughout an organization. On the one hand, she must understand risk management, scheduling, and cost control; but on the other, it is essential that she be highly organized, possess superior communication skills, and maintain a professional comportment. At the same time, it is the project manager's responsibility to coordinate and manage the technology, support services, and details of the project plan. The project manager working in the legal business will not be able to do any of these things or make informed strategic decisions if they do not understand the context, the environment, and the nature of the legal process.

Litigations in particular have discrete parts or phases. In general,

Figure 1: Phases of the Litigation Process

Pleadings	Motions	Discovery	Motions	Trial	Appeal
• Complaint • Answer • Petition • Reply • Subpoena • Indictment	• Dismissal • Quash • Discovery conferences	• Document requests • Interrogatories • Admissions • Depositions	• Summary judgment • Pretrial conferences	• Jury Trial • Bench Trial • Arbitration • Settlement	• Intermediate appeal • Final appeal

the following are phases of a typical litigation:

A case or legal action is commenced by the filing of a complaint and answer, a petition, or the handing down of an indictment. This is commonly known as the pleadings phase. Almost all litigation begins when one party (the "plaintiff") files a formal complaint with a court or other tribunal, and the opposing party (the "defendant") files a response or answer to the complaint. Depending upon the geographic location and the court involved and the type of proceeding, a petition can also be a pleading, and if the government is the complaining party, the pleading might come in the form of a subpoena or, in criminal cases, an indictment. Pleadings, then, are the allegations of the complaining party or plaintiff and the answer, response or plea of the responding party or defendant.

Following the pleadings phase, there may be a motion practice phase. Generally, depending again upon the jurisdiction and the type of proceeding, this is the phase in which one party seeks to either dismiss or amend the complaint, or possibly to move the lawsuit to another court or to join other parties.[8]

There typically follows a discovery or disclosure phase, during which each party exchanges information, documents and electronically stored information (ESI) relevant to the dispute and takes depositions –oral questions answered under oath—from important witnesses to memorialize their sworn testimony for future use. There are several other discovery mechanisms as well, including written interrogatories or questions, and requests for admissions of undisputed facts.

Following discovery, there may be another round of motions seeking to dismiss the case or refine the claims, and then the case moves into the trial phase. A trial of course usually results in a verdict

---

8   Some actions, like intellectual property litigation, for example, have additional phases or proceedings that take place after a complaint is filed. A claims construction hearing – also known as a "Markman hearing" after the Supreme Court decision of the same name—is a proceeding in patent infringement cases in which the court and the parties determine the precise meaning of terms related to the patented product in issue. There are, of course, other types of hearings and proceedings in other litigations as well. The phases outlined above are the most typical stages of a litigation.

or judgment finding in favor of one of the parties to the action. After a trial, there might be one or more appeals to a higher court to challenge either a decision of the court below or the outcome of the case. In between each of these phases, the parties may participate in settlement negotiations.

These are the principle phases of legal process in the American legal system –laid out here in an admittedly rudimentary manner. As will become clear, many of the core principles of project management can be applied across this framework. Although it is in the best interest of law firms, corporate legal departments, and government agencies to integrate project management concepts into all of their case management workflows, this book focuses on project management during the discovery phase of litigation –a subject discussed in more detail shortly.

But before applying project management principles in discovery, it is important to understand the structure and organization of law firms and legal departments and take a detailed look at the discovery process.

Law Firm and Legal Department Structure

In keeping with traditional project management principles, it is necessary to consider the environmental and organizational factors, as well as the roles and responsibilities of stakeholders, when preparing to perform project-oriented work in a legal environment. For this reason, it is important that the project manager have an understanding of the general structure, culture, and workings of a typical legal environment.

Law firms are usually set up as partnerships or professional corporations. They are owned and generally run by the partners or principals, some of whom may have founded the firm, and others who buy in to the business as equity partners. There are usually different partnership levels within a firm. In the most typical scenario, equity partners are the primary stakeholders in a firm. These are the experienced senior partners who own a stake in the firm. Some of them may have their name on the door; most, if not all, have a book of business consisting of clients who bring legal work to the firm.

Equity partners bring in clients, maintain existing client relationships, and manage the clients' cases and transactions. Most firms have a leadership committee, which usually elects one partner to be the managing partner of the firm. The managing partner generally runs the firm on a daily basis. There may also be administrative partners who serve as leaders of particular practice areas, such as litigation. The administrative partners may have clients and practice law, but they are also responsible for various administrative duties related to firm operations, finances or staffing.

Many firms also have nonequity or service partners. Despite having the title of "partner," service partners are essentially employees of the firm, albeit at the top of the firm. Service partners may not yet have clients of their own and are reliant upon equity partners for work. They are usually younger and either working to build a client list of their own, or they may be more senior, having joined the firm from another firm or legal organization.

Every year, law firms announce new partners. Most commonly, they come from within the ranks of the firm's most senior associates— junior attorneys at the firm. Partner candidates typically have been at the firm for at least 7 years and have demonstrated their value to the firm leadership. After a period of between 7 and 10 years, an associate may be invited to join the partner ranks.

Associates may actually begin working at law firms before they even finish law school. Many work as interns or summer associates during their last year of school. Every year, big law firms send recruiting personnel to law school campuses in an effort to recruit graduates to work at the firm. The process can be quite competitive, but those who are selected usually start as summer associates and most are offered jobs as first-year associates upon graduation. First-year associates become second-year, then third- and fourth-year associates. If they remain with the firm, perform well, and either cultivate additional clients or bring in new business, they may be invited to join the partnership after several years. Associates perform much of the legal work on client cases and transactions brought in by the partners.

Paralegals have become essential and profitable employees

within law firms as well; this is a huge change from a few decades ago. Historically, paralegals were viewed as necessary, but usually nonbillable clerical staff. They did not bill their time like lawyers, and clients considered their work to be overhead. Today, paralegals are fully billable and, in many instances, provide important services at billing rates lower than associates. And they are quite profitable as well, typically billing hours and earning billable dollars in excess of their salary and benefits. Generally, paralegals are responsible for keeping pleadings, client documents, and discovery materials organized. They might keep track of court dates and filing deadlines, perform research, or draft documents for attorneys.

Law firms also have nonlegal administrative staff. At large firms, these may include marketing, accounting, human resources, technology, and litigation support. Each of these departments have a department head—usually a director or manager—who is responsible for administrative and operational aspects of their department, and for the development and implementation of firm policy related to their department. Depending on the size of the firm, a director may have one or more managers whose responsibilities are to oversee the day-to-day operation of the department and the staff working within the department. Directors or department heads may report to an executive director, who in most instances will be the administrative leader of the nonlegal staff. In larger firms, directors may report to C-level officers, such as a chief information officer, chief operations officer, or chief executive officer. In the end, regardless of the size or structure of a firm, the partners are the ultimate owners of the firm and both the legal and nonlegal personnel are accountable to the partnership.

One of the more recent developments at many firms has been the introduction, growth and development of litigation support departments.[9] There is usually a director or manager who leads the

---

9   The phrase "litigation support" is used in this book to describe the class of legal support personnel who specialize in providing consultative services and applying technology tools to various aspects of legal practice. It can be somewhat

department. Project managers are responsible for managing cases and projects arising within cases in much the same way as paralegals. Project managers meet with case teams and clients to discuss, plan, and provide support and technology services necessary to the case. There are also likely to be one or more technical analysts, specialists, or trial technicians who support the project manager and are responsible for maintaining databases and performing many of the highly technical tasks necessary to complete a discovery project.

Corporate and government legal departments are not very different from law firms, although most lawyers will say that being an in-house corporate attorney is very different from work at a law firm, particularly when it comes to litigation work. Like law firms, legal departments within an organization or within the government have a chief legal officer or general counsel who is an attorney, and more junior attorneys and paralegals who work within the department. In large corporations, there may also be additional legal administrative staff, or even a litigation support department.

The lawyers and paralegals within a corporate legal department manage the cases and legal affairs of the corporation. Many companies used to rely more heavily on outside counsel for their legal needs, but over the past few decades corporate legal departments have increased in size. Today, corporations still rely on outside firms for many things, but the chief legal officers within corporations have become more involved in company management and they have hired more lawyers to manage day-to-day legal business. Still, corporations rely pretty heavily on outside law firms to manage litigation tasks like discovery, document review, and trial-related work.

---

of a misnomer because in many instances these legal support professionals provide services and use technology in practice areas other than litigation. For this reason, some firms have taken to calling them "practice support," "technology support" or "legal technology" personnel. Either way, Litigation Support is used here to refer to them all.

Challenge to the Law Firm Business Model

The challenges facing law firms today are not related to how they are structured or organized, how lawyers are compensated, or whether they should or should not have professional litigation support personnel on staff. The partnerships of most firms are incredibly stable and firms generally run smoothly. Rather, the challenges today relate to the changing legal services market and whether firms can continue to conduct business in the same manner as they did during booming economic conditions. Litigation is expensive and corporate legal departments are doing more of the litigation work at the same time their budgets to pay for this work are shrinking. Large firms are seeing clients take litigation work to smaller, less costly firms, and alternative fee arrangements are squeezing the higher margins out of the profitability of litigation work, which is typically based on the billable hour. Amidst a shrinking and more competitive litigation market, clients expect law firms to be more efficient and to employ the latest technological tools. This is a sea-change for many established firms.

One answer to the challenges facing the modern firm is whether and how to apply and implement project management principles. As noted previously, law firms have generally struggled in recent years to adjust to the changing economic landscape, technological innovations, and more competitive business operations. Some firms are embracing the change and adjusting appropriately; others are having difficulties. Lawyers are generally not overly interested in being project managers and, make no mistake, attempting to introduce and implement new processes for them to organize and manage their clients and cases requires high-level support that many firms are not prepared to provide.

What is going to drive the adoption of project management principles in a legal setting? And will lawyers be able to dictate the terms of any such adoption? The primary motivation for adopting project management has to be client satisfaction, which any partner at a law firm will tell you is her primary responsibility. If clients are not satisfied, they will simply take their business elsewhere. Related to client satisfaction is pressure and a desire on the part of lawyers to find efficiencies in order to maintain a client's satisfaction. Legal support personnel have been asked for several years now to do more with less, and they have discovered and implemented new efficiencies as their staffs and budgets have been reduced. Newer, faster and more advanced technologies have begun to play a larger role at most firms and service providers, and along with these tools come the professional and technical staff needed to implement them. So, while an adapt-or-die mentality might be overstating the issue, surely in the years to come, law firms—like other businesses—are going to have to find new ways to work in order to remain competitive. Project management provides one clear path to greater efficiency.

The new reality in the legal world—fewer clients, less work, reduced resources—tends to explain why, at least among large firms, only a few firms have had success in integrating project management into the practice of law itself. But this should not stop individual business units within a firm or corporation from using project management principles to further the needs of their department, particularly in a process-oriented business unit, such as a litigation support department. There are opportunities in litigation support departments to fully exploit traditional project management principles, particularly when it comes to projects related to discovery.

Conclusion

Understanding the organizational and environmental factors that affect the work of a project manager in the legal business—whether it is within a law firm, a corporate legal department, or another legal setting—is critical to successfully managing a discovery project. It is necessary to know the phases of a litigation, the roles and responsibilities of the primary stakeholders, and the structure and organization of a law firm so that a project manager working in a litigation support setting may have the appropriate context for their work.

CHAPTER ONE SUMMARY

KEY POINTS

- Understanding the body of work and, in particular, the work of lawyers and the phases of a litigation, are essential to providing effective project management services in the legal industry.
- Project management in a legal environment has unique characteristics that differentiate it from other industries.
- The legal services industry is a service-oriented business that delivers advice and advocacy to clients rather than a physical product.
- Legal work is less predictable, takes place amidst an adversarial process, and can be quite bureaucratic.
- The economic downturn and new and disruptive technologies have dramatically changed the legal industry.
- One answer to the challenges of contemporary legal practice is the implementation of project management methodologies.
- Emerging and more advanced technologies have begun to play a role in firms, corporations, and service providers and the implementation of these tools require professional and technical staff.
- Knowledge of the key people and the structure and organization of law firms and legal departments are equally important to the project manager.

The Discovery Process: Narrowing the Issues, Avoiding Surprise and Uncovering the Truth

Much of the work of lawyers involves drafting legal documents, performing research, meeting with clients, developing case strategy and dispensing legal advice. Lawyers investigate facts, interview key people, and appear as advocates for their clients in court, at depositions, or other formal proceedings. But the most resource-intensive aspect of civil litigation is discovery.

What Is Discovery?

Discovery, also known as disclosure, is the phase in a litigation or lawsuit in which lawyers and the parties to a lawsuit have an obligation to share information, documents, tangible items, and the identities of persons who may have information relevant to the lawsuit. Discovery takes place when the parties demand that an opponent produce documents, answer written questions or give sworn testimony in a deposition. The purpose of exchanging this information during discovery is to narrow the disputes in the case and avoid surprise at trial. Prior to the adoption of formal rules of discovery procedure in 1934 —and in many instances even after the adoption of the rules— the general practice was "trial by ambush" in which the parties revealed all their evidence in court during trial. While ambushing opposing counsel with an incriminating document or statement may have added drama to the proceedings, it clearly did not lend itself to very efficient courtroom procedures.

Parties to a litigation may obtain discovery of any relevant, nonprivileged information relating to the claims and defenses in the case. Included in these discovery obligations is the requirement that parties identify, collect, review, and produce documents and electronically stored information (ESI) relevant to a case. Discovery occurs in civil litigation, government inquiries and investigations, during transactional and bankruptcy matters and in antitrust litigation. Discovery is compulsory in criminal cases (at least for the government),[10] and it takes place in domestic relations matters, trust and estate matters, and even in tax disputes. In short, anytime there are adverse parties, the discovery process may be invoked to gain access to information that may be relevant to the case. And although not technically discovery, the need to gather and review documents and ESI may also arise during internal corporate investigations.

The largest single contributor to the explosion in the volume of discoverable information is the development of technology and the use of that technology to create and store electronic information. Thus, discovery has become electronic discovery. Given all the moving parts involved in discovery, the resources needed, the people, and the large volumes of data—not to mention skyrocketing costs—it makes perfect sense to apply project management principles to discovery projects. First, it is important to understand some of the discovery process and how technology has impacted discovery.

Technology Transforms Discovery

Discovery is governed by formal rules in both state and federal jurisdictions, which seek to ensure that the process of exchanging

---

10   Discovery in criminal cases is governed by different, more stringent rules of procedure. Constitutional and statutory provisions guarantee a defendant in a criminal case the fundamental right to inspect and confront all evidence against them, and the government is obligated to disclose to the defendant not only incriminating evidence, but also any exculpatory evidence.

documents and information during discovery is fair, efficient, and proportional to the case or amount in controversy, and that the information exchanged remains relevant. Emerging technologies are, however, changing the discovery process. The advent of technology has disrupted the American litigation process that had existed for hundreds of years, especially as it relates to discovery.[11] Formerly, parties engaged in large-scale discovery projects poured through boxes and boxes of paper documents, made multiple copies of those documents, and transmitted them to other parties via courier van or truck. Today, in a world where nearly all documents are created on a computer, parties still exchange documents, but they do so on CDs, DVDs, or external hard drives, or transfer them over secure FTP sites and then view the documents in a database on a computer screen. Boxes and expanded folders have been replaced by databases and electronic folders in a Windows-based file directory structure. Attorneys now search for and designate or code documents "responsive" on a computer rather than following manual processes and using the colored Post-it flags they once used to affix to documents. Technology and the need for litigants to access and organize electronic documents efficiently have given birth to an entire industry, known as litigation support.

Some argue that discovery today, and electronic discovery in particular, threatens the integrity of the legal process because the costs put smaller firms and organizations with fewer resources at a distinct disadvantage. Whether this is true is not the point; rather, the point here is that applying project management principles and adhering to some basic organizational concepts enables any organization to meet their discovery obligations in a cost-effective and efficient manner.

Given that discovery plays such a large role in the civil system of jurisprudence, one would imagine that the processes involved would

---

11   Large-scale discovery and disclosure of information before trial is a uniquely American litigation trait. In most other countries, whether common law or civil code states, the notion of gathering and disclosing millions of pages of documents is unusual.

be more standardized and uniform across cases. But the fact is, both large and small organizations that create and maintain documents and electronically stored information do so in remarkably disparate ways, across very different systems, and each has its own procedures for responding to discovery requests. There is no one-size-fits-all in the creation, storage and disposition of ESI.

The Federal Rules of Civil Procedure (FRCP) have been in place since the 1930s to govern the course and conduct of discovery. But, like most rules, the FRCP can be a two-edged sword. When the rules were amended in 2006 to specifically authorize discovery of electronically stored information, it became clearer to attorneys and to the legal industry as a whole that a new form of discovery was emerging. At the same time, the rules were noticeably silent on some important aspects of electronic discovery; for instance, the rules do not require a company or its attorney to implement a litigation hold to preserve electronic documents. A *litigation hold* is a notice circulated to appropriate personnel within an organization that directs them not to delete, alter, or destroy documents. This requirement is instead governed by the common law or court decisions, which require a party to a lawsuit to preserve any potentially relevant evidence.

Notwithstanding the FRCP, lawyers have conducted discovery in very different ways and for different purposes for many years. Some operated with impunity and, instead of being a tool in the litigator's arsenal for learning the facts of a case, they propounded expansive discovery requests seeking every shred of paper and electronic information remotely relevant to the claims in a case. Discovery, in some instances, became pure sport and an effort to impede and overwhelm opposing counsel by either burying them in overly broad document requests or dumping enormous volumes of documents on them. The small company and solo practitioner could indeed be said to be at a disadvantage.

Discovery-related projects are the one area of civil jurisprudence where technology and the law collide directly with the business need to identify, collect, review, and produce documents, sometimes on a very large scale. And so, the discovery process has become known as the *electronic* discovery process, mostly because the vast majority of discoverable material is now stored electronically. But it is important to emphasize that, while it is called *electronic discovery*, the process of discovery itself has not changed; only the sources of the discoverable information and the forms in which it is produced have changed.

Given these changes in discovery and the development of technological tools to assist in discovery, it make sense that a new, technical framework for discovery has emerged.

The Electronic Discovery Reference Model

Attorney George Socha and technologist Thomas Gelbmann developed the Electronic Discovery Reference Model (EDRM). The pair had worked together at a law firm, and later formed a consulting firm. They produced the well-known Socha-Gelbmann Survey, an annual review of software and service providers in the electronic discovery industry.

In 2003, while preparing their annual survey, Socha and Gelbmann began to realize that providers across the country were each claiming to be the only proficient providers offering "real" electronic discovery services. What emerged was a widespread lack of consensus on standards, which, in turn, led to confusion among buyers of legal support services, including law firms, who were struggling at the time with this new concept of electronic discovery.[12] By 2004, no organization had addressed the lack of standards in electronic discovery. A national think tank comprised of mostly lawyers and jurists called The Sedona Conference had issued some

---

12 The earliest known case involving electronic discovery —that is, the exchange of digital information in litigation—appears to have taken place in the early 1970s when information from an IBM computer was sought in discovery. See *United States v. IBM*, 58 F.R.D. 556, 559 (1973). What followed in the 1980s, with the adoption of the personal computer, was small-scale discovery of electronic documents or databases on computer hard drives. In the 1990s, email— although still somewhat primitive—and the ubiquitous use of computers in office settings, led to a natural desire to seek electronic documents and information created on these machines.

guiding principles for practitioners, and the *Zubulake* cases –which were among the first high-profile court decisions to address electronic discovery requirements—had been decided, but there was no solid, uniformly accepted process framework. Electronic discovery prior to 2003 was indeed the Wild, Wild West.

In 2005, Socha and Gelbmann brought together representatives from law firms and corporate legal departments with the service providers who were offering the various forms of electronic discovery software and services. Corporations and law firms were the ultimate consumers of these offerings, so it made sense that they have a seat at the table in the development of standards in this emerging area. The goal was simply to discuss standardization in the electronic discovery industry.[13]

The first meeting of the EDRM membership took place in May of 2005, and this set in motion the development and design of the EDRM. The EDRM membership has been meeting semi-annually since 2005 to review and update its standards and to plan and

Figure 2: The Electronic Discovery Reference Model

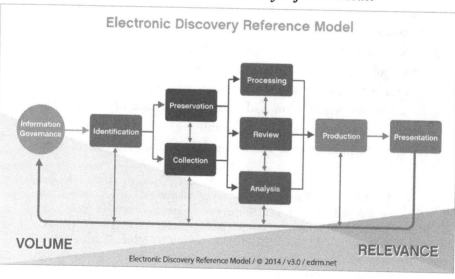

13   George Socha (co-founder and principal of EDRM), in discussion with author, June 2013.

undertake new initiatives.

The beauty of the EDRM is that its model framework predates the 2006 amendments to the FRCP, so those rules played little or no role in the development of the EDRM. This is important because, rather than focus on complying with rules, EDRM members focused on developing a process framework specifically related to the handling of electronic discovery projects. The spirit of the federal rules is very much present, however. Workflow, organization, and standardization were primary goals of the EDRM.

What precise role does the EDRM play, and how does a project manager use this framework to manage a discovery project? The answer to those questions are discussed in detail in the chapters that follow. For now, it is important to understand the basic component parts of the EDRM.

Information Governance

All corporations, nonprofits, government entities, businesses, and individuals create and store information. Indeed, due to federal statutes such as the Sarbanes-Oxley Act of 2002, the Dodd-Frank Act of 2010, the Stored Communications Act of 1986, and a maze of federal and state regulations, publicly traded corporations and companies in heavily regulated industries such as finance or insurance are required by law to create and maintain certain information. The information governance node of the EDRM, then, relates to the manner in which an entity creates, stores, organizes, manages, secures, and disposes of information created in the course of its business operations.14

---

14   Definitions of "information governance" vary depending upon who one asks. The Information Governance Initiative, an organization focused on advancing information governance, defines it as "the activities and technologies that organizations employ to maximize the value of their information while minimizing associated risks and costs." This book discusses information governance only insofar as it relates to an organization's maintenance of records and information needed in litigation and the role of the project manager working on an e-discovery project. See, Chapter 6, *infra*.

Every business is responsible to develop and maintain records and information management (RIM) policies. Such records could be paper documents, electronic documents, and data in an accounting database, or personnel files in the human resources department. Across the world, nearly all information is created on a computer or other electronic device and, given the volume of such data, it is in the best interest of every business to have information governance policies in place that guide and control the retention, security, and disposition of its business records. Additionally, companies in highly regulated industries have formal compliance procedures. The way in which an organization creates, stores, and manages this information can be critical to the success or failure of a discovery project.

While the responsibility to develop RIM and information governance policies within a client organization may not lie directly with a project manager working on an e-discovery project, it is important that the project manager and the attorneys involved understand the client's policies, or lack thereof. After all, it is the client's information that will be subject to discovery and, therefore, the project manager and attorneys should have a firm understanding of the client's policies so that they may work with the client to identify and collect potentially discoverable materials.

Identification

The identification node of the EDRM is where a project manager's work typically begins on a discovery project. The goal is to identify potentially relevant ESI in the clients' possession, custody, and control. RIM policies within a client organization will aid in this process. Therefore, attorneys and/or project managers should first inquire whether the organization has such a policy. But whether a RIM or information governance policy exists or not, it is still the project manager's responsibility to work with attorneys and the client organization—particularly their IT personnel—to identify the locations of, the people who possess, and systems that contain relevant documents and ESI. Although it can vary widely from one organization to another, and it is difficult to develop an exhaustive list because technology is constantly changing, the project manager should identify the sources and locations of ESI potentially relevant to the matter, including the names of custodians, the data assets involved, and a date range or other limiting characteristics that identify the needed documents and ESI.

Preservation and Collection

Once an organization has notice of or reasonably anticipates legal action, it should identify and preserve potentially relevant documents and ESI. Preservation implicates several responsibilities. First, the necessary personnel should be notified via a litigation hold notice, or memorandum instructing them that documents and ESI may not be altered or deleted. Second, the organization should suspend any records disposition policies, cease any automatic deletion policies, and stop backup media rotation if such processes affect preservation. Third, the potentially relevant documents and ESI should be preserved or collected for further use later in the case.

Collection is the process of physically gathering unaltered copies of documents and ESI identified as relevant. The importance of proper collection procedures cannot be understated. When paper documents are collected, no one writes on them. Electronic documents and other ESI should likewise be collected in a way that preserves the metadata associated with those documents. Electronic data can be preserved with software and tools that prevent writing to the individual files while they are being copied. To collect ESI otherwise runs the risk of altering the metadata, and this may invite claims that the ESI has been spoliated during collection.

Processing, Review, and Analysis

Processing ESI involves converting electronic documents to a uniform format so that they may be analyzed and reviewed. During processing, specialized software is used to extract and index the metadata and text of documents; this renders the documents searchable. Next, a combination of dates, keywords, or file type extensions may be used to search for or filter out documents that may not be relevant. Deduplication, or removal of duplicate documents, also typically takes place during processing. System files are also usually removed from the document collection during processing.

Once processed, documents are most commonly loaded to a document review platform, which is a database that stores either the *native file*—the format in which a document was originally created or last saved—or a tagged image file format (TIFF) rendering of each page of a document and the metadata and text associated with each document. *Review* and *analysis* are an iterative process that involves reviewing the documents and making determinations regarding their relevance. Documents may be coded responsive or nonresponsive to a particular document request or subpoena, or they may be coded privileged, which means the document will not be produced because it contains privileged attorney-client information. During the review, attorneys usually evaluate the documents and their relative importance to the case, or they may discover a new fact or learn about additional personnel whose documents may be relevant. Through this iterative process of review and analysis, the attorneys determine which documents need to be produced, or decide that further investigation of the case is necessary.

Production

Producing documents involves physically exchanging the responsive, nonprivileged documents with the other parties to a litigation. Preferably, the parties agree in advance to the format of the production, but the most common format for production of electronic documents is TIFF, with appropriate image load files. This is so because TIFFs are static, smaller than native files, and difficult to alter. TIFF is also preferred because of the ease with which most document review platforms allow for the redaction of images and the endorsement of Bates numbers on each page for later reference. An image load file and a delimited data file, which separates fields of metadata—such as author, recipient, and date—by comma or semicolon, may also be delivered if the parties have agreed to exchange metadata.

Presentation

During trials, arbitrations, depositions, and court hearings, or while preparing for any of these proceedings, documents may need to be displayed. Digital presentation is more efficient than lugging numerous boxes with multiple copies of each document for distribution in the courtroom. More and more courtrooms are equipped with projectors, screens, or monitors to enable the judge, jury, and the parties to view evidence in a digital form.

Generally, *presentation* of documents, graphics, or other digital information involves materials that were exchanged in discovery. Typically, production documents are exported from the document review platform to a presentation software, where they may be renumbered as deposition or trial exhibits. A trial technician may be engaged to prepare the documents for presentation, although litigation support project managers or the attorneys themselves often perform this function.

Conclusion

Knowledge of the discovery process is essential to the work of project managers working in a litigation support environment. Technology has impacted legal discovery more than any other area of the law, and the growth of the volume of ESI has changed the way technology is used in legal practice. The EDRM outlines the typical stages of a discovery project. The framework functions as a lifecycle for discovery projects in much the same way that the project management process groups discussed in the coming chapters guide all projects. At each successive stage, the project manager must bring to bear the appropriate project management tools to make the identification, preservation, collection, processing, review, production, and presentation of documents more efficient.

CHAPTER TWO SUMMARY

KEY POINTS

- *Discovery* is the process of opposing parties sharing of information in order to avoid surprise at trial.
- The discovery process is the most resource-intensive and costly aspect of litigation.
- The use of technology to create and store documents has caused an explosion in the volume of information parties must share during litigation.
- Electronic discovery is the result of the collision between technology, the law, and the business and legal requirement to produce information in litigation.
- The *Electronic Discovery Reference Model (EDRM)* is a process framework for the discovery project lifecycle.
- Managing information and identifying, preserving, collecting, processing, reviewing, producing, and presenting that information is the standardized lifecycle of a litigation discovery project.

CHAPTER THREE

The Fundamentals of Traditional Project Management

TO this point, the focus has been on introducing the reader to the legal environment and discovery processes in litigation matters. The preceding chapters revolve around the idea that having a solid foundation in the litigation process –whether at a law firm, corporate legal department or service provider– is paramount to providing sound, defensible discovery processes, particularly in the context of electronic discovery. Now the discussion shifts to a relatively new way of thinking about and organizing the processes involved in the discovery aspects of legal practice.

There has been much discussion of late about the use of Legal Project Management (LPM). More than a few books have been written that touch on LPM and the use of project management principles in the context of legal practice. The general idea is that LPM, when for instance applied to the entire operation of law firm practice –from matter intake through appeal in litigations—results in more efficient processes through proactive planning, identification and assignment of tasks, use of budgets, schedules, and quality controls. This in turn will translate into lower legal costs and, ultimately, better legal services for clients. While certainly a laudable goal and one that is worthy of exploration, the fact is that many firms are deeply entrenched in their culture and current processes and it is difficult to penetrate and change the status quo. Introducing LPM across the many practice areas and operations of an entire firm can be an arduous, costly, and time consuming undertaking, and if the support of the firm's top management is not strong or pockets of resistance arise there is a legitimate concern that an LPM initiative may not succeed. This is not to say that firms should not try LPM; indeed, it has been implemented at several firms. The point is that firm-wide LPM initiatives are not something to be undertaken lightly.

The good news is that few of the risks associated with a firm-wide LPM initiative prevent the individual business units within a firm or any organization from adopting project management principles and applying them to their day-to-day work. As it happens, project management principles are well-suited to the operation of a litigation or practice support department and to discovery projects in particular because much of the overall processes and many tasks are easily standardized. Application of project management to discovery projects is particularly appropriate given the abundance of repetitive and dependent tasks, the variety of people and organizations involved, and the need to find efficiencies that help better manage the timing and delivery of discovery projects and reduce costs. Moreover, the sometimes massive volumes of disparate types of information and data involved in discovery today strongly suggest that discovery projects and the clients for whom they are undertaken will benefit significantly from the use of project management in electronic discovery.

This book will next explore the basic principles of traditional project management, explain what traditional project management is, and lay a foundation for how it may be used in practice-oriented support services in the legal business. It is important to first say that project management is not a "thing," a single practice, or specific tool, that one simply picks up and transposes over the work performed in a particular industry. Rather it is an operational theory and series of practices; it is a way of thinking; a methodical and disciplined approach to outcome-oriented work. To be sure, there are principles, defined practices, tools and techniques involved, but more than any one thing, project management should be viewed as an organizational tool or framework geared toward effectiveness, efficiency, quality, cost and risk containment, and the management and leadership of people, process and technology.

What is Project Management?

Project management, defined, is the structured application of skill, knowledge, tools and techniques to organize processes, activities and tasks designed to bring about a desired outcome that efficiently meets a project or business need.15 While this may seem a somewhat amorphous or abstract concept, it is really quite simple: In the business world, in manufacturing, even in a service industry like the legal business, there are business needs or goals that an organization may be interested in achieving. Typically, the person with the right skills, knowledge and talent is enlisted to achieve these objectives and manage the necessary work. That person brings her industry experience, education and training, understanding of the resources, tools and workflows required to complete discrete tasks and the overall project work, and the ability to interact with different people and organizations needed to perform the actual work. That person is a project manager.16

A *project* is a temporary, non-routine endeavor limited by scope, time, and cost that creates a unique product, service, or result that meets the specified requirements or a customer need. The fact that a project is temporary in nature necessitates that there be a clear

---

15   The focus in this book is on traditional project management. Other project management methodologies include: *Agile*, (a more nimble, iterative version of traditional project management); *Lean* (which emphasizes eliminating waste and increasing efficiency through improvements in speed and cost); and *Six Sigma* (a continuous improvement methodology that seeks to measure and improve operational performance by identifying variations and eliminating waste, leading to less defects and increased quality).

16   A quick word should be said about project management education. Many project managers, particularly in the legal industry, are either self-taught or mentored by a certified project manager. There are, however, colleges, universities and credentialing organizations that teach project management and provide certification credentials. Readers must decide for themselves whether formal instruction or certification is what interests them.

beginning and end. Just because something is temporary does not necessarily mean it is short in duration. Indeed, projects can be small and brief or very large and last for many years, involving seemingly unlimited resources.

Projects have primary characteristics that distinguish them from other work. All projects, have an established objective and a defined scope. The business need and requirements necessary to meet that need are defined in a project plan, and typically require a variety of resources across multiple areas of an organization. Projects generally are undertaken in response to a customer or organizational need. The end of a project is reached when the project objectives have been met, the project is terminated because the project objectives can no longer be met, or the business need for the project ceases to exist.

In contrast, while projects are part of the operations of an organization, it is important to distinguish them from operations. Unlike projects, *operations* involve the everyday, routine, or repetitive tasks an entity does to sustain itself. For example, taking a parts order is something an automobile parts manufacturing company may do many times each day; but each order is not a project. Designing and building a system or program to manage those orders, maintain inventory, and feed information to an accounts receivable system, however, would be considered a project. Similarly, the design and building of the part itself would be a project, but the sale of each part is part of operations.

In the legal business, projects may emerge within each case or matter. Indeed, a transaction or a lawsuit might be a project, or some part of the case may be a project. Preparing a motion and brief, for instance, can be broken down into subordinate parts and dubbed a research or writing project. Lawyers may not know all of the controlling statutes and case law applicable to a particular legal issue. Typically, they have to perform research to find the leading authorities. They identify the issues to be raised and argued in a motion or brief, perform the research, draft the motion, quality-check the brief by proofreading and cite checking, and then file the motion with the court and serve it on opposing counsel. There may even be a team involved, depending upon the number and importance of the issues or size of the brief. This is a typical high-level project workflow for preparing and filing a motion or brief. Other projects may arise in the legal industry as well. Preparing for and using technology during a trial or a hearing to more efficiently and effectively present digital evidence is also a project. And, most relevant here, collecting and processing a company's documents and ESI for attorney review in a litigation or as part of a transactional matter—these are legal projects that combine the need for organization and efficiency with technology, and the expertise of attorneys and litigation support professionals, any of whom may also be project leaders.

Legal projects may come to fruition in a number of ways. There may be a business need—such as merging two companies—or one company may be using another's proprietary information without license, thus resulting in a patent or trademark lawsuit. In the context of litigation in particular, a project arises once a complaint is filed, a subpoena is served, or the government launches an inquiry or investigation. On the transactional side of the law, a merger or bankruptcy could also be considered a project. Regardless of the origin of the project, like any project, it is typically a project sponsor—in the legal business, the client—who identifies the business need and provides the financial resources, most commonly by engaging a law firm to provide legal advice and services.

Who is a Project Manager?

A project manager is the person possessing the applicable skills, knowledge, and talent who is assigned by an organization and responsible for overseeing and actively managing, among other things, the scope, time, and cost of a project to achieve project objectives. The project manager must manage the interests and expectations of the people and organizations involved and ensure that the project is completed at scope, on time and within budget. Along the way, project managers measure and manage risk, ensure the quality of deliverables, and manage the personnel and other resources associated with a project—sometimes in a politically charged, stressful, or time-sensitive environment.

The employment of project managers in the legal industry might seem confusing at first. Exactly what role should a project manager play in an industry dominated by lawyers? To begin with, a project manager could also be a lawyer or a paralegal, or—yes—even a judge. A project manager leads, guides, and manages project tasks and stakeholder expectations. Who better to lead a legal project team than a person with the necessary authority, legal skills, and knowledge of a case and of legal process?

More commonly, though, a project manager in the discovery context is part of the administrative staff and non-lawyer professionals in a firm or corporate legal department. She plays a supporting role. Project managers in the litigation support industry are individuals who, on a daily basis, orchestrate the use of technology in the practice of law and assist lawyers with discovery and trial-related tasks. In the past decade or so, we have seen not just the formation and growth of this entirely new industry, but along with it, expansion of the role of the project manager.

One very important thing a project manager in a litigation support setting must keep in mind is the notion that it is the lawyer's job to practice law; it is the project manager's job to provide support and help them practice—to help them be more effective and efficient using technology. This is a core value a project manager in the legal business must understand. A litigation support project manager who is not a lawyer does not—indeed should not—practice law and would therefore not presume to tell a lawyer how to do so; however, the project manager must also be able to tactfully advise the attorney on best practices and the efficient use of technology in his practice.

The mechanics of project management—knowing how to initiate, plan, schedule, estimate, and close—are not all that is required of a project manager. Almost anyone can be taught bottom-up estimating or scheduling—it is basic math. And nearly anyone can sit in a planning meeting to scope out what needs to be done on a project. Similarly, performing quality checks on data loaded to a database is not incredibly difficult work if you know what to look for and what could go wrong. It is not enough just to know industry best practices related to the preservation, collection, processing, review, and production of ESI. Project management involves subtlety and nuance, soft skills, and tact. Project managers must be articulate, have a good command of the written word, and exude confidence—not too much confidence, but enough to make a first- or second-year attorney comfortable with the task at hand. Strong project managers are able to put things in perspective and quickly grasp context. They are decisive, they know what they do not know, and they are able to marshal needed resources. Equally important, they have general business, organizational, and management skills, strong interpersonal skills, and a pleasant demeanor. It may be too much to expect that a project manager command all of these skills, or that he develop them on the job, but these are some of the basic characteristics of project managers who are successful in the legal industry.

All project managers must have experience in the industry in which they work and general project knowledge; that is, an understanding of the body of work within an industry such that they are able to place in context the significance of the work before them. Thus, it is critical that the project manager understand the lifecycle and phases of litigation and transactional legal matters. But experience alone—even combined with initiative or ambition—will only get one so far. Becoming a project manager in a legal setting requires a special blend of other skills or traits that, if they are taught or even capable of being taught, are not taught frequently.

Successful project managers in the legal industry have people skills. They are able to listen when problems arise and persuade others when suggesting or implementing solutions. They have team-building skills, they display empathy, and they motivate other people. They have coping skills as well, enabling them to be patient, to think critically yet creatively, and to understand the plight of project stakeholders and sponsors. They are also tactful and possess the temperament to deal with a wide array of people and personalities. Project managers are analytical and methodical, but also flexible and adaptive to the inevitable changes in scope and plan that accompanies legal practice.

Project managers are also leaders. They identify and communicate the project vision, give direction, and establish key processes and expectations. *Leadership*, quite apart from management, is the art of influencing others to achieve results. Almost anyone can be trained to oversee or perform daily administrative tasks; leaders, however, see the future, how the future might be better, and help others to see the same things. Leaders see business needs and opportunities where others see obstacles and problems, and they know that they can meet those challenges. Leaders take initiative, set an example, and inspire others by rallying enthusiasm around a project. Leaders take the long view and allow their vision to take root. Leaders take on the roles of coach, communicator, listener, and source of advice. Although they are passionate about their work, leaders care about more than just results; leaders also care about those who follow them.

Many project managers in the legal business have succeeded without formal project management education. They learn the essential skills and develop the necessary characteristics over time by doing the work and managing people and processes. As the litigation support and electronic discovery industry matures, however, it is natural that a higher level of competence is expected.

The typical project manager in a litigation support role today is someone with a legal or technology background, or both. They come from the ranks of paralegals, from positions in records management, and from a variety of IT roles. It is also not unusual for young attorneys—mostly those who were unable to land the coveted few and highly competitive first-year associate jobs at law firms—to become involved in litigation support, electronic discovery, and project management. In the end, regardless of their background, it is essential that project managers have a full understanding of the legal process, technology, and—of course—project management. They must have an interest in helping attorneys practice law and in integrating technology into their practice.

Project Management Roles and Responsibilities

Project managers in a litigation support environment understand their role in relation to the other stakeholders on a project. Stakeholders are the driving force behind any project. A stakeholder is any person or organization involved in a project whose interests may be affected by its outcome. Stakeholders may include a project sponsor, who typically provides financial support and resources for a project, or a customer or end-user who will actually utilize the finished product or service.

Other stakeholders include the project manager, whose role is to shepherd the project forward from beginning to end; project team members, who apply their individual expertise and skills to carry out the project work; and functional managers within an organization. These managers may be from administrative departments such as human resources or finance, who, while they may not be directly involved in the project work, provide ongoing administrative or support services to the project team. Lastly, stakeholders may include service providers, vendors, or business partners who are typically external companies that provide materials or services needed for a project

In the legal world, stakeholders are no different than in any other setting. The general counsel of a corporation may be the sponsor of a project. As the client, they typically pay the law firm's bills. But, in many cases, an associate general counsel will be the client stakeholder who is substantively involved in day to day decisions on a project. On the law firm side, the engagement or billing partner is typically the lead stakeholder, but again, there may be any number of other attorneys involved in a case, and each of them is a stakeholder as well. Paralegals are also stakeholders and, in some circumstances, they may play a large role in managing a case.

It is important to understand these different roles and responsibilities. In a corporate setting, the general counsel is usually the chief legal officer, and he or she plays a role both in management of business affairs as well as in the legal decisions affecting the company.

Depending upon the size of the organization, the general counsel may have other legal staff, such as associate general counsel, staff attorneys, and paralegals who report to the general counsel. Smaller companies may have just one attorney who serves as counsel to the company. In either event, the role of general counsel and the legal department within most organizations is to protect the organization, give advice to management, measure and manage risk, and ensure it complies with applicable laws. General Counsel also manages transactional legal affairs, and defends or prosecutes lawsuits involving the company.

Law firms, on the other hand, have one thing that most corporate legal departments do not have a lot of: lawyers. For this reason, most corporations rely on law firms as outside counsel to supplement their legal department attorneys and staff, and to provide substantive legal services, legal advice, and expertise on matters that cannot be handled internally.

In the end, and quite apart from the titles individuals may have, it is important that a project manager in a litigation support environment understand and remember the roles and responsibilities of each person involved in a project. It is the project manager's responsibility to manage and meet stakeholder expectations, and to interact with all of the people involved in a project.

Organizational and Environmental Factors

Stakeholders are not the only influential forces on a project. A number of cultural, political, and other enterprise environmental factors influence projects. The structure and culture of an organization can affect how projects are chosen, funded and supported throughout the project lifecycle. Critical to the success of a project is understanding how an organization works, the vision and values of top management, and who within the organization can influence such things as allocation of resources. In short, having buy-in and support from top leaders within an organization can strongly influence not only whether a project is completed, but also whether it gets off the ground in the first place.

And while the internal structure of an organization can affect the nature and substance of projects, many external factors can influence projects as well. Government regulations, the political climate, the economy, and the broader marketplace may affect not only current projects, but also the risk tolerance of an organization when evaluating project initiatives. It may be that these factors do not directly impact the project manager working in the legal business, but certainly factors such as the economy can and will affect whether a lawsuit is even filed. The point here is that both internal and external organizational and environmental factors may affect project work in any organization and the project manager must be sensitive to these facts whether they work at a law firm, corporation, or a service provider.

Project management as we know it today probably would not exist if some enterprising workers had not determined that certain tools, standards, guidelines, policies, and practices were necessary to carry out standardized project activities. Thus, every organization engaged in project-oriented work develops or adopts organizational process assets to ensure the success of its projects.

Organizational process assets consist of historical information, tools, or other resources that are available to the project team during a project. A simple standardized form that is completed before part of a project may be outsourced is one example of an organizational process asset. Templates, network schedule diagrams, standardized instructions or checklists for performing a task, and written guidelines or best practices are all tools used during project work. There may also be policies and procedures for safety and health, requirements for measuring and ensuring quality, or standards for ethical business or personal practices. Numerous software tools on the market help project managers track project activities, monitor the schedule and cost of a project, and prepare real-time reports on the status of a project. These, too, are process assets in the project management arsenal.

Organizational process assets should be developed, maintained, and stored in a *knowledge base*—a database that contains the process assets of an organization, including not only standard procedures or instructions, but also historical information about past projects for use as precedent to guide current and future projects. A knowledge management system can be as simple as a spreadsheet with hyperlinks to appropriate documentation, or it might be as elaborate as a relational database that shares information across multiple departments.

The legal industry is no different from others in this regard. The legal business—and the litigation support industry in particular—has developed process standards and best practices that guide attorneys, paralegals, and litigation support personnel, and that provide for quality assurance throughout the lifecycle of a project. Every firm and corporate legal department is different, but as discussed later in this book, standardized and defensible practices and procedures guide successful project outcomes for project managers. Whatever the work an organization is performing, it is important to develop process assets—such as best practices, checklists, and forms—to ensure that the work performed is repeatable, defensible, and that it meets the project's objectives.

Conclusion

The broad strokes outlined in this chapter are intended to lay a foundation for project management and to introduce project-oriented thinking in a legal setting. Understanding the nature of project management, the roles and responsibilities that people play, and the organizational issues unique to project work in a legal environment, is prerequisite to understanding how project management may be integrated into legal discovery projects.

CHAPTER THREE SUMMARY

KEY POINTS

- *Project management* is the application of knowledge, skills, tools, and techniques to activities designed to meet a particular project's specifications
- The pillars of traditional project management are the management of the scope, time, and cost of a project.
- A *project* is a temporary, non-routine endeavor limited by scope, time, and cost that creates a unique product or service to meet a business need. A project has an established objective and a defined scope.
- In the legal business, projects emerge with each case or transaction. A transaction or a lawsuit itself might be a project, or some sub-part of the case may be considered a project.
- A *project manager* is the person assigned to oversee a project and achieve the project's objectives, manage stakeholder expectations, and ensure the project is completed at scope, on time, and within budget.
- Project managers must understand the body of work within an industry, and possess leadership qualities as well as general business, organizational, and management skills.
- Project managers also need strong interpersonal and communication skills, and are persistently dedicated, assertive, confident, analytical, methodical, and decisive.
- A project manager in litigation support must know industry best practices related to the preservation, collection, processing, review, and production of ESI.
- Only attorneys are licensed to practice law; non-attorney project managers may not practice law, but instead provide support services to help attorneys practice.
- A *stakeholder* is any person or organization involved in or whose interests may be impacted by the outcome of a project.

CHAPTER THREE SUMMARY (cont'd)

- Stakeholders in the legal business include the client organization, their in-house attorneys, the partner, associates, and paralegals at the firm representing them, and litigation support personnel, including vendors and consultants.
- Internal and external organizational and environmental factors may affect projects in any organization or firm, including the culture of the firm, the political climate, and the economy.
- Organizational process assets help organize and control project work and ensure project success. These include tools, standards, guidelines, policies and practices, templates, forms, schedules, checklists, and instructions—all assets that are needed to carry out standardized project activities.

CHAPTER FOUR

The Project Management Lifecycle

Projects have a life. They have a beginning; they have an end. How a project progresses from start to finish is the essence of project management work. Understanding the concept of a *project lifecycle*—the processes that a project passes through, including the requirements of each process, task, their internal dependencies, and the context in which those processes take place—is essential to the project manager.

Project Management Process Groups

Within different organizations, there are many variations on how a project progresses from start to finish. Indeed, some in different industries and in academic circles might argue that there are varied definitions of the project lifecycle. Generally, the lifecycle of a project moves sequentially through ordered and sometimes overlapping process groups. The most common process framework is that which has been developed by the Project Management Institute (PMI), as illustrated below in Figure 3.

Figure 3: Five Project Management Process Groups

INITIATING	PLANNING	EXECUTING	MONITORING & CONTROLLING	CLOSING
(Start a Project)	(Organize a Project)	(Perform Project Work)	(Check Project Work)	(End a Project)

These five process groups are necessary to any project, and they are followed in the same sequence on each project, regardless of the industry, business, or application area. The process groups are not project phases, per se, but instead are the main components of a framework for organizing a project.

Management and project leaders in litigation support may debate whether the five process groups above represent an overly complicated view of the project management lifecycle. Some might suggest a more simplistic structure to a typical legal project, especially for smaller projects. Whatever we call the process groups in the lifecycle of a project, it is important to ensure that project work is aligned with the strategic goals of the organization or client and that the methodology deployed is consistently applied to achieve project success. Process has no regard for the type or size of project and, as far as can be determined, no one is clinging to labels as a means of defining the lifecycle of a legal project. The point here is for all projects to have consistent structure and strategic organization, and these five process groups achieve that objective.

Initiating, the first process group, requires that the necessity and purpose of a project are identified. Next, in the Planning stage, the project begins to take shape. The scope is defined, cost and time estimates are developed, and necessary resources are identified. In the Executing process group, project work begins. During Monitoring & Controlling, the fourth process group, the focus is on regulating the scope, schedule, cost, and quality of the project, and on managing changes to the project. Finally, the fifth process group is Closing, during which a project ends and post-project review is undertaken.

More important than the names we use to identify the process groups of a project, it is essential that a project manager understand the meaning and purpose of process. And so, from the definition of a project itself, and from the understanding gained earlier of the role and characteristics of the project manager and stakeholders, we move into the essence of traditional project management: identifying the inputs, tools and techniques, and the outputs required to produce results.

This is what project managers refer to as *process*—a series of steps, actions, or operations used to achieve an objective. As this definition makes clear, in order to finish a project, a common sense, orderly approach to the component parts of the project must be assessed and carried out. As one might expect, process is one of the keys –a core principle—to project management.

Each of the five project management process groups focus on three things: inputs, tools and techniques, and outputs. Project managers use these three components to analyze, build, and organize project-oriented work. *Inputs* are the information, tasks, actions, and documentation or requirements necessary to a project. *Outputs* refer to completed tasks, deliverables, and—ultimately—the final product, service, or result that is the objective of the project. *Tools and techniques* refer to the systems, methodologies, equipment, and resources necessary to the process that will achieve the desired outcome. *Process*, then, in project management terms, refers to the discreet steps one might take to achieve project completion, the tools used to get there, and an understanding of what the completed project will look like.

Project Management Knowledge Areas

In addition to the five process groups that govern the lifecycle of a project—Initiating, Planning, Executing, Monitoring & Controlling, and Closing—PMI's project management model also teaches that there are ten areas of focus with which project managers are primarily concerned throughout a project:

1. Integration Management
2. Scope Management
3. Time Management
4. Cost Management
5. Quality Management
6. Human Resource Management
7. Communications Management
8. Risk Management

9. Procurement Management

10. Stakeholder Management

Known as *knowledge areas*, they help the project manager categorize and navigate the necessary order of project work. These ten knowledge areas require a project manager's attention throughout a project; they must be consistently integrated, managed, and monitored during a project.

The first knowledge area, Integration Management, includes processes and activities needed to unify and coordinate project management activities across the five project management process groups. Integration Management includes consolidation and integrative actions that are crucial to project completion. The goal is to more successfully meet customer and stakeholder requirements and manage expectations. Integration Management causes the project manager to think about the larger picture of the project and all of its component parts as a whole. As will be seen, project managers who understand Integration Management are more apt to grasp the inputs and outputs necessary to keep a project on track.

The remaining knowledge areas, each of which is addressed below, represent the core areas of focus for any project. A project manager is responsible for each of the inputs, tools and techniques, and outputs in each of these knowledge areas.

To illustrate the point, table 1, on page 43, shows the intersection of the five project management process groups with the ten knowledge areas, and a high-level view of the primary outputs required for each area during a project.[17]

---

17   This table and the one reproduced in full in the appendix with all inputs, tools and techniques, and outputs included is adapted from a table designed by and is presented here courtesy of PMI. See, Project Management Institute, *A Guide to the Project Management Body of Knowledge, 5th Ed.* (the "PMBOK Guide"), Table A-1-1, p. 423 (Project Management Institute, Inc. 2013). Copyright and all rights reserved. This table and material from this publication are reproduced pursuant to an agreement granting the permission of PMI.

Table 1: Project Management Process Groups and Knowledge Areas

KNOWLEDGE AREAS	INITIATING	PLANNING	EXECUTING	MONITORING & CONTROLING	CLOSING
Integration Management	Develop project charter	Develop project management plan	Direct and manage project execution	Monitor and control project work Perform change management	Close project
Scope Management		Collect Requirements Define scope Create work breakdown structure		Verify Scope Control scope	
Time Management		Define activities Sequence activities Estimate activity resources Estimate activity duration Develop schedule		Control schedule	
Cost Management		Estimate costs Determine budget		Control costs	
Quality Management		Plan quality	Perform quality assurance	Perform quality control	
Human Resource Management		Develop human resource plan			
Communications Management		Plan communication	Distribute information Manage stakeholder expectations	Report project performance	

KNOWLEDGE AREAS	INITIATING	PLANNING	EXECUTING	MONITORING & CONTROLING	CLOSING
Risk Management		Plan risk management Identify risks Perform qualitative risk analysis Perform quantitative risk analysis Plan risk response		Monitor/control risks	
Procurement Management		Plan procurements	Conduct procurements	Administer procurements	Close procurements
Stakeholder Management	Identify stakeholders	Plan Stakeholder Management	Manage Stakeholder Engagement	Control Stakeholder Engagement	

As the table above illustrates, each process group and knowledge area requires certain outputs or deliverables. The process groups and knowledge areas provide the framework for successful project completion. Each of the inputs (requirements), tools and techniques (methodologies), and outputs (deliverables) necessary to successful project completion are laid out in the larger table include in the appendix and are discussed in greater detail below.

Initiating: The Project Charter and Stakeholder Identification

When initiating a project, the business need or necessity for a project is identified and initial thought is given to the development of a project scope statement. Although projects are initiated in a variety of ways and for many reasons, a project sponsor, client, customer, or other stakeholder typically requests or recommends a project. Alternatively, a business need, opportunity, or a legal requirement may be the impetus for a project. Regardless of how a project arises, the objectives when initiating are to develop a project charter, including a project scope statement, and identify stakeholders.18

Developing a project charter

A project charter is a document that formally authorizes a project to move forward within an organization. It identifies the scope, milestones, resources, and timeline of a project. The project charter contains the client or sponsor requirements; a preliminary scope statement; a high-level description, purpose, or justification for the project; the roles and responsibilities of key personnel; any organizational or external assumptions or restraints, including finances; and the business case justifying the project. Stakeholders are identified in the charter, and a project manager is usually assigned to lead the project.

It is common in the legal services market for an attorney and client to reach some agreement about the nature and scope of the legal services to be provided. This is typically achieved with an engagement letter between the attorney and the client, which may serve as the project charter. An *engagement letter* is an agreement between a client and attorney to provide professional legal services. The letter commonly contains a high-level description or scope of the legal work to be performed, and may provide for the billing rates or fees and the resources to be assigned to the matter. Ideally, the engagement letter *should* outline the scope and cost of anticipated discovery, particularly since discovery can be the most costly and time consuming aspect of litigation. Rarely, however, is this the case. In practice, such details do not find their way into an engagement letter. For this reason, it is prudent for a project manager to develop a project charter and scope statement at the time he becomes involved in a discovery project. Certainly, if a service provider is engaged to provide services related to a discovery project, a charter or statement of work detailing the scope

---

18   Referring back to Table 1, above, one can easily see that "Develop project charter" and "Identify stakeholders" are the two outputs that are required in the Initiating process group. Each successive process group similarly has output requirements (see the Project Management Process Groups table reproduced in the appendix).

and cost of the services would be a necessity. Project work at a firm or corporation should be no different.

Preparing a project scope statement

Essential at the outset of any project is the development of a project scope statement—a short, concise statement that identifies the purpose and goals of the project. The project manager uses his expert judgment in consultation with other stakeholders to examine and begin to define the scope of the project. Sometimes referred to as scoping, determining the parameters of a project usually occurs in a meeting or discussion led by a sponsor or by the project manager. At the beginning of a project, the scope statement may evolve and change but, at some point, it must be agreed upon and fixed because it defines when the project is completed. Clearly defining when a project is complete is another core principle of effective project management.

Writing a scope statement may sometimes be more difficult than it seems. Technically, a scope statement can be any imperative-style sentence that identifies the project's overall objective. But the scope statement should also bind the project manager and provide enough detail to allow for the development of cost and time estimates. Writing something such as, "Erect a single-story retail building" qualifies as a scope statement, but a better description of the project might be: "Design and build to code a single-story, 25,000-square-foot commercial real estate building at 123 Smith Street for ABC Retail Corp.; including all electrical, plumbing, and HVAC; with a storefront façade and three retail outlets at a cost not to exceed $750K and complete for inspection within 180 days."

In a legal setting, one might prepare the following scope statement for a discovery project: "Collect and produce documents in litigation." But the client and stakeholders would better understand the project if the scope statement were more detailed: "In connection with XYZ litigation, identify potentially relevant ESI from client's systems; defensibly preserve and collect the ESI for processing to uniform tagged image file format (TIFF) with extracted metadata and text; and prepare for attorney review and production the responsive, nonprivileged material on or before January 14th." A scope statement might also go on to include: "One project manager and one technical analyst will be assigned and report progress to attorney and client stakeholders as EDRM milestones are achieved. Project to be completed within 65 days at a cost not to exceed $75K."

A project manager in a litigation support setting is not going to begin a discovery project without guidance and instruction from the lead attorney on a case, and therefore the project manager should develop the project scope statement with input from the case team and then and seek authorization to move the project forward.

Identifying stakeholders

Identifying the stakeholders on a project requires that a project manager analyze the project and its scope to determine who may have an interest in the outcome of the project. This stakeholder analysis examines whether there is someone to whom the project manager or the project organization is ultimately accountable. The project manager here is not just considering the project requirements, but also the organizational requirements and environmental factors that may affect completion of the project. He is also considering initial resource requirements, pondering questions such as: Who will work on the project? What internal resources are available and when? Whose authorization or cooperation is required to complete the project? Are any external resources required and what are the politics of procuring those resources? The answers to these questions inform the project manager's determination regarding exactly who are stakeholders.

As can be seen from the three tasks above –developing a charter, preparing a scope statement, and identifying stakeholders—the inputs during initiating are no more than the general project requirements, a high-level overview of the nature, scope, and outcomes desired, and any documentation that may affect development of the project charter and scope statement. Tools and techniques used during the Initiating phase are mostly the project manager's expert judgment, tempered by input from stakeholders. The project manager will attend meetings, communicate with stakeholders, and begin thinking about the timing and resources necessary to complete the project. The output at this stage is of course the project charter or perhaps an engagement letter, including a project scope statement.[19]

At the conclusion of the Initiating process, the organization will make a decision whether or not to proceed with a project. It is important that this decision is made before committing additional resources to the next stage of the project – the Planning process.

Planning: The Project Management Plan

A project begins to take shape during the Planning stage. It is the most important part of any project. There are many things to accomplish during the planning process. It is typically the busiest and—short of missing a deadline—is perhaps the most frenzied part of a project, as the risks to project outcomes can be difficult to overcome if the project manager does not plan properly.

The primary objective when planning is to develop a *project management plan* (PMP), in which the project manager refines the scope of the project, identifies specific resources, prepares cost and time estimates, and develops both a schedule and a budget. The project manager must also develop quality policies and practices and identify the points at which quality checks will be performed. Establishing a clear chain of communication—who will communicate project metrics and status and to whom—is also critical during the Planning phase. Risks to the project's success must be assessed, and outsourcing decisions made.

A project management plan identifies the inputs, tools, and outputs across the five process groups and ten knowledge areas that are necessary to define, prepare for, and coordinate all components of a project. It integrates into a single place all of the requirements of the project. Whether a formal project management plan is required is at the discretion of the project manager.[20]

---

19   It is not absolutely necessary in all cases that a project charter be so formal. The key principle here is for the project manager and the project team, including the attorneys and the client, to have a plan. A sample project charter form may be found in the appendix.

20   A sample project management plan is included in the Appendix.

There may also be detailed subordinate plans or documentation regarding, for example, quality management or scheduling. These, too, are prepared at the discretion of the project manager. But whether or not these plans are formalized, each of the knowledge areas must be addressed in the planning process and the necessary project components should be included in the project management plan.

Scope Management

Scope management is primarily concerned with collecting all project requirements, defining, and then controlling, what is included in and what is excluded from the project. It may be necessary on a large, complex project to create a separate scope management plan documenting how project scope will be defined, verified, and controlled, and how the work breakdown structure will be structured but, for most projects, a detailed scope statement inserted in the project management plan is more than adequate.

Several inputs are necessary to collect project requirements and build a project's scope. This may include conducting interviews, holding meetings, or analyzing what the finished product or service must look like. Relevant documentation—such as questionnaires, checklists, or best practices protocols—should be reviewed and considered during the Planning process, and consideration should also be given to organizational and environmental factors. The use of questionnaires or checklists to gather information and prepare the project specifications is a preferred practice and provides historical documentation for the project. The project manager also uses his expert judgment to evaluate these inputs and refine the project scope.

When considering scope management, it is important to understand that changes in scope do not occur in a vacuum. When scope changes, it affects cost and time as well. Known as the *Triple Constraint*, the scope-time-cost relationship is a hallmark of traditional project management and another core principle. Quite simply, if any one of these three factors expands or contracts, that change impacts the other two factors.

Figure 4: The Project Management Triple Constraint

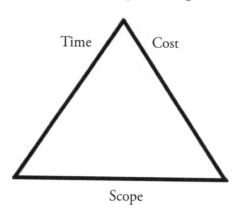

Controlling the scope of a project is of paramount concern to the project manager. It involves managing the influencing factors that create changes to the project scope and the impact of those changes.

Changes in scope should be expected during the lifecycle of any project. The stage at which such changes are implemented, however, can affect a project very differently. Changes to scope during the initiating process are likely to have little impact on the project. Changes during the planning process will likely require some additional planning. Scope changes implemented after project work has begun generally have the greatest impact on the project schedule and cost. It is therefore necessary to carefully plan a project and thereby minimize the need for change.

A project manager must ensure that changes to project scope are processed through a change control process—what is referred to as "change management." *Change management* is the establishment of procedures for implementing changes to a project, associated project documentation, or deliverables. Uncontrolled change or scope creep must be monitored and mitigated, if possible. If the nature of the work expands or contracts, it impacts the time needed to adjust to the change and this, in turn, affects the cost of the project. Most importantly, when scope changes are necessary, they need to be vetted and communicated to stakeholders to assess any impact the project deliverables, schedule, and cost.

Creating a Work Breakdown Structure

One key component of the planning process is the creation of a work breakdown structure (WBS). A WBS is an outline, chart or list identifying the deliverables, subdeliverables, activities, and tasks involved in a project. It defines the relationship between project deliverables and identifies tasks that are dependent upon the completion of other work. A WBS breaks down project phases and tasks into their constituent or component parts once the project scope is clearly defined. A WBS can be formal in scope and involve complex diagrams, tying together each part of a project, singular tasks, and their dependencies, or it may be less formal and involve an ordered checklist of tasks that, when complete, meet a project goals.

The WBS is also helpful in developing cost and time estimates. In order to provide stakeholders with accurate estimates, the project manager should understand all of the tasks, materials, and resources required to complete the project. Knowing each of the tasks associated with a project enables the project manager not only to control the scope of a project, but also to create a schedule of resources and costs.

When creating the WBS, the project manager's inputs are the project scope statement and supporting documentation. The project manager is using expert judgment and a process called *decomposition*, which is essentially subdividing activities and deliverables into smaller more manageable components. The project breaks down into phases, each phase into a subproject, each subproject into work packages, and each work package into tasks. In this way, a graphical representation of the project is created that will guide the project work, not just for the project manager, but also for the entire team.

Time Management

Managing the time it takes to complete a project involves identifying the processes, tasks, activity sequencing, and dependencies required to accomplish the necessary project work. The primary inputs in time management are the project scope statement, the WBS or an activity list, a calendar, and an understanding of any organizational factors. The project manager may use several planning tools and techniques, including project management software, diagrams, templates and the project manager's own expert judgment to define and schedule activities.

The most significant aspect of defining and scheduling project activities is ensuring that *mandatory dependencies*—those tasks that must be completed before another task starts—are identified. One way to do this is to develop a network diagram or flow chart to illustrate the dependencies. For instance, you would not start framing a new house until after the foundation is complete. And the roofing shingles should not be delivered until the framing and sheathing is complete. Likewise, on a discovery project, one cannot process documents and ESI until after they are collected.

When estimating the duration required to perform each scheduled activity, a project manager may use expert judgment, published data on estimating particular tasks, and estimating techniques such as bottom-up estimating. The decomposition technique is used to break the project into parts and tasks that can more easily be used to estimate duration. Expert judgment, or the project manager's prior experience working on similar projects, is an appropriate measure on which to base an activity duration estimate; that is, how long an activity took and the resources required to complete it in prior similar circumstances. A project manager may also seek to consult with other project managers who have worked on similar projects to gather their expertise, or, when the information is available, it is appropriate to use data from prior projects to inform estimates on later projects, known as *analogous estimating*.

Project managers must also consider the lead and lag time between activities and tasks. For example, if a necessary resource or material must be ordered and takes three days to arrive, the project manager should schedule three days' lead time. Many factors influence schedule change. Determining when the project schedule has changed, managing and controlling those changes, and reporting them to stakeholders is much of what a project manager does daily.

Cost Management

Cost management is the processes of estimating and controlling costs to complete a project within the approved budget. Naturally, in order to prepare a cost estimate, the project manager should identify the scope of the project and the time, resources, and materials necessary to complete the project. Other inputs are the cost of the people performing project work, including any vendors.

When estimating the cost of resources needed to complete project activities, project managers have several tools and techniques at their disposal. Analogous estimating provides a good estimate early in the planning process, but once the scope of a project is defined, a project manager should prepare a more accurate cost baseline. *Bottom-up estimating* is one of the more accurate estimating tools. Similar to time management, when applied to cost, bottom-up estimating involves examining the cost of each individual task and work package and then aggregating the costs up through the larger activities and deliverables of a project. This is done using the deliverables, activities, and tasks outlined in the WBS. This cost estimating technique is quite common, and it usually results in a fairly accurate cost estimate because, unlike analogous estimates, it takes into consideration all of the tasks involved in a project.

Many project managers, especially those overseeing large, complex projects, use project management software to estimate costs so they may consider various alternatives. But effective software must have valuable data that project managers may use; solid metrics, defined pricing, and clear task descriptions are necessary.

Project managers should consider reserve analysis when estimating costs. *Reserve analysis* involves adding a line item to an estimate or budget for costs to be allocated, at the discretion of the project manager, to deal with anticipated but not certain events or known unknowns. It is an accepted practice to include a 10% management reserve in project cost estimates to account for such unanticipated events.

The output here is a cost estimate and project budget. The *cost estimate* for a project consists of the aggregated costs of all the tasks as scheduled. The project manager should review the costs and schedule with the project's sponsor or high-level stakeholders and the project team because no two factors dictate expectations during a project more than time and cost. The cost estimate essentially becomes the budget for the project.

Quality Management

Quality is the degree to which a project fulfills project requirements. In other words, quality management ensures that the deliverables and final product meet not only the specifications of the project but, more importantly, the expectations of the stakeholders and/or customer. Quality management planning involves identifying the policies, objectives, and responsibilities that ensure the project will satisfy the needs for which it was undertaken. A quality management system should place emphasis on customer satisfaction, prevention over inspection, and continuous improvement. Quality must be planned into a project, not just inspected during or after a project.

The inputs necessary to making quality determinations are the project scope statement, the project schedule, and the points during the project's timeline at which quality may be checked. To begin to analyze the quality requirements of a project, the project manager should first know all the project requirements and understand the risks inherent in the project. Several tools and techniques may be used to assess, monitor, and measure quality during a project. The project manager may use charts and diagrams that illustrate how various factors may be linked to problems. Diagrams such as the classic cause-and-effect, or Ishikawa diagram, control charts, or histograms that measure variances that are outside of acceptable limits or show patterns or trends pointing to defects by frequency of occurrence, are commonly used to track quality.

Benchmarks for measuring quality during a project are most useful to a project manager. During the planning stage, the project manager should identify potential problem areas and establish a baseline for achieving quality at those points in the project. Benchmarks should be set for points in the project at which deliverables are checked and measured. The outputs from the quality planning process include checklists or fixed metrics and a process improvement plan, should the quality of a deliverable be deficient.

"Document what you do and do what you document" is a favorite adage of quality management specialists. The concept of *Kaizen*, the Japanese word for "continuous improvement" (継続的改善) is a modern-day theory of quality management that looks at constant process improvement in small increments over the course of many similar projects.

Entire books have been written on quality management. It is beyond the scope of this book to delve into the science or methodologies behind quality management. The basic principles outlined here provide a starting point and sufficient guidance to the project manager in the context of electronic discovery projects.[21]

Human Resource Management

Managing people, or human resource management, is the process of identifying, organizing, motivating, and managing a project team to complete project work. Every project manager must do it, and it can be the most complex part of managing a project—in part because human beings are generally the least predictable component of a project.

The principle inputs in human resource planning are the project schedule and activities, and knowledge of the available resources. In

---

21   It is important to understand general notions of quality. The International Standards Organization (ISO) has developed standards that complement current notions of quality assurance. The ISO standards provide some of the best-known guidance and tools for organizations that want to ensure their products and services consistently meet customer quality standards. See http://www.iso.org/management-standards/iso_9000.htm (and visit the "Standards" page). See also http://asq.org (and visit the "About" page) (the American Society for Quality is a global community of people dedicated to quality who share the ideas and tools that make our world work better) .

staffing, a project manager brings her understanding of not just the necessary skills and competencies required for the project, but also the best judgment of whether or not a particular person possesses the required skills. The first objective of a human resources plan is to define the roles and responsibilities of team members. Failure to clearly define roles and identify the work that each team member is expected to perform can lead to confusion, overlap or turf battles, and rework. In short, it is most efficient if every member of a project team knows what every other member of a project team is doing or is expected to do. Second, for similar reasons, authority should be clearly defined on a project: who reports to whom, and who has the right to apply resources, make decisions, and grant approvals for project work. Third, and just as important, is project team competence or, more specifically, matching people to the processes at which they excel. There is nothing worse than miscasting a person in a role for which he is unprepared. A project team leader must be sensitive to the abilities of each member of the project team and match the right person to the right role to ensure the highest quality deliverables.

When planning for human resource management, the project manager must be familiar with the knowledge, skills, and talents of the project team members. This does not mean that every single team member is an expert; the project manager may identify training needs or require team members to freshen their knowledge of a particular aspect of a project prior to execution.

Team members should be involved in early project planning and decision making to add their expertise during the planning process, to strengthen their commitment to the project, and to ensure project continuity. Developing a WBS is a useful team-building exercise, it helps the entire team better understand and maintain continuity on the project, and it gives meaning to the team members' work.

Communications Management

Communications management requires that a project manager coordinate the timely and appropriate collection, storage, retrieval, and distribution of project information. Poor communication is often the root cause of many obstacles to successful project completion. For this reason, the project manager needs to develop a communication plan.

Planning communications involves determining the information needs of the project stakeholders. The inputs while developing a communication plan are an understanding of the project stakeholders' communication requirements and any organizational factors that may affect communication. A project manager must determine what information is to be communicated, who will communicate the information, the frequency of the communications, and the best method for communicating. In addition, there needs to be an escalation process in the communication chain for issues that cannot be resolved at a lower level.

In the communication planning process, the output is a plan for communicating project information, whether individual instructions or project status. The project manager should identify the milestones at which he will report the status of the project to stakeholders. At the same time, a project manager must be prepared to communicate project information, both good and bad, at any time during the project.

One of the strengths of a successful project manager is the ability to communicate clearly, succinctly, and without interference. Knowing what to say, to whom, when, and how is essential to successful communication on a project. Understanding the personalities and agendas of stakeholders and keeping in mind the culture, hierarchy, and politics of the project organization are all integral to effective communication. The communication process provides the critical links among people and information necessary for successful projects. Project managers spend a lot of time communicating with the project team, stakeholders, vendors, customers, and sponsors. Everyone involved in a project should understand how communications affect the project as a whole.

Risk Management

Risk management is an essential part of project planning and requires that team members make proactive attempts to recognize and manage internal and external, uncertain or chance events that may affect the outcome of the project. What could go wrong and how might a project manager minimize the risk event's impact? The risks to a project may be recorded in a formal risk management plan on a larger project or, on a smaller project, the project manager may have a less formal risk register or list of documented risks to project outcomes. The project team should be made aware of the risks to the project.

The objectives in risk management are to increase the probability and impact of positive events and to decrease the probability and impact of events adverse to project objectives. One way to do this is by performing a risk assessment at the outset of a project. The inputs in assessing risk management are the scope statement, schedule, and cost analysis. Ideally, the project team should identify risks and determine how they might affect the project scope, cost, and schedule. The project manager may document the characteristics of these potential risks and prepare a risk response plan that outlines options and actions to either reduce or respond to these obstacles to project success.

There are several useful tools and techniques for managing risk. The project manager should assess the potential risks to the project by meeting with the project team to analyze what could go wrong on the project. From these planning meetings, the project manager may develop a risk register or list of issues that could affect project outcomes and deliverables. A corresponding list of contingency response strategies should also be developed that guides the team in responding to events that may arise during the project. When faced with negative risks, the project manager should consider changing the project plan to eliminate the risk (e.g., reduce project scope, extend project schedule), a process known as *avoiding risk*. But a project manager may also shift risk from the project team or organization to another party, called *transferring risk*. Risk transfer is usually accomplished by securing liability insurance, bonding, or by contracting with an organization or vendor better suited to perform a specific task. Finally, *mitigation of risk* is the act of minimizing the impact of risk on a project. If there is concern that a project may be delayed due to a hurricane, for example, a project manager might plan to begin the project out of hurricane season.

Whichever strategy is used, the output in the risk planning process is a contingency response strategy that may be executed if certain events occur. The project manager must manage risk proactively, and all team members should be involved and encouraged to identify and plan for risks. In the end, the project manager must use his expert judgment to identify risks, the root causes of the risk, and the potential responses.[22]

Procurement Management

Procurement management is the process of purchasing or acquiring products or services needed from a third party outside the project team to perform project work. One of the early steps in the planning process is performing a make-or-buy analysis. As noted previously, outsourcing all or part of a project may be a strategic decision tied to the project organization's tolerance for risk.

The inputs that guide the outsourcing decision-making process are the project scope statement, the availability of internal resources, the project schedule, the project budget, and an assessment of project risks. Among the tools and techniques the project manager will use are her expert judgment, research and meetings with stakeholders and vendors. Considering the outcome of the project, the activities, tasks, and deliverables involved, the project manager determines whether it is more efficient and cost effective to have another organization perform some part or all of the project work. Once a decision to procure products or services from a third party is made, the project manager must identify potential vendors who may contribute to the project and enter into contractual arrangements with them. The

---

22   Risk management, like quality management, has become its own specialty, and there are specialists in the field of risk analysis that span much of commercial industry. The discussion here is intended to provide a high-level overview of the topic to ensure that the project manager is aware of and plans for the management of risk on a project.

project manager must then administer the contracts and any change control processes necessary to fulfill the contracts.

The outputs from the procurement planning process are agreements or contracts with third parties. There are different types of contracts and, depending on the nature of the project, the degree of tolerable risk, and the budget for the project, the project manager should choose the option that best meets the needs of the project. A fixed fee agreement, for instance, typically incorporates all work in exchange for a lump sum payment. This type of arrangement exposes the project organization to the least risk. A time and materials agreement, or an agreement that provides incentives for meeting or beating a performance objective may also be appropriate. In either event, when outsourcing, the project manager should ensure the necessary agreements are in place, including any confidentiality or non-disclosure agreements.

Stakeholder Management

During the planning process, a project manager must consider how he will manage stakeholder expectations. This includes not only the subordinate project team members, but also higher-level stakeholders, sponsors, and management. High-level buy-in and approval often affects the course and outcome of a project and, for that reason, stakeholders need to be involved in the planning of a project.

Again, with all of the project requirements in mind, and with knowledge of who the stakeholders are and their roles and authority within the project organization, the project manager will schedule strategic discussions or meetings with stakeholders to review the project and the stakeholder's expectations. How the project will proceed, the scope, the cost, and the timing are all of particular importance to stakeholders. Additionally, agreement should be reached on the substance and frequency of status reports throughout the project.

At the conclusion of the Planning stage, the primary output is a project management plan addressing each of the knowledge areas. The PMP will serve as the roadmap for the project. Input from the stakeholders is of course necessary, and the plan should be shared with the entire project team.

Executing: Directing and Managing Project Work

When Executing project work, the project manager is directing and managing people and processes to complete necessary tasks. He will acquire and develop the project team, assess and identify the quality metrics that will be measured during the project, and distribute project-related information to the project team and primary stakeholders.

The project management plan is the primary input when executing a project. The PMP serves as the roadmap for executing all project activities. The project manager is using his or her expert judgment to kick off the appropriate tasks and get the project moving forward. Outputs during the execution process are the task and/or project deliverables; any change requests that alter project scope, time, or cost; and updates to any project-related documentation.

Performing Quality Assurance

Quality assurance is the process of analyzing the project quality requirements, identifying and implementing quality policies, and reviewing the results of quality control measures to ensure appropriate quality standards have been instituted on a particular project. Quality control, on the other hand, is the process of monitoring and recording the outcome of quality checking activities to assess performance and making any necessary changes.

During the execution phase of a project, the project manager is applying the planned systematic quality activities identified during the planning process to ensure that deliverables meet project quality standards. Quality metrics and project performance information are compared at this point, or the project manager may use audits or other analysis to ensure that project work is meeting or exceeding quality standards. The project manager is constantly monitoring specific project results to determine whether they comply with the relevant quality standards and identifying ways to eliminate causes of unsatisfactory performance. Project team members must also examine their output to ensure deliverables are meeting quality specifications, record any deficiencies, and update project documentation.

Acquiring, Developing, and Managing the Project Team

When acquiring a project team, the project manager reviews the work to be performed and makes informed judgments regarding the staff needed on a project. The project manager determines not only the number of people needed, but also the skill sets and competencies of those staff. Obviously, it is in the project manager's best interest to recruit the most qualified personnel.

The inputs here are the PMP, a resource calendar, staff performance reports, and any organizational issues that may affect project staffing. Roles and responsibilities having been defined earlier, the project manager must now coordinate staff assignments and resource allocation based on availability, experience, interests, and cost.

A project manager must also review and assess project team members. A successful project manager looks not just for the work to be completed, but also to improve competencies and the interaction of team members to enhance project performance. Improving feelings of trust and cohesiveness raises productivity, reduces staff turnover, and leads to project success. Therefore, skilled project managers communicate ground rules at the outset of a project and attempt to transparently and consistently apply those rules throughout the course of a project. Simple things such as assisting one another when workloads are unbalanced, or recognizing desirable behavior, can all go a long way toward developing a team. Even team-building exercises, such as bringing the project team together to build the WBS during planning, can be a valuable experience for both the project manager and the team. The outcome of this continuous assessment and development may be additional training, staffing changes, and either informal or formal performance reviews of project staff.

The project manager must also provide feedback, resolve issues, and coordinate staffing changes to enhance project performance. Managing conflict resolution is part of the project manager's responsibility. Many things contribute to conflict between project team members, but none are more prevalent than scarcity of resources, scheduling priorities, and personal issues. Clearly communicated ground rules; established role definitions; and a collaborative, team approach to resolving issues usually result in greater harmony and productivity. Remember, differences of opinion are healthy and facilitate creativity, but everyone involved in a project must understand their own role and where to turn when conflict arises.

Managing Communications

During the execution process, it is vital to make needed information available to the project team and stakeholders in a timely manner. Clear, consistent, and transparent communication with the project team during a project enhances project performance. The project manager should provide regular status reports to all stakeholders, preferably at project milestones identified during the planning process. This ensures that everyone is aware of the project's progress, current cost, and schedule.

In addition to reporting on the general status or progress of a project, the project manager's communications should include any issues that have arisen, as well as any material changes to project scope, cost, or schedule. Stakeholders—particularly anyone with a financial interest in the project—expect to hear about these developments throughout the course of the project.

Coordinating Procurement Activities

During the execution stage of the project, the project manager must decide which vendors, if any, will be used to help complete the project. This involves reviewing vendor responses to requests for information or requests for proposal that may have been solicited during the Planning phase. The project manager reviews quotes, bids, offers, or proposals made by vendors, and will choose the vendor or vendors who are best for the project. The project manager will also negotiate written contracts, pricing, or the terms of statements of work with the vendors.

Once the project begins moving forward, it is the project manager's responsibility to manage each vendor. This includes communicating regularly with each vendor, monitoring costs and the timing of deliverables, and reporting project status to stakeholders.

Managing Stakeholder Engagement

As noted previously, communication with the project team during a project is key to project success. Communication with primary stakeholders, sponsors, and management can be particularly important. Keeping leadership informed and managing their expectations appropriately—with tact and in a consistent, transparent manner—garners support for the current and future projects and increases the likelihood of successful project outcomes.

The classic scenario most project managers face is communicating project performance, especially where cost or time estimates are not meeting projected forecasts. Addressing, clarifying, and resolving issues like these, anticipating future issues and project risks, and knowing the expectations of stakeholders, enhances not only commitment to the project, but also the level of engagement, trust, and respect that primary stakeholders have for the project manager.

A project manager engages stakeholders and, more specifically, the project team, through meetings, informal discussions, and other forms of communication. It is during these interactions that the project manager's interpersonal skills, experience, and knowledge of the industry will be of paramount importance. The goal of the project manager should be to engender confidence—to make stakeholders and the entire project team feel comfortable and confident that the project is in the right hands. To state the obvious, once a high-level stakeholder or sponsor loses confidence and trust in the ability of a project manager, the project outcome becomes increasingly uncertain and the project itself may be more difficult to manage. Plus, the project manager then has to regain the trust and confidence of stakeholders and upper management.

In the executing phase of a project, it is the project manager's responsibility to arrange, execute, and manage the processes defined in the project management plan, including all project activities, staffing, training, and managing the project team; coordinating procurement activities; managing change and the quality of project deliverables; and establishing and managing communication channels.

Monitoring & Controlling: Analysis and Verification of Project Work

It is the fundamental responsibility of the project manager to monitor and control the overall scope, schedule, and cost of a project. Analyzing, tracking, and monitoring project scope risks; providing status reports on progress, cost, and schedule estimates; and implementing changes are all responsibilities of the project manager during the Monitoring & Controlling phase of a project. This is also when quality control measures will be implemented.

Monitoring and controlling project work involves taking preventative and corrective action to control project performance. Inputs at this stage include the PMP as the project roadmap, the WBS as a task list, and any organizational factors that may affect project performance. The primary tool the project manager uses here is her expert judgment to assess and compare actual performance to the projected schedule and costs to assess whether corrective action is necessary. Quality measurements will be taken and considered as well to ensure deliverables are meeting project objectives. This may result in change requests or updated project documentation.

Performing Change Management

Change is an inevitable part of every project. Stakeholders change the scope requirements, quality issues arise, and organizational priorities sometimes shift. Reviewing, approving, and controlling changes to a project's scope, cost, schedule, activities, and deliverables are among the most important responsibilities of the project manager. The challenge is not in knowing when or where a change may arise, but in how the project manager responds to the change. The project manager must be prepared to recommend and adjust the project's scope, time, and cost, and to communicate the effect of any changes to the stakeholders. Developing a clear process for submitting, vetting, and managing change requests across the project management process groups can ensure that all stakeholders are prepared to handle change seamlessly when it does arise.

Verifying and Controlling Project Scope, Schedule and Cost

The project manager continuously monitors the scope and progress of a project so that, in the event change is necessary, she is prepared to respond. As a practical matter, this means that, during the monitoring and controlling process, the project manager and team are examining deliverables as they are completed and comparing the finished product to the project management plan, the WBS, and the quality standards in place. At this point, the project manager either accepts a deliverable as complete or recommends corrective action. This process does not occur in a vacuum and on complex projects with many deliverables an undertaking like this can consume an inordinate amount of time. For this reason, it is vital that the project manager take the time during the Planning phase to understand what completion looks like at the end of each stage of the project so that it is easier to verify scope and to understand when the project or any part of it is complete.

Schedule control involves managing threats to the project timeline. The project manager must monitor the schedule of the project and any recommended corrective action or change requests, and update the project management plan with any deviations. This is done by monitoring project performance and, using the scheduling tools outlined in the planning process, adjusting the project schedule as needed. If, for example, a particular task is taking longer than anticipated, it is the project manager's responsibility to examine and document the issue and to take corrective action to regulate the project schedule (e.g., resource leveling, schedule compression). Staffing issues frequently affect a project's schedule, and a project manager should not only set clear work expectations up front, but also make adjustments to staff work schedules, if necessary, to meet the needs of the project.

Diligent forecasting and budgeting cannot account for the unexpected events that may arise on a project. Things break, people make mistakes, natural disasters interfere, and changes are part of every project undertaking. Cost is one aspect of project work that can determine the success or failure of a project. Monitoring and controlling the cost of a project is vital to effective project management.

Keeping in mind the inputs from the PMP—including cost estimates, the budget, and general project funding requirements—the project manager should monitor project costs to date and forecast the cost at complete if the project progresses at the current pace with the current resources.

When it comes to monitoring cost, a project manager's communication skills are of paramount importance. Sensitivities to cost, particularly on the part of a project sponsor, can be difficult to navigate. No one on a project likes surprises, and financial sponsors enjoy them even less. Because no one can anticipate every single and the various unknown events that may arise, project managers use contingency planning and reserves to cover unknown events that affect cost. It is the project manager's responsibility to communicate to top-level stakeholders—sometimes with great delicacy and tact—that a cost overrun is anticipated, the cause and nature of the overrun, and the impact on the overall budget and project outcomes.

Performing Quality Control

The project team uses quality checklists and any metrics or performance reports that may be applicable to a project to examine quality and validate project deliverables. As noted earlier, the benchmarks established in the Planning stage form the basis of the quality management plan or checklist. The project team is measuring project performance against these benchmarks. If a defect is discovered while performing quality control, a recommendation for corrective action should be considered and a change request should be prepared. The corrective action and change request are put into action as part of the defect repair process and, once the defect is corrected, the deliverables are examined and validated again to ensure quality.

Through this process of corrective action, change, and defect repair, it should be apparent that preventative measures may be taken to avoid this defect in the future. If so, then the project manager should ensure that this improved process is added to the organizational process assets for use on future projects.

Reporting on Project Performance, Risk and Procurement

Managing communications during a project involves collecting and distributing project performance information. Performance reporting requires the project manager to prepare and deliver to stakeholders the status of the project; progress measurement; and forecasts on scope, schedule, cost, and quality. This may be accomplished in an informal email; a memorandum to all stakeholders; or formal reports with charts, tables, and histograms.

There are no better communication tools than transparency and honesty. Great project managers do not hesitate to share news and project developments—both good and bad—on a project. A project manager should never be fearful of sharing project mishaps, mistakes, or problems. It is far better to communicate bad news and devise a plan for dealing with it than to conceal a problem and deal with the almost certain backlash at some later point.

A project manager must track identified risks, identify new risks, and execute risk response plans as necessary throughout a project. Work performance information, change requests, and quality control issues raise the specter of risk and place project success in jeopardy. The project manager must stand ready to take preventative or corrective action to avoid, transfer, or mitigate risk events. At the same time, the project manager must evaluate the effectiveness of risk response activities.

Contract administration—managing the contract and the relationship between a vendor and the project organization—is necessary whenever all or part of a project is outsourced to a third party. Reviewing and documenting how the vendor is performing is critical to project success, and provides a basis for future relationships with that provider.

The project manager uses performance evaluation and quality tools to audit and inspect project deliverables from the vendor. The fact that some part of a project is outsourced to a vendor does not relieve the project team of the obligation to ensure quality metrics are being met. It may also be necessary for the project manager to coordinate vendor payments during this process.

Controlling Stakeholders

Maintaining control of the project team, sponsors, and high-level stakeholders begins in the planning process of a project. The project management plan should clearly outline the roles and responsibilities of stakeholders and identify communication channels throughout the project so that stakeholders understand how and through whom they should funnel project-related issues, questions, and concerns.

Ideally, the project manager is the conduit for communication throughout the duration of a project. It is important that all stakeholders understand this, and that the project manager be assertive but tactful about enforcement of this rule. Whether reporting on project performance, implementing a change request, or addressing a personnel problem, the project manager must establish himself as the leader. This is most effectively done during the planning process, team meetings, and discussions with high-level stakeholders.

Closing: Documenting and Learning from a Project

Finalizing activities across all project management process groups to close a project is the responsibility of the project manager. A project comes to a close when it is complete or when it cannot be completed. The inputs for Closing will be the PMP, all project documentation, and the completed deliverables. Tools used in closing are a project manager's expert judgment, audits and analysis, meetings and negotiations, and a records management system. Of course, the output following closing is the completed product, service or result, but there should also be a complete project file. There are several objectives to consider during the closing stage of a project.

Administrative Closure and Documentation

The first objective in closing a project is administrative closure, which involves memorializing the details, activities, interactions, roles, and responsibilities of the team and stakeholders. The project manager must verify customer satisfaction with the deliverables and then release project resources. Project records and documentation are collected and archived, and performance metrics related to the scope, time, and cost of the project should be memorialized for future use. As part of the administrative closure, the project manager should also assess the work performance of project team members and record information that may be helpful for staffing future projects.

Another objective in the project closure process is to settle and close contract agreements. This involves verification of product and/or service deliverables from vendors to ensure that all outsourced work has been completed correctly and satisfactorily. It also involves reviewing, verifying, and paying any outstanding vendor invoices. All documentation related to procurement and outsourcing activities will also need to be archived.

Post-Project Review

Lastly, a post-project review session should be conducted, during which time project team members can share lessons they have learned during the course of the project. The project manager or other leader within the organization will typically initiate and lead this discussion. During a post-project review, the entire project team should be brought together to discuss any issues that arose during the project. This can be a very valuable part of a project. A project manager may learn, for example, that insufficient resources exist to undertake projects of a particular type, or he may learn the strengths or weaknesses of a particular team member.

Perhaps the most valuable information learned from the completion of a project is how the team might better handle similar projects in the future. Project managers cherish metrics that measure the effectiveness and efficiency of their processes. For a project manager to learn and to know that a particular process, task, or resource is going to cost X amount of dollars and take Y amount of time is a valuable piece of information that make project management as a whole a worthwhile undertaking. Stakeholders flock to project management teams with metrics and information on this level.

Conclusion

This chapter outlines a fairly high-level view of the project management lifecycle. Instead of delving into the more technical aspects of project management, the goal here is to build a foundation and explain the basic, commonly understood principles and process of project management –enough to enable a project manager in the legal industry to implement basic structured processes on assigned tasks. Through an understanding of the five process groups, ten knowledge areas, and inputs, tools and techniques, and outputs in each area, a project manager has the basic tools to make effective use of project management in a legal setting.

CHAPTER FOUR SUMMARY

KEY POINTS

- The project lifecycle is a series of five process groups that provide a consistent structured framework. They are: *Initiating, Planning, Executing, Monitoring & Controlling*, and *Closing*
- Within each process group there are ten knowledge areas on which the project manager must focus attention during a project:

Integration management	Human resource management
Scope management	Communication management
Time management	Risk management
Cost management	Procurement management
Quality management	Stakeholder management

- The five process groups intersect with the ten knowledge areas to structure project activities with primary emphasis on scope, schedule and cost – the pillars of project management.
- *Process* is a series of steps, actions, or operations formulated to bring about a desired result. It is a core principle of project management.
- Project processes revolve around three concepts: *Inputs, Tools & Techniques*, and *Outputs*.
- Initiating a project requires the development of a project charter and identifying stakeholders.
- A *project charter* contains a preliminary scope statement, the sponsor and stakeholders, and the justification for the project.
- A *scope statement* is a short, concise statement identifying what is/is not included in a project; it is a core principle of project management to clearly define what "done" looks like.
- In the planning stage a project management plan is developed, integrating into one document all project components across the five process groups and ten knowledge areas.
- A *work breakdown structure* (WBS) identifies all project activities and task durations.

CHAPTER FOUR SUMMARY (cont'd)

- The project planning process ends when each of the five process groups and ten knowledge areas are considered and incorporated into a project management plan.
- Executing involves a project manager directing and managing project work as the project team begins to perform project-related tasks.
- The roles and responsibilities of project team members are clearly defined before project work begins, and any decisions regarding outsourcing are made in the Executing stage of a project
- It is the fundamental responsibility of a project manager to monitor and control project work for adherence to the planned scope, schedule and cost; to manage quality and changes to the project plan; and to communicate the impact of any changes to stakeholders.
- Effective communication skills are necessary to report project performance; and transparency and honesty are part of the best communication policies.
- Closing a project involves finalizing and memorializing all project activities, collecting and archiving project documents, releasing and evaluating project resources, closing contracts and paying invoices, and verifying satisfaction with project deliverables.
- Post-project review is a valuable tool used to learn what went right or wrong on a project and how similar projects may be handled in the future.

CHAPTER FIVE

Preparing for the Discovery Process

To properly manage the scope, time, and cost of a discovery project, a project manager must understand not only the context in which discovery takes place, but also the general facts of a case, the applicable discovery rules, and the tasks and deadlines that lie ahead. Accordingly, at the outset of a discovery project, the project manager should read the complaint, answer, document requests and interrogatories, and any other relevant documents, court orders or correspondence in a case. These documents inform the project manager about the basic facts of the case and the information sought in discovery. They also aid in developing the scope of the discovery project.

It is essential that the project manager meet with the case team at the beginning of the project to discuss planning for discovery and any specific case strategy that may be pursued. In addition, although it is the responsibility of the legal team to adhere to applicable legal rules of procedure, the project manager should also be familiar with the legal rules and procedures. In civil litigation, these rules are generally referred to as civil practice or procedural rules, and the federal courts and every state court system has such rules.

Applicable Federal, State, and Local Rules

The obligations of parties involved in litigation are governed by federal and state rules and case law. The Federal Rules of Civil Procedure (FRCP) apply to civil actions filed in federal courts.

These rules "should be construed, administered, and employed by the court and the parties to secure the just, speedy, and inexpensive determination of every action and proceeding."23 Many states also have rules and procedures that apply in their courts and judges have local rules, all of which affect the course and conduct of discovery in almost all cases.24

Several provisions of the FRCP outline the discovery tools or mechanisms that are available to litigation attorneys. Rule 26 governs the general scope and limitations on discovery, while Rules 30, 33, 34, and 36 govern specific discovery tools—depositions, interrogatories, requests for documents, and requests for admissions. Rule 37, which governs a party's failure to comply with discovery, is also implicated in discovery projects.

Rule 34, related to requests for documents, is perhaps the most common discovery tool, particularly as pertains to electronic discovery. Rule 34 provides that a party may serve upon any other party a request to produce or inspect documents, ESI or other tangible items (see Rule 34). Requests for production of documents under Rule 34 are typically served by the parties to litigation following the filing of a complaint and an answer. In federal court and in some state courts, however, the parties to an action are required to make initial disclosures, without having received a document request from an opposing party. Under Rule 26(a), for instance, a party to litigation must produce certain information as part of their initial disclosures, without a request having been made.

The project manager may be called upon to help the attorneys

---

23 Fed. R. Civ. Proc., Rule 1 (as amended December 1, 2015). Excerpts from the Federal Rules of Civil Procedure referenced here are included in the Appendix.

24 California and Florida, for example, have enacted statutes specifically to address issues involving electronically stored information. See, Cal. Civ. Proc. Code § 2031.010 (West 2010); Fla R. Civ. P. 1.351 (West 2013). In New York, although it lacks a specific statute, the courts have developed administrative rules governing some aspects of electronic discovery. See, 22 N.Y. COMP. CODES R. & REGS. § 202.70(g) (2010) (Rule 8(b), Commercial Division of the Supreme Court).

compile information that must be disclosed, particularly if ESI has already been collected and received from the client. This is typically the first opportunity for the project manager to communicate with her attorneys and the client regarding their computer systems. It is also an opportunity to inform opposing parties and counsel about the format and types of ESI or other information relevant to the matter.

When it is determined that initial disclosures will be made, or, once requests for discovery are received, the project manager, attorneys, and client should begin thinking about limiting the scope of the information to be collected. For instance, by identifying specific custodians under the initial disclosure provisions of Rule 26(a)(1)(A) (i), or by limiting the sources of data to certain categories or locations, or to a specified time period, the scope of the discovery project and the volume of data may be reduced.

The Scope and Limits of Discovery

Rule 26(b) of the FRCP governs the scope of discovery. The rule provides that discovery may be obtained of any nonprivileged information relevant to a party's claims or defenses and proportional to the needs of the case. It also prescribes when discovery is permitted and how discovery may be limited.

It is important to read these provisions carefully because they contain language that should guide the course and tone of discovery in general. For instance, the repeated use of the words *reasonably* throughout the FRCP strongly suggests that reasonableness is a general standard applicable to discovery requests. Likewise, other provisions requiring "good cause" and references to "undue burden," "costs," "expenses," and "duplicative" or "cumulative" discovery material all suggest that the discovery process is intended to be a cooperative, cost-effective and efficient process. Additionally, the three subparagraphs of Rule 26(b)(2)(c) can specifically be read to mean that discovery must be proportional to the value of the potential recovery in the case. In other words, it does not make a lot of sense to spend $100K on discovery in a case where the potential damages are valued at only $50K. Indeed, in 2015, the word "proportional" was inserted into Rule 26(b)(1). Doing so reminds parties to consider proportionality when preparing and responding to discovery requests. Additionally, the FRCP advisory committee, which proposed the 2015 amendments, suggests that courts will also specifically consider proportionality when ruling on discovery disputes.

Another 2015 amendment to the FRCP allows parties to make early requests for discovery. See, Rule 26(d)(2); Rule 34(b)(2). Previously, parties were limited to serving discovery requests until after certain court hearings. Parties may now deliver discovery requests to any other party 21 days after the complaint has been served. The reasoning behind this amended rule is that delivering earlier requests will get the lawyers and their clients talking about discovery sooner in the process. It will also encourage the parties to prepare for the Rule 26(f) meet and confer conference.

As soon as possible after commencement of an action, the project manager and the attorneys should begin to consider and discuss a means for narrowing the volume of potentially discoverable materials. It may be possible, for example, to limit discovery to only specified custodians or to a distinct time period. Search and processing tools may be used to search for and deduplicate ESI, and to reduce the number of documents to be collected, processed, and reviewed. Perhaps the need to search data sources that are unlikely to produce relevant information (e.g., personal files, employee PDAs, archived material) can be eliminated. In cases involving large volumes of ESI of questionable relevance, it may be prudent to agree to perform searches to test or sample the contents of a large universe of ESI. The parties may also agree to conduct discovery in stages, deferring certain categories of discovery until later in the case. Parties may agree to use advanced technology or analytic tools to parse through the documents. Whatever the case may be, the scope of discovery should usually be defined by limiting criteria designed to reduce the volume and cost of discovery.

Rules 26(c) provides for another limitation on discovery: permitting a party to make a motion for a protective order. This rule is often used when a party to litigation seeks to protect information sought in discovery from disclosure to other parties. As the rule lays out, there are several grounds for protecting otherwise discoverable information, and a recent amendment gives the court the option to consider the allocation of expenses associated with discovery. However, before a party requests a protective order, it necessary for parties to first confer with one another to resolve the dispute prior to bringing a motion for a protective order. See, Rule 26(c)(1).

Planning for the Discovery Meet and Confer

Nearly all jurisdictions require that attorneys for all parties plan to meet and confer to discuss the scope, form, and costs of discovery as these relate to the production of ESI. Cooperation during the discovery process is encouraged because it makes the process more efficient. In July of 2008, a working group of attorneys, judges, and e-discovery practitioners gathered to publish the Sedona Conference® Cooperation Proclamation, an advisory paper on cooperation among parties to discovery.[25] Project managers should familiarize themselves with this document.

Rule 26(f) of the Federal Rules of Civil Procedure requires that parties meet and confer on a variety of topics relating to discovery, including the development of a discovery plan. A project manager should be prepared to assist attorneys in preparing for the meet and confer. This requires an understanding of the effort made to identify and preserve documents and ESI, as well as an understanding of the client's computer systems, document retention policies, and the litigation hold procedures put in place to preserve potentially relevant information. Working with the client, a list of the names of personnel who may possess potentially relevant documents and ESI should be prepared. The sources or locations of the ESI should be prepared as well, including but not limited to email systems, file servers, workstations, peripheral devices, personal and business smart phones, Blackberries,

---

25   See, *Cooperation Proclamation*, 10 The Sedona Conference Journal, p. 331 (Fall 2009).

instant messages, text messages, websites, and social media sites. It is also prudent to identify the relevant time period and the procedures that may be used for identifying and collecting potentially relevant materials.

An inquiry should also be made regarding whether or not the ESI is *reasonably accessible,* which is generally understood to mean ESI from a client's systems that would not be difficult to access or that would not cause an undue burden or cost to a party. Indeed, Rule 26(b)(2)(B) and applicable court decisions specifically limit discovery of ESI on these grounds. ESI that is not reasonably accessible is not ordinarily required to be produced, absent a showing of good cause by the party seeking the information. In general, reasonably accessible is best understood in terms of the format of the data or the type of media on which the ESI is stored. Thus, active data, data in near-line storage on servers or hard drives, or data that is archived but is still accessible, are likely to be deemed reasonably accessible. But data that is stored on backup media; data for disaster recovery purposes; data that has been deleted, fragmented, or damaged; and data that is only temporarily stored may be considered inaccessible. If ESI is accessible, but the cost of retrieving it is prohibitively high or will disrupt business operations, this, too, may lead to the conclusion that it is inaccessible. As part of the Rule 26(f) Conference, attorneys for all parties should be prepared to discuss and agree upon how accessible the client's sources of data are and whether ESI will be collected from them.

It is important to remember, just because ESI is deemed inaccessible does not relieve a party in litigation of the obligation to preserve such data. Indeed, as the rule itself points out, a court may order a party to produce ESI for good cause shown even though it is not reasonably accessible.

At the same time, parties should consider their options related to cost shifting. Consistent with the general notions of proportionality in Rule 26(b)(1), it is possible for a producing party to ask a court to direct the requesting party to share in the cost of production of ESI. Indeed, Rule 26(c)(1)(B), was recently amended specifically to allow for "the allocation of expenses" among the parties.

In an effort to help attorneys prepare for the Rule 26(f) discovery conference, the project manager should also help develop an estimate of the volume of potentially relevant documents and ESI (by custodian, location, data system or time period); the procedures for retrieving such materials; and the expected cost and timing of collecting, processing, and reviewing such information, including whether and how searches will be performed and how duplicate documents may be handled. This information is essential to the attorney appearing at the meet and confer.

During the meet and confer, the format in which ESI and other documents are produced should be discussed. This requires the project manager to provide the attorney with the necessary technical specifications for how and in what format to exchange the ESI between parties. The court expects and the attorney should be prepared to agree with opposing counsel upon the following decisions:

- The scope of the preservation and collection of documents and ESI
- The format of the production (e.g., TIFF or native format, with or without metadata)
- The specifications for processing ESI (e.g., search terms, de-duplication, date filter)
- The timing of discovery
- Whether a confidentiality or non-disclosure order is necessary

Recently, courts have been encouraging attorneys to enter into a stipulation governing the discovery requirements for a particular case. In fact, some courts, such as the Northern District of California, the Delaware Federal Court, the Eastern District of Texas, and the courts of the Federal Circuit, to name a few, have implemented model rules and prepared model stipulations intended to help the parties agree upon the handling of ESI. In the Southern District of New York, a pilot program requires the parties to use court-designed forms and work together to develop a joint discovery plan. A stipulated ESI protocol should include discussion of at least the following topics:

- Sources of ESI to be preserved and collected
- Limitations on the scope and volume of discovery
- Searching, filtering, and deduplication processes
- Forms of Production (e.g., TIFF or native) and technical specifications
- Metadata fields to be produced
- Claw-back of inadvertently produced documents

These proposed ESI protocols or stipulated orders governing ESI have gained prevalence as the industry matures, and attorneys and courts tend to favor such agreements because they identify the parties' responsibilities relating to electronic discovery and they reduce the need for extended motion practice or satellite litigation regarding discovery issues.[26]

Certification of Discovery Requests and Responses

Certification of discovery requests is an often overlooked but essential requirement of the parties in discovery. Rule 26(g) requires every discovery request, response, or objection be signed by an attorney of record or a party. By signing his or her signature, an attorney "certifies . . . to the best of the person's knowledge, information, and belief formed after a reasonable inquiry" that the discovery response is complete and that requests for discovery are in compliance with the rules and existing laws.

The implications of this certification for the individual signing the discovery request or response are that as a matter of professional responsibility the individual truly understands the nature and scope of the discovery in a case, particularly as it relates to ESI. This is consistent with the recently amended Comment 8 to the American Bar Association's Model Rule 1.1 governing competence. Attorneys are under these rules required to "keep abreast of changes in the law and its practice, *including the benefits and risks associated with relevant technology*." For the project manager, it is of course her responsibility,

---

26   A sample proposed stipulation and order governing discovery of ESI is located in the appendix.

to the best of her ability, to help the attorneys to understand it.

Rule 37 and Discovery Sanctions

If, in the course of discovery, a party fails to preserve ESI, fails to produce ESI, provides evasive or incomplete discovery responses, or fails to cooperate with other parties in the discovery process in general, any other party may make a motion to compel the party to respond and a party may request that the court sanction the recalcitrant party.

FRCP Rule 37(a)(3) outlines the several circumstances in which a motion to compel discovery or for discovery sanctions may be filed, and there are several behaviors that may invite a motion to compel. If the motion is granted or the discovery material is produced after the motion is filed, the court may order the party resisting discovery to pay the other party's expenses related to the motion. Likewise, if the motion to compel is denied, the court may order the moving party to pay the other party's expenses related to responding to the motion to compel. See Rule 37(a)(5).

Motion practice related to discovery abuses has increased in the years since ESI has become the larger focus of discovery. While the imposition of discovery sanctions on the parties to litigation is still relatively rare, some courts have imposed very significant monetary sanctions.[27] Frequently a court will enter an order directing a party to respond to a discovery request. A failure to comply with such an order can be very damaging to the party's case and have an economic impact as well. Under Rule 37(b), the range of possible sanctions a court may impose for not obeying a court order range from a limiting instruction to very severe preclusion orders. These sanctions are serious. Precluding a party from presenting evidence on a particular subject or limiting a party from pursuing a claim can change the course and outcome of a case. Likewise, giving a jury an *adverse inference*

---

27   See, *Sanctions for E-Discovery Violations: By The Numbers*, 60 Duke Law Journal 789, 803-23 (2010) (cataloging cases in which outright dismissal, adverse jury instructions, and monetary sanctions have been imposed, for failure to preserve or produce ESI or for failure to comply with discovery orders).

instruction –essentially a directive to the jury that they may conclude a party intended to withhold, hide or destroy evidence in discovery–may effectively convince a jury not to find for that party.

A court may also impose the most serious sanction – outright dismissal of the lawsuit—if a party's behavior warrants it. Called *terminating sanctions*, this most severe sanction is typically reserved only for the most recalcitrant party, those who intentionally destroy dispositive evidence or who attempt to defraud the court. And finally, in addition to the sanctions outlined above, under Rule 37(b)(2)(C), both a party and their attorney may also be made to pay attorney's fees and related expenses for resisting or disobeying discovery orders.

Failure to disclose documents, to respond to admissions, or to attend one's own deposition during the discovery process can also result in sanctions under Rules 37(c) and (d).

A new provision, added in 2015, relates to the parties obligations to preserve ESI. New Rule 37(e) addresses the consequences when a party fails to take "reasonable steps" to preserve ESI and the information cannot be obtained through additional discovery.[28] The court, upon finding a party has been prejudiced by another party's failure to preserve ESI, may take measures to cure any such prejudice. Additionally, if a court finds that a party *intended* to deprive another party of discoverable information, more severe sanctions may be imposed, including an adverse inference instruction or outright dismissal of the action.

As can be seen, the rules require parties to litigation to participate in the discovery process. Under Rule 37(f) if a party or its attorney fails to participate in good faith in developing and submitting a proposed discovery plan as required by Rule 26(f), the court may,

---

28   New Rule 37(e) replaces what was known as the "safe harbor provision." Under the former rule, if ESI was lost as a result of the routine, good faith operation of an electronic information system, a court was not supposed to impose sanctions absent some extraordinary circumstances. The new rule appears to make preservation more of an affirmative duty and, by introducing the intentional state of mind component, it seems the new rule will make it more difficult for courts to impose the most severe sanctions.

after giving an opportunity to be heard, require that party or attorney to pay to any other party the reasonable expenses, including attorney's fees, caused by the failure.

Each of the rule passages above make clear that attorneys clearly should be familiar with the provisions of Rule 37, particularly as it relates to the preservation of ESI. A project manager should also be aware of the potential impact of missteps in the preservation of ESI because the consequences can be quite severe. As a general rule, it may be prudent to over-preserve ESI because, regardless of what happens later in the case, a party may always return to properly preserved ESI.

Forms of Production

Rule 34 of the FRCP is the most common discovery mechanism used to request documents and ESI from parties to a litigation. Under the rule, a party may request documents, ESI, or other tangible things relevant to the claims and defenses in the pleadings and proportional to the needs of the case.

Rule 34(b) outlines the procedural requirements for requesting and responding to requests for documents. Documents must be produced as they are kept "in the usual course of business," or a party may organize and label the documents to correspond to the categories outlined in the document request. If a requesting party does not specify a form for producing ESI, the producing party must produce it in the form in which it is ordinarily maintained, or in a "reasonably usable" form. A party is not required to produce the same ESI in more than one format. Because a party who is requesting documents or ESI may not know how another party maintains its ESI, it is important to discuss with opposing counsel the forms and format of production in order to avoid making requests with which the producing party cannot comply.

In the end, though, ESI must be produced in a form that is "reasonably usable." This is a phrase for which the definition may vary dramatically, depending on the resources of each organization or law firm involved. For firms with advanced document review platforms, a *reasonably usable* production may mean single-page TIFF, native or near-native format files, an image or native load file, a data file containing the commonly understood fields of metadata, and the extracted text of the documents. For smaller firms or solo practitioners with limited resources, it may be appropriate to produce documents in Adobe PDF format, or even in paper form. Ideally, parties should state the form in which they prefer to receive document productions in their requests for documents, which is specifically provided for in Rule 34(b)(2)(E). Alternatively, parties should simply confer with one another and agree upon a suitable format prior to production.

The project manager's responsibility during production is to identify the form in which documents are to be produced, to help the attorneys communicate with other parties in the case regarding the selected form and any related technical issues, and of course to manage the mechanics of the production itself.

The project manager should also encourage her attorneys to decide early in the case whether metadata will be produced. *Metadata*, simply put, is data about data, or the mostly hidden properties associated with electronic documents. The term most commonly refers to the data elements, attributes, or properties of an electronic document. Some metadata is easily identified (e.g., the name of the file, its size, the author and date created), while other metadata is hidden or embedded and cannot be viewed (e.g., some dates and times, changes to the file, location of the file, and BCC information).

There are different types of metadata as well. In a typical office setting, metadata may be generated by a network system or by a document management system (the system date) or by an individual software application (an application or document date).

There are hundreds of fields of metadata associated with electronic documents and the computer systems that store them. The most common fields of metadata in electronic documents are those pieces of data that represent the bibliographic information about a document—for example, who created the document, when it was created, and the file name. For typical Microsoft Office documents, such as Outlook, Word or Excel files, parties usually exchange some of the following fields: Author, Recipient, Title, Date Created, Date Last Modified, File Name, and File Extension fields. For email documents, some of the most common fields exchanged are: To, From, CC, BCC, Subject, Date Sent, and Time Sent.

These lists of metadata fields are by no means exhaustive. Electronic documents and email files have many other fields of metadata that may be necessary depending upon the circumstances of each case. For example, if a party is going to use email threading to group together emails representing an email "conversation" or string of emails, it will be necessary to extract the message ID or conversation thread metadata that identifies the relationship between related emails. However they are organized, these and other metadata fields are extracted from electronic documents and email during processing. The parties should agree in each case which metadata fields need to be exchanged.

Paper documents that are scanned to image format files have no metadata, strictly speaking. But once they are scanned, these documents do have a File Name and Date Created.

It may also be necessary to produce the searchable text of documents. There are two forms of text produced in discovery. First, there is the text or body of an electronic document, which, like metadata, is extracted from the document during processing. Second, text can be generated using an *optical character recognition (OCR)* program, which reads the characters appearing on the face of a document. OCR is typically needed for image-type files from which text may not be extracted. Whether extracted during processing or generated using OCR tools, the text is then either converted to a text file or captured in the data deliverable itself, usually in a data field named "Text." The extracted text or OCR is then either loaded to a field in a document review platform or database, or the text files are mapped or linked within the database to the associated files via a unique document identifier.

Parties may agree to produce some or all ESI in native format, in a near-native format, or in TIFF image format. *Native* format means giving the other parties the files in the format they were maintained and as they were collected from the client's systems. In other words, turning over, for example, the Microsoft Word or Excel files or the Outlook PST or Lotus Notes NSF files without altering them. There are arguments against producing documents in purely native format. Documents produced in native format are subject to alteration because, unlike TIFF images, native files are not static and may be changed. It is also difficult to apply sequential Bates numbers to each page of a native file, which precludes later citation to a page of that native file.[29] And it is not possible to redact privileged or work product information from native files without altering the file, and therefore producing in purely native form may result in the disclosure of privileged information. The metadata embedded in native files may also contain privileged information or work product—data that may need to be "scrubbed" or removed from the file prior to production, which also alters the document. That said, some files (most notably Excel files) frequently need to be produced in native or near-native form because the design and formatting of such files often makes rendering a TIFF difficult.

Near-native format is essentially a modified form of the native file. A near-native production of ESI means producing files in their native format, but only after modifying the file. For instance, a party may choose to scrub metadata from a file, or to produce only certain fields of metadata. Or, it may make sense to rename a file to reflect a Bates number. Similarly, a WordPerfect file or a spreadsheet or database file might be converted to another more useable format. With respect to email, producing anything other than the complete PST container file might be considered near-native, although some might argue that at least for Microsoft Outlook the true native file is the .MSG file type. In the end, withholding or modifying any data or component of a

---

29   Bates numbering is the process of stamping each page of a document with a sequential number, either physically for paper documents, or electronically for ESI. The process is named after Edwin Bates, who invented a hand-held, self-inking stamping machine that was used to stamp paper documents with Bates numbers. Now, of course, the Bates numbering process is performed by endorsing image-based electronic documents with an over-laid number that is generated by a computer.

native file effectively renders it a near-native file.

The most common format for producing documents is the non-native *TIFF image* format. TIFF images are a graphical rendering of each page of a document—a sort of picture of each page. These images are typically produced with agreed upon metadata fields and searchable text, thus giving the parties all the necessary information about the actual file. But not all documents render to TIFF image format well, and therefore many parties produce a combination of TIFF images and near-native files.

Most modern document review platforms today can accommodate both TIFF and native files, and it is up to the parties to agree upon the format of the production.

Inadvertent Production, Waiver and Claw-back Provisions

Rule 26(b)(5)(B) of the FRCP provides that a producing party can request the return of an inadvertently produced, privileged document pending determination of the claim of privilege. Generally, it is preferable not to wait until a privileged document has been inadvertently produced before agreeing on procedures for dealing with such inadvertent productions. As part of the Rule 26(f) meet and confer discovery plan in a federal case, or by stipulated agreement or court order, the accepted practice would be for the parties to agree upon a procedure for dealing with inadvertent production and privilege waiver, and ask the court to ratify that procedure as part of a stipulated court order.

Rule 502 of the Federal Rules of Evidence supplements Rule 26(b)(5), and specifically provides protection against waiver of the attorney-client privilege and work-product doctrine. The attorney-client privilege and work-product doctrine protect documents from discovery or disclosure if the documents contain legal advice or legal strategy. If a party inadvertently produces a privileged document, that disclosure does not operate as a waiver of the privilege if reasonable steps were taken to prevent the disclosure and rectify the error. "Reasonable steps" to prevent disclosure generally require that an effort be made to carefully review the documents and prevent the disclosure of privileged materials.

The best practice to ensure preservation of the attorney-client privilege and to safeguard attorney work product, is to enter into a stipulation with opposing counsel or seek a court order providing that inadvertent disclosure of privileged communications or work product does not constitute a waiver.

Cost Expectations in Electronic Discovery

Preparing for a discovery project also means preparing for the costs associated with the project. Costs related to electronic discovery are driven by a variety of factors. Identifying, preserving, and even collecting documents can be relatively inexpensive, as they largely involve people and the reasonable time to collect the documents. Absent the need to collect an extraordinary volume of documents from numerous sources or remote locations, these costs are fairly predictable and easily contained, and several economical tools are available to collect ESI.

On the other hand, processing documents and converting them for use in a document review platform—including searching, filtering, and deduplicating—is driven almost entirely by the volume of the data. Processing ESI is typically priced based on volume, so it can be costly if a large volume of ESI is collected. Some organizations and law firms have been able to control these costs by purchasing the processing software and performing the processing in-house, but many others regard processing ESI as highly technical processes that corporations and law firms should not undertake. Consequently, many firms outsource ESI processing to vendors, and most vendors charge for processing based on the volume of data in gigabytes.[30] That

---

30   Recently, there has developed a movement in the industry towards what is known as *managed services*. Although there are several different models for these services, managed services is essentially outsourcing electronic discovery processes –the services, the people and the tools—to a vendor pursuant to a long-term agreement for bundled services. Collection, processing, hosting and review of ESI, as well as expensive software licenses and personnel are typically

said, the cost of processing has come down considerably. At one time, it was not unheard of to pay $2,500 per gigabyte. Market forces and advances in technology dramatically changed this. Today, processing costs are well over 90% cheaper. Keep in mind, too, as discussed later in this book, that the best way to control processing costs is to in the first instance collect only the ESI that is needed and take additional steps during processing to reduce the volume of ESI.

By far, the largest expense associated with electronic discovery is the cost of attorney review time. Attorneys at law firms, even junior attorneys who typically perform document review tasks, can have high hourly billing rates –sometimes these rates are hundreds of dollars per hour. For this reason, many organizations and firms use vendors or staffing agencies that offer contract or temporary attorneys at lower rates. Additionally, some service providers offer managed review services for which they charge per document or offer bundled fees, depending upon the level of service and resources required.

Budgeting and forecasting for electronic discovery has become a common practice. A project manager should be prepared to help develop cost estimates and a budget, and to discuss the budget with the engagement partner and client if necessary. The budgeting process does not need to be a painful experience, either. Gathering the costs for each stage of a discovery project and aggregating them together – known as bottom-up estimating—is frequently sufficient and there are several tools available, including popular spreadsheets, that are helpful in this process. In the end, stakeholders are going to be concerned about the cost of discovery and, therefore, every effort must be made to control the costs.

---

offered at lower rates, often for a fixed monthly fee. The fact is that some services may be streamlined or commoditized and completed more cost-effectively when combined and offered together. Frequently, such agreements also include data storage, which, in a legal industry teeming with high volumes of data, can be a more attractive alternative to organizations struggling to purchase the IT infrastructure needed to keep up with the growing volume of ESI in discovery. Managed services providers also attempt to leverage lower-cost personnel by offering talent in geographic locations where the cost of living and salaries are lower.

Another factor to consider in discovery is the notion of cost shifting. If, during the course of discovery, production of ESI is particularly costly or it is burdensome to retrieve the ESI, it may make sense to ask the court to consider shifting the cost to the requesting party. Different courts have different rules when determining whether to shift the cost of production to a requesting party. The early cases on this issue suggest that the courts consider some of the following factors when deciding whether cost shifting is appropriate:

- The extent to which the discovery request is specifically tailored to obtain relevant information
- The availability of the requested information from other sources
- The total cost of production compared with the amount in controversy
- The total cost of production compared with the resources of each party
- The relative ability of each party to control costs and its incentive to do so
- The importance of the issues at stake in the litigation
- The relevant benefits to the parties of obtaining the information[31]

Keep these factors in mind when planning a discovery project or when attorneys are asking a court to order cost-shifting.

Lastly, it will likely become necessary at some point to engage a service provider or consultant for some aspect of or even an entire project. The project manager should not only be consulted when vendors are to be hired, but should be the point of contact with the vendor. This removes from the attorneys or the client the burden of managing the vendor. It is the project manager's responsibility to outline the scope of work to be performed by the vendor, help the vendor to prepare cost estimates and establish a timeline for

---

31 *Zubulake v. UBS Warburg LLC*, 217 F.R.D. 309, 322-23 (S.D.N.Y. 2003) (relying on the earlier decision in *Rowe Entertainment, Inc. v. William Morris Agency, Inc.*, 305 F.R.D. 421, 429 (S.D.N.Y. 2002)).

completion of the project, and to generally oversee the work of the vendor.

Before engaging a vendor, however, the project manager must put in place several safeguards to preserve the confidentiality of information exchanged during a project. First, vendors must sign a confidentiality and nondisclosure agreement before performing any services. This agreement protects the confidentiality of client documents and data, specifically, any privileged or proprietary information. Second, it is essential that the vendor perform a conflict check to ensure that the vendor is not currently engaged in work with opposing counsel or any party adverse to the client in a given litigation.

When engaging electronic discovery vendors, the project manager must make every effort to ensure that the vendor:

- Is properly staffed with the necessary project management and technical personnel to support the needs of a given project
- Has sufficient capacity, processes, and infrastructure in place for the project
- Has not only safeguards in place to ensure the physical security of the client's data, but the hardware and software necessary to ensure the integrity of the data as well
- Has standardized practices in place to validate and measure the quality of its services, processes, and procedures

Service providers should be required to prepare a statement of work and a formal cost estimate that details the nature and scope of the work to be performed and the costs of each product or service to be used during the course of the project. It is important to ensure that vendor costs are reasonable at the outset of a project, and care should be taken throughout a project to ensure that vendor costs do not spiral out of control. Project managers will be relied upon to manage the vendor engagement process and they must review the project with the lead attorney or case team and secure permission to move forward with a vendor.

Conclusion

Proper planning for a discovery project and understanding the procedural rules applicable to discovery in general are essential to the success of the project. The emphasis in this chapter has been largely placed on the rules that apply in the federal courts. It is equally important to understand that most states and local jurisdictions have similar rules governing discovery. And although legal decisions regarding the application of and adherence to the federal and state rules governing discovery are exclusively the responsibility of the attorneys on the case, it is important that project managers know and understand these rules, not only so they may be prepared to tactfully remind attorneys of the rules when necessary, but also so that they may recognize situations in which the rules are impacted.

To this point, the book provides an introduction to the legal process, basic principles of project management, and the nature and scope of the discovery process and applicable rules. The objective is to lay a good foundation for the more detailed discussion that follows. Next, this book begins to explore the fundamentals of the electronic discovery process in much more detail and how project management may be used during this process.

CHAPTER FIVE SUMMARY

KEY POINTS

- To be effective, a project manager must understand some of the facts of the case and the applicable federal or state discovery rules.
- The Federal Rules of Civil Procedure (FRCP) govern civil discovery in federal courts; each state and local jurisdiction may also have rules.
- Parties are expected to make a reasonable effort to identify, preserve, collect, and produce documents and ESI in discovery.
- The discovery process is intended to be proportional, meaning the cost of complying with a request for production should be relative to the value of the outcome of the case.
- Parties are required under most rules to meet and confer and to be cooperative in planning the discovery process.
- A project manager's role in preparing the legal team for a meet and confer conference is to help the attorney understand technical issues and specifications related to the collection and production of ESI.
- ESI that is not reasonably accessible due to undue burden or cost is generally considered not discoverable.
- Written ESI agreements between the parties are favored because they identify each party's discovery obligations.
- Failure to preserve ESI, to comply with discovery orders or rules, or to participate in the discovery process, can result in sanctions.
- From the outset of a litigation, attempts should be made to reduce the volume of ESI to be preserved and collected.
- The format in which documents will be produced should be determined as soon as possible, and the format must be reasonably useable.
- Costs related to electronic discovery are driven by the volume of ESI.
- Attorney review is the largest expense associated with electronic discovery.
- If privileged documents are inadvertently produced, a claw-back agreement between the parties may protect privileged documents and may prevent the waiver of privilege for those documents.
- Project managers are best suited to manage project that are outsourced to vendors.

CHAPTER SIX

Information Governance: The Foundation of Legal Discovery Projects

Information governance in the context of litigation or a discovery project involves managing the creation, storage, access to, and archiving or disposition of records and information maintained by an organization. The management of information has never been more important than it is today. In a world where the volume of information created by human beings in the past few years exceeds the volume of information created by all of humankind prior to 2012,[32] one can begin to estimate the importance of properly and efficiently managing information. The management of records, data and information has therefore become the very foundation of electronic discovery.

Another way of characterizing information governance in the context of e-discovery is to consider documents, records, files or other data –indeed all ESI—as potential evidence in a lawsuit or investigation. Both the attorney and the client are going to consider the likely costs associated with gathering, reviewing, and producing these records. Records and information management, therefore, becomes critically important in the context of litigation not only because the

---

32   SINTEF, *Big Data, for Better or Worse: 90% of World's Data Generated Over Last Two Years*, Science Daily, www.sciencedaily.com/releases/2013/05/130522085217.htm (accessed June 24, 2015); See also *Data, Data Everywhere*, The Economist, Feb. 25, 2010, last accessed at http://www.economist.com/node/15557443.

records of an organization provide insight into the past activities of that organization that may be evidence relevant to a lawsuit, but also because the discovery process is the most costly aspect of litigation. The less time spent looking for discoverable information, the less impact such activities have on the overall time and cost of the project.

Information governance is a broad and growing discipline encompassing ideas, concepts, and practices related to but not exclusively about electronic discovery. It involves not only managing paper and electronic documents, but also an organization's compliance with laws and regulations pertaining to records retention, security, privacy, and the use and disposition of information. Some industries, such as banking or insurance, are highly regulated and are required to maintain certain records to comply with federal, state, and local laws. Other smaller organizations may be entirely unregulated. In either instance, managing information has become a critical task for most companies.

Still, varying definitions of "information governance" abound. The Information Governance Initiative, a cross-discipline organization and think tank focused on advancing the field, defines information governance as "the activities and technologies that organizations employ to maximize the value of their information while minimizing associated risks and costs." Other organizations have similar definitions; some are broader and some are narrower, and some include electronic discovery processes. Information governance is a holistic view of the value and the efficient, collaborative use of an organization's records and information. It is not a technology or a tool; it is not just managing risks or costs; it is an enterprise-wide practice designed for the benefit of the organization. And every organization is different and will have a different approach to information governance. The point here is not to define or redefine information governance. Instead, what is important is that project managers and legal teams have some understanding of information governance. The principles underlying information governance are discussed here only insofar as they relate to the role of the project manager working on an e-discovery project.

Information Governance Meets eDiscovery

How an organization creates, stores, accesses, and disposes of information is critical to a legal discovery project. One objective of information governance in this context is to help a client prepare for litigation. Being "litigation ready" means that an organization knows (or can easily determine) what information it has, where that information resides, and what needs to be done to preserve and collect it, if necessary. The benefits of effective information management practices are not only that it aids in the efficient and cost-effective operation of entities in general, but they also facilitate efficiency in discovery projects. Whether a multinational conglomerate with offices around the globe or a small business owner with one office, it makes good business sense to know what information you have and where you have it. Similarly, having effective information management policies in place enable an organization to make good faith claims in the event the policies are challenged during litigation. The importance of these principles cannot be overemphasized, because sound information management practices enable an organization to determine what it has done in the past and, sometimes, guide what it will do in the future.

At the outset of a discovery project, the project manager and attorneys should begin to consider the client's information governance maturity. The attorneys should inquire of the client whether or not formal information governance policies exist, the nature and substance of the policies, and the extent of compliance with the policies. For the project manager assigned to a discovery project, it is essential to understand records and information management and to have more than a basic knowledge of information technology and data management systems and processes in order to help the client organization respond to litigation. Traditional project management principles weave their way into the information governance phase of litigation in the form of initiating and planning activities. The project manager and attorneys must begin to develop a preliminary scope statement and plan for discovery. The project manager should:

- Define and refine the scope of the project and the ESI relevant to the discovery project;
- Identify activities and tasks and their sequence and timing;
- Clarify the scope and timing of the project and begin building information that will enable the development of a cost estimate;
- Gain an understanding of the client organization's IT infrastructure;
- Prepare to staff the ESI collection effort and consider outsourcing options;
- Assess risks associated with the project, particularly given the information and records management aptitude of the client.

Understanding Records and Information Management

ARMA International, formerly known as the Association of Records Managers and Administrators, is the world's largest professional association of records managers. They have developed a series of principles, called "The Principles," that have come to be known as the Generally Accepted Recordkeeping Principles. ARMA maintains that:

"Records and recordkeeping are inextricably linked with any organized activity. It is only through the information an organization records in the normal course of business that it can know what it has done and effectively plan what it will do in the future. As a key resource in the operation of any organization, records must be created, organized, secured, maintained, and used in a way that effectively supports the activity of an organization, including:

- Facilitating and sustaining day-to-day operations
- Supporting predictive activities such as budgeting and planning
- Assisting in answering questions about past decisions and activities
- Demonstrating and documenting compliance with applicable laws, regulations and standards"[33]

---

33   See, http://www.arma.org/r2/generally-accepted-br-recordkeeping-

These foundational principles should guide an organization in the development and maintenance of a records and information management (RIM) policy. Principles involving accountability, integrity, security, and accessibility are among those that govern effective RIM practices. Additionally, an efficient RIM process incorporates proper retention and disposition policies geared toward the needs of the organization and compliance with applicable laws.

But what exactly is a record? A *record* is any document or information, in paper or electronic form, created in support of, on behalf of, or about an organization. Records capture and memorialize the business activities, transactions, and correspondence of a company. They include corporate documents such as financial statements, board minutes, and accounting documents. Email, memoranda, instant messaging logs, and even information posted on a social media site are all records. In addition, information stored in less structured forms, such as data in a company's financial software, other databases, time-keeping information, or content found on an internal or external webpage—all of these are records. Conversely, documents and information that are unnecessary to the operation of an organization are not records. An email to a friend saying, "Meet you in five minutes for lunch," or a menu circulated from the latest eatery are not considered records.

Records have a life. They are created, used, maintained, or stored and perhaps revised. Once a record is no longer needed or useful to an organization, it is important to dispose of the record properly. Some records might be kept forever—such as founding documents, final contracts, or agreements. But most records may be archived or destroyed once the business need for the document is reduced or ceases to exist.

Components of an Information Management Policy

Effective RIM policies generally include three components: (1)

principles (last accessed 6/26/2015).

an inventory of records, (2) a retention schedule, and (3) a process for disposing of records. The development of a RIM policy begins with an organization taking an inventory of the records they create, maintain, and store, in both paper and electronic form. In order to organize the information, one must first know what one has. So, for the first component, every department, business unit leader, or individual within an organization should be consulted regarding the records created and maintained. The various types of documents should then be grouped into categories of documents useful to the organization. For example, employee files might be categorized as human resources records and financial data and accounting files might be categorized as finance records.

The next component requires that an organization prepare a retention schedule that identifies how long each type of record or information need be retained. Several factors come into play here. First, a retention schedule must incorporate the legal requirements to retain certain records. Tax records, for example, are generally retained for 3 years from the filing of the tax return. The legal requirements will vary from one industry to the next and from department to department within an organization. Human resources records must be retained longer than, say, the records of the marketing department. For every source or type of record within an organization, the appropriate legal retention period must be identified and included in the retention schedule. Second, the business needs of an organization must be considered. A company may not be required to retain a certain record, but that does not mean they must dispose of it. There may be an internal or business need to retain a record. Lastly, the users of records may have a reason why they retain certain records. In developing a retention schedule, it is important to ask users how long they need to retain information that is useful to the company. The retention schedule should incorporate the various categories and types of records identified during the inventory and the period of time that each record will be retained.

The third component of an effective RIM policy is identifying a process for disposing of records. Upon reaching end of life, records should be disposed of properly. For paper documents, this typically means shredding and recycling. For electronic information, there are several ways to manage the disposition of information, including archiving, backup, and deletion of records. The key to effective RIM policy is to consistently dispose of records that are no longer needed for legal or business reasons. Maintaining a consistent, standard operating procedure for disposing of records enables an organization to make a good faith argument that it destroyed information in compliance with its written policy.

Additionally, the consistent disposition of records –sometimes referred to as *"defensible deletion"*— reduces the overall volume of information an organization maintains, and will thereby reduce the time and cost associated with collecting, reviewing, and producing that information in discovery.

Preparing a RIM policy requires buy-in at the highest levels of an organization. The investment is necessary not only in the financial commitment required, but in the time and resources needed to develop and execute the policy itself. And, it is essential that the IT leadership of an organization be involved in the development of a RIM policy because they will ultimately be responsible for managing the storage and disposition of electronic records within the organization.

Preparing and executing a proper RIM policy can also be time consuming, and it requires recruitment of professional records managers. To ensure proper levels of accountability, upper management must not only approve of but also actively support the development and execution of an organization's RIM policy.

Understanding a Client's RIM Policies and Technology Infrastructure

With these core ideas about RIM in mind, it is necessary to examine the role of the project manager as it relates to records within an organization that may be relevant in litigation. Project managers working in e-discovery need to help attorneys and their clients understand records management and information governance and their importance to the discovery process, particularly as it relates to ESI. To do this, a project manager should understand the client's records keeping practices and information technology infrastructure. This is particularly true today, because nearly all records are created on a computer. A project manager should also understand that, although it is the client's responsibility to maintain effective RIM policies, there may be situations in which the client does not have a RIM policy and the project manager must guide the client or at least refer the client to resources that may help structure RIM policies. Regardless of whether or not the client has a RIM policy, in discovery, a project manager will likely need to collect the client's ESI and documents; for this reason, understanding best practices and the client's RIM policy and IT infrastructure is crucial. The project manager working in discovery with a client that does not have a RIM policy should encourage that client to design and implement such a program. There are any number of organizations that specialize in information governance and records management that would be willing and able to assist the organization with the development of sound RIM policies.

Assuming the client does have a RIM policy in place at the outset of a discovery project, the project manager and attorneys need to understand the policy. This will aid significantly in the preservation and collection phases of the project. As noted previously, a client's adoption of and consistent adherence to a sound RIM policy can demonstrate reasonable and good faith compliance with discovery obligations. And it can result in more efficient and cost-effective discovery projects. If, for instance, documents or ESI are no longer available because they were disposed of pursuant to a formal RIM policy prior to any obligation arose to retain them, then an organization should in theory be freed of the obligation to preserve and collect or produce that information. Defensible deletion like this can result in huge savings in connection with e-discovery processes.

In this planning stage of a discovery project, the project manager and attorneys should review the client's RIM policies. If the policy is in writing, a copy should be included in the case file. Then, like any project, the project manager, attorneys, and client need to begin scoping out the nature of the data and systems in place within the client organization. They must collect information and identify tasks and activities that must be completed. These include identifying key players who might possess and systems that may contain ESI relevant to the litigation. Next, they should confirm the extent to which the RIM policy has actually been followed with respect to potentially relevant paper documents and ESI. If the policy has not been followed, the degree of noncompliance should be determined and exceptions to the policy should be documented. At this point, all parties also need to understand any deadlines for completion of project work.

As a project manager, it is important to understand how a client creates, stores, and disposes of ESI within an organization. It is necessary to learn the types of hardware, software, data processing, and data storage devices the client uses. This includes the client's network configuration, operating systems, workstations, laptops, file and email servers, and other storage devices and backup systems. A data map or network diagram is helpful in learning about a client's computer systems. A *data map* is a tool that is used to diagram an organization's IT infrastructure in an effort to visualize and identify the location of all the different types of electronic records maintained. A simple *network topology* may be used as well. The project manager should ask the client's IT personnel for a data map or topology of their systems. As illustrated in Figure 5, a simple topology provides an easy and effective way to quickly identify which sources of data may contain relevant information.

Ideally, attorneys and the project manager should have a scoping call with the client's IT and records management personnel. This discussion should involve other stakeholders as well, such as the client's inside counsel and any attorney overseeing the litigation or discovery project. A good practice is to use an infrastructure questionnaire or checklist to ask the IT personnel about their systems to identify the data assets that may contain potentially relevant information.[34] Doing so not only provides a record of the details of the conversation, but

---

34   A sample IT infrastructure questionnaire is located in the appendix.

Figure 5: Simple Network Topology

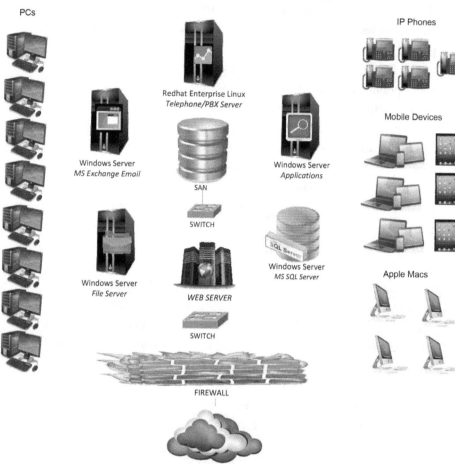

also enables attorneys to make informed decisions regarding the best course of action for preserving and later collecting the documents. The project manager will want to learn not just about the sources of data, but how records are created, who creates them, and when and where records are created and stored. Accordingly, a good questionnaire or checklist must, at a minimum, inquire about:

- Network configuration, storage, and operating systems in use
- Types and number of file servers in use and the contents of each

- The email application, number of servers, and mail stores
- Software applications that are in use
- Databases and proprietary applications in use
- Types of workstations and/or laptops in use
- Remote access, home use, and personal device polices
- Backup systems in use; backup policies, frequency, and retention
- Legacy or retired systems no longer in use
- Policies on former employees, data retention, and device imaging
- External media, hard drives, CDs or DVDs, and flash drives
- Internal or external websites, intranets, and social media pages
- Text messaging programs and unified voicemail systems

It is also important to identify the relevant date range for events in the case, the names of key personnel who may possess relevant ESI, and any specific categories of documents that may be relevant (i.e., sales or marketing information). These pieces of information guide many future efforts on the project.

One person within the client's organization, preferably from the IT department, should be designated to testify as a deposition witness regarding ESI, if necessary. It is common to receive from opposing counsel a request to identify the person most knowledgeable regarding the company's IT systems and processes. For this reason, the designated individual should possess comprehensive knowledge of the client's network systems and policies.

Equally important, the project manager should determine early on if the company has experienced any problems that would interfere with or prevent the proper preservation of relevant ESI. Some of the most common data preservation problems involve:

- The absence of a document management or retention policy
- Recently implemented policies that limit access to older data
- Network upgrades or system changes that affect the storage or movement of data
- Computers of former or recently departed key personnel
- Auto-deletion and network user policies

An organization's backup systems must be understood as well. Backup systems are generally designed for disaster recovery in the event of a total loss of system resources; they are usually not designed for retrieval of documents in connection with litigation. Restoring old backup tapes can be costly and time consuming. Nonetheless, if documents cannot otherwise be obtained, it may be necessary to restore and process data from a backup system. Therefore, it is important to know the client's backup policies, including the timing of system backups, the rotation of backup tapes, and the processes necessary to prevent data disposal from these systems. If backup tapes must be retrieved, consider analyzing tapes that relate only to particular custodians, or pulling only the last full backup or just that backup tape closest in time to the events in question.

Client policies on former employees often present preservation issues, particularly if the relevant time period is years prior to commencement of the litigation. The project manager and attorneys involved should learn from the client's IT personnel what happens to the documents of former employees, including email and loose documents, whether stored on the network or on each employee's workstation or laptop. Remember, it is not improper to dispose of ESI if there is no legal obligation to retain it.

Conclusion

The information management stage of a discovery project involves initiating and planning the discovery project. There are not a lot of process requirements here, but gathering and documenting information at this stage is critical to the success of a discovery project. Without some basic understanding of how a client's information is maintained, it is difficult for a project manager to assist the client and advise attorneys in the latter stages of the discovery project. The project manager's objective here is to learn as much as possible about the organization's policies and practices so that potentially relevant ESI may be properly identified and preserved. What should result from a review of a client's RIM policy is a preliminary project plan for identifying and preserving ESI.

The information governance stage of a discovery project—learning how a client creates, stores and manages its documents and ESI—provides the foundational underpinnings for many decisions that will be made later in the case. While the responsibilities associated with information governance rest for the most part with the client organization, it is important that the project manager and attorneys who advocate for the client know and understand the client's policies.

CHAPTER SIX SUMMARY

KEY POINTS

- Information governance relates to the creation, storage, access to, security, archiving, and disposition of records and information; it is the foundation of an electronic discovery project.
- The Information Governance phase of a discovery project is a planning and information-gathering process.
- Organizations should be prepared for litigation by knowing what records and information they have and where it is stored.
- Effective information governance and records management practices increase efficiency, save money, make good business sense, and aid in the discovery process.
- When a lawsuit is filed, the information possessed by a company becomes potentially relevant evidence.
- Project managers need to understand not only GARP and RIM policies, but also storage, retrieval, and general IT practices.
- Creating a sound RIM policy involves:
    - Taking inventory of organization records and information
    - Preparing a retention schedule for each type of record
    - Developing a defensible disposition practice for records
- A data map or network topology is a visual representation of an organization's IT systems and infrastructure that aids in identifying potentially relevant ESI.

Key Information Governance Tasks	Documentation
Review pleadings/motions/discovery requests and meet with legal team.	Complaint, answer, discovery requests, subpoena
Ascertain client's IT infrastructure and systems/software in place.	Litigation readiness plan/ Data map (if available)
Obtain and review for compliance records/information management policies.	Client RIM and IT policies
Establish firm and client's contacts related to discovery.	Contact list
Understand client organization's IT infrastructure.	Infrastructure questionnaire

CHAPTER SEVEN

Identification and Preservation of Electronically Stored Information

After gaining insight into the client organization's information management practices, next it will be necessary to identify and preserve potentially relevant ESI. As observed earlier, FRCP Rule 26(b) identifies the scope of discovery as "any nonprivileged matter that is relevant to any party's claim or defense and proportional to the needs of the case . . . ." The rule lists a number of factors to consider in making the proportionality determination, and it is important to remember that information need not be admissible in evidence to be discoverable.

Once an organization or individual reasonably anticipates or becomes aware of threatened or actual litigation, a legal duty arises to identify and preserve potentially relevant documents and ESI in their custody or control. To comply with this duty, a party to litigation is obligated to do two things: (1) identify and either preserve in place or physically sequester relevant documents and ESI, and (2) implement a *litigation hold*—a formal notice to individuals and departments within an organization directing that they preserve any documents or ESI they possess or control relevant to the facts and circumstances involved in a litigation. These two actions are intended to prevent the loss, alteration or deletion of potentially relevant materials, and to satisfy a party's legal obligation to preserve documents and ESI.

The types of documents and ESI and the scope of the information to be preserved will ordinarily depend upon the nature of the litigation or investigation, the substance of the claims and defenses, and the legal and factual issues of the case. Requests for documents or subpoenas and any responses or objections to those requests may also further guide the preservation effort. But document requests are typically not served until after the obligation to preserve information has lapsed, and it is therefore important to begin identifying and preserving information as soon as the duty to do so arises.

In addition, parties to litigation are under the applicable rules regarding the scope of discovery obligated to consider whether the information sought in discovery is proportional to the needs of the case, considering the importance of the issues, the amount in controversy, the parties' access to the information and the importance of the information to the issues in the case. Also to be considered are the resources available to the parties and the burden and expense of the proposed discovery. These guidelines should be kept in mind by both the party requesting documents and ESI and the party producing documents and ESI.

Project Planning in the Identification and Preservation Stage

Attorneys and clients are ultimately responsible for meeting discovery obligations. A project manager working on a discovery project is responsible to the attorneys and the client for helping to meet these obligations. Failing to properly identify and preserve data, and failing to implement a legal hold, can have severe consequences if relevant documents and ESI are lost or discarded as a result. For this reason, the need for planning is of paramount importance.

Identifying and preserving relevant documents and ESI is not only a logical extension of the information governance phase, it is also the primary planning stage of the discovery project. Here, the scope of discovery is finalized. The plans made here will guide nearly every future decision the attorneys and project manager make on the project. Specifically, a project manager should:

- Participate in meetings intended to identify the client's sources of discoverable information;
- Obtain a final list of custodians and data sources in preparation for the collection of ESI;
- Consider staffing the project directly or outsourcing to a vendor;
- Prepare an estimate of the cost to collect ESI from the client's systems;
- Develop a preliminary schedule for the collection of ESI, including the sequence and timing of the collection;
- Assess all risks associated with the collection and prepare contingency plans if necessary;
- Develop a plan for quality assessment of the collection process;
- Establish firm lines of communication between stakeholders, the project team, and any vendor;
- Prepare a status report for all stakeholders.

The plan here is to identify and preserve documents and ESI and implement a litigation hold. The attorneys and the project manager involved should understand the basic facts of the case and the dates or date range of the events leading to the dispute. In addition, either the attorney or the project manager should have some understanding of the client organization's IT infrastructure.

Identifying Documents and ESI

The next steps are to identify the key people or custodians within the organization who were involved in the events and who may possess relevant facts, information, and documents, and to identify the sources and locations of documents and ESI that may need to be preserved. These pieces of information not only aid in the identification and preservation effort, but they also help to establish limits on the scope of discovery from the outset of the case. Clients are not required to preserve every single document ever created by every person within the organization, but it is necessary to conduct a reasonable inquiry and preserve relevant information.

In most civil matters or investigations, the project manager, attorneys, and client work together to develop the parameters for identifying and preserving documents and ESI that are relevant to the case. This targeted approach is best because it limits the scope and size of the data to only those sources that may yield potentially relevant ESI. Limiting the scope of the ESI by custodian or source in the beginning helps to keep costs down.

On the other hand, if there is uncertainty regarding which sources contain or which custodians may possess potentially relevant data, or if the circumstances of the case warrant a wider scope, it may make sense to preserve entire servers or workstation hard drives through full-disk acquisition. However, full forensic acquisition of a client's email, file servers, and workstations is rarely warranted, mostly because forensic preservations that are broad in scope can be costly and time consuming. Typically, forensic preservations are reserved for cases involving suspected criminal activity such as fraud, theft of intellectual property or other proprietary information. Forensic preservation may also be used when it is necessary to trace the computer use or activities of a particular individual, to analyze computer code, or to collect and review deleted data. This is not to say that forensically preserving ESI is not a useful activity. A full-disk forensic acquisition might be appropriate, for instance, if the client organization is very small and their overall volume of ESI is small. Small amounts of data can be forensically collected fairly quickly and inexpensively. This way, a complete, pristine set of the data is available and you may return to it at any time to identify additional relevant ESI.

Whether using a targeted approach or full-disk acquisition, it is best for the attorneys on both sides to reach agreement regarding the scope of the preservation effort. Indeed, one purpose of the Rule 26(f) meet and confer requirement of the federal rules is for the parties to agree on what ESI will be preserved. It is always preferable to reach consensus and preserve only information that may be relevant, rather than to continuously revisit the preservation and collection process, or to over collect documents and ESI that will need to be reviewed and potentially produced at a later date. Addressing the scope of the preservation effort with opposing counsel in an effort to limit the volume of the ESI and the cost and time to retrieve it will not only benefit the parties involved, but will also demonstrate to the court that the parties are cooperating in discovery.

The parties may consider several criteria to limit the scope of preservation, including:

- Agreeing to preserve data from only active sources such as email, file servers, and workstations;
- Agreeing that preservation of inaccessible data (e.g., backup tapes, archives, ephemeral and deleted data) is not necessary;
- Agreeing to limit the preservation of ESI to a specific number of key individuals;
- Agreeing to limit preservation of ESI to a specific date range;
- Agreeing to use keyword searching or other filtering techniques to limit the data to only those documents responsive to a search or filter;
- For large data collections, agreeing to process a sample set of data and then analyze the potential relevance of documents in the sample;
- Exploring the use of advanced search and analytical tools to further reduce the volume of the ESI.

Any agreement reached by the parties should be put in writing. If the parties do not reach an agreement, or if opposing counsel appears to be making unreasonable discovery demands, it may be advisable to ask the court for guidance on limiting the scope of discovery. This is particularly true if the burden of discovery falls disproportionately upon one party.

Implementing a Litigation Hold

Even before the advent of computers and ESI, parties to litigation were obligated under the common law to preserve information and documents related to litigation. Given the ubiquity of court decisions discussing the issue, it would be unusual for anyone in the legal community to assert that they did not know a legal or litigation hold was necessary in a given case. As mentioned, the rules of discovery have not changed; only the locations from which one retrieves discoverable information have changed.

What does it mean to implement a litigation hold? As soon as possible after identifying the custodians and sources of documents and ESI, a litigation hold or document preservation memorandum should be circulated within the organization. This notice should inform appropriate personnel, senior management, and the IT and records departments that the company anticipates being or has been named in a legal action, and instructing them to preserve all documents and ESI relevant to the matter. The contents of a litigation hold notice should include:

- A brief summary of the nature and circumstances of the dispute;
- A statement of the obligation to preserve relevant information;
- A directive not to delete, alter or destroy any potentially relevant documents and ESI;
- The sources and types of documents to be preserved, how to properly handle them, and the consequences for failing to do so;
- A request that each recipient of the litigation hold acknowledge receipt of the notice;
- A person to contact if there are any questions.

The litigation hold notice should outline the reasonable steps to take to identify and preserve relevant information, and create a mechanism for someone other than the document custodians themselves to search for or identify potentially relevant the documents. If third parties are involved in the events of the litigation, a preservation letter should be sent to those parties requesting that they preserve the information pending the outcome of the lawsuit.

It is advisable when distributing a litigation hold to obtain confirmation from each custodian that he or she has read and understood the litigation hold notice. And, working with the client's legal and/or IT personnel, it is also advisable to monitor the hold and circulate periodic reminders, or to revise the scope or sources of potentially relevant ESI to be preserved when additional information is learned. Finally, when the lawsuit is over, it is important to remember to release the litigation hold so that the organization may resume its usual RIM practices.

Ideally, someone within the organization should be designated as the point person, responsible to oversee the preservation process and answer any questions that may arise within the organization. In-house counsel may be best suited to this role, but whoever is chosen should have clear authority to direct all personnel within the client organization and have the knowledge and ability to deal effectively with outside counsel, litigation support professionals, and IT personnel.

It is also important to take affirmative steps to safeguard against the inadvertent loss of relevant information, if necessary. This means, if it is practical, reasonable and proportional, that parties should suspend any information management, network or computer policies that require the automatic deletion or destruction of documents or ESI possessed by the custodians who possess relevant information. And lastly, IT personnel within the client organization should consider at least temporarily ceasing backup media rotation and records management personnel should be alerted that usual procedures for document disposal should be suspended until further notice. As an alternative to full cessation of backup tape rotation, it may be reasonable to pull only backup media containing potentially relevant ESI out of rotation. A client and their attorney should discuss whether or not backup media would be wholly duplicative of ESI that is available elsewhere. Similarly, with respect to auto-delete policies, it may be that by the time a litigation hold is in place some documents were disposed of before any obligation to preserve them existed and future documents may simply not be relevant. In such circumstances, it may not be necessary to suspend auto-delete policies. The point here is to have a discussion with the client, document the course of action that is taken, and alert opposing counsel and the court if necessary of the steps taken to implement a hold and preserve ESI.

Unfortunately, relevant ESI is frequently deleted due to human error, inadvertence, or the automatic operation of a computer or network systems. Such losses of data can have adverse consequences, both for the client and for outside counsel. Even the innocent deletion of ESI can potentially give rise to claims of spoliation. Conversely, the intentional destruction of discoverable information can lead to the most severe consequences, including adverse jury instructions, outright dismissal of the action, and monetary sanctions. These are a few of the reasons it is important for organizations to have information management policies governing the retention of documents and ESI.

In the end, the most important thing an organization can do to protect against the adverse consequences of accidental data loss is to impose an effective litigation hold on relevant sources of information from the outset of the case and consider suspending any backup practices and automatic deletion policies as soon as it has notice of the litigation.

Preserving Documents and ESI

Preserving documents requires that no documents or ESI related to the litigation or investigation are altered, destroyed, or deleted—including the metadata associated with electronic documents. This is accomplished first by implementing a litigation hold, which gives notice to appropriate personnel not to alter or delete ESI. The litigation hold must be directed to all people within or outside of the organization who were involved in the events or transactions leading to the litigation, and who may possess or control potentially relevant documents or ESI.

At most companies, there are several sources of potentially relevant electronic documents. Inquiry should at least be made about each of the following:

- Computer workstation or laptop hard drives (Windows and Mac);
- Email systems (e.g., MS Outlook, Lotus Notes, GroupWise);
- Personal or home directories on the company network for

each user;
- Database servers or proprietary systems and applications;
- Group or department shared drives on the company network;
- Peripheral devices (network attached devices);
- Business and personal smart phones or devices, including text messages;
- Home computers or laptops, if used for business purposes;
- Web servers, company webpages, and/or social media sites;
- ESI stored in any cloud-based applications;
- Instant messaging programs;
- Web-based news feeds and Bloomberg messages;
- External storage devices (e.g., CD/DVDs, flash drives, external drives);
- Voicemail systems (if retained);
- Archive, backup, compliance retention, and disaster recovery systems;
- Retired legacy systems.

While preservation is conceptually the same for paper and electronic documents, preserving ESI does present some unique challenges that frequently require knowledge of and skills relating to the internal operation of computers or computer forensics. ESI is stored on networks and in computer systems that sometimes make it difficult to preserve. Databases containing tables of data that are related but when view alone are often indecipherable, for example, present particularly difficult challenges. Other ESI, such as deleted data stored in a hard drive's unallocated space, frequently in a fragmented state, require a high degree of technical skill to retrieve. The complexities of a given case will often dictate how this and other types of data will be handled. Therefore, if a company is not equipped to preserve data, it is advisable to engage the services of an expert or consultant trained in preserving ESI.

Preservation also entails physically sequestering documents in a secure location with limited access by other people. ESI may be preserved in place, a process referred to as "preservation in place," by either leaving the files in their original location or, if the company has the technology to do so, by "locking" the files to prevent access to them. ESI may also be physically copied from its location and stored in a separate location or on separate media such as an external hard drive or DVD.

When moving or copying files in this way, it is essential that write-blocking software or hardware be used so that the process of the copying the files does not alter the system or file metadata. There are several cost-effective software tools on the commercial market that will enable client organizations to properly move or duplicate ESI that needs to be preserved.

Some organizations may also have a document retention or compliance system in place that automatically stores a copy of email and other documents. These systems are more common in heavily regulated industries such as banking and finance, where companies are required to retain all communications inside and outside of the organization. Generally, these retention systems are adequate at preserving ESI for litigation purposes. In such circumstances, the company is also likely to have personnel who are trained in the handling of ESI. For other companies with no such systems or personnel in place, it may be best to engage trained personnel or an outside expert to preserve the ESI properly.

It is generally considered unacceptable to simply drag and drop files to a CD, DVD, or other external storage medium. It is also generally unacceptable for a client to email potentially discoverable documents to their outside counsel or vendor. These practices alter the metadata of the documents and destroy the original file path location of the files. If an organization does not possess the software and trained personnel to preserve documents without altering them, a vendor should be engaged to perform this service.[35]

---

35   There are of course cases and circumstances in which strict preservation protocols are neither required nor warranted. For example, in small disputes where parties may have limited resources, it may be appropriate to simply copy a file or email it to one's lawyer. The origin of the file or its metadata may simply not be an issue in the case. In much the same way that forensic collection determinations are made, attorneys and their clients need to make this assessment on a case-by-

It is a good practice to document the steps undertaken during the preservation stage of a discovery project. The project manager, attorney, or client should prepare a memorandum memorializing the steps taken and the locations searched to find and preserve relevant ESI. This memorandum should also record instances in which client personnel report that they do not possess any requested material. Such a record will later aid in the determination of whether the search for and collection of ESI was reasonable and when it was completed. It will also help defend against a future claim by opposing counsel that a client's preservation effort was deficient.

Interviewing Potential Custodians

As in any lawsuit, it is necessary to debrief potential witnesses, key personnel, executives, and managers to determine their proximity to the events at issue. Such interviews are also used to inquire about the location of potentially relevant documents. Sometimes, witnesses do not recall that they have relevant information in their possession and, for this reason, it is best to conduct interviews as part of the ESI preservation effort.

Custodian interviews should be conducted by either counsel within an organization or by the company's outside counsel. Potential witnesses and custodians should not be left to identify and preserve their own documents and ESI. If a custodian indicates he may possess relevant discoverable information, proper steps should be taken by appropriate personnel to preserve that information.

Interviews should focus on custodian knowledge of or involvement in the events that are the subject of the lawsuit or investigation and the location of any potentially relevant paper or electronic documents. It is important that each interviewee understand that documents and ESI relevant to the case are sought, and they should generally be asked to err on the side of overinclusion. The types of electronic documents to be preserved will vary from client to client and case to case but, in

case basis. One recommendation is to discuss the issue with opposing counsel to determine the requirements for a particular case.

general, counsel should be interested in preserving any documents created by individuals, such as email communications, word processing documents (e.g., memoranda, letters, reports, faxes), spreadsheets, presentations, PDF-formatted documents, and documents created by client databases or proprietary systems (e.g., accounting or human resources software). There may be situations when it is necessary to collect and process audio or video files as well.

The substance of conversations with custodians should generally be documented. One practice is to use a custodian interview form[36] to record responses to questions, such as the location of specific ESI, network user names, and computer names.

From these custodian interviews, a list of key players or custodians will emerge. These are likely to be the primary individuals whose documents and ESI need to be preserved and collected. It will become obvious which divisions or departments within the company are likely to possess relevant documents. It will also become clear from witness interviews who else in the organization may possess relevant information. Be sure to include assistants and secretaries in the interview process, because these personnel often maintain files for their superiors.

Lastly, consider whether any documents or ESI from nonparties (e.g., agents, vendors, or experts) may need to be preserved and collected. There is no exception to preservation obligations because an individual or entity is not direct employed by the company. Third parties generally need to preserve ESI relevant to a lawsuit as well. To meet preservation requirements, it is advisable to send companies or individuals outside the organization a preservation letter alerting them to preserve documents and ESI relevant to the subject matter of the lawsuit.

Reasonably Accessible Data

Whether ESI is "reasonably accessible" is a question that arises

---

36   A sample custodian interview form is included in the Appendix.

in almost all electronic discovery projects. Under Rule 26(b), parties "need not provide discovery of electronically stored information from sources that the party identifies as not reasonably accessible because of undue burden or cost." This means that, if gaining access to, retrieving, restoring, or producing documents or ESI would be overly difficult or extraordinarily costly, then it may not be necessary to preserve or collect that information.

The undue burden or cost rule contemplates two classes of ESI: accessible and inaccessible. There are no precise definitions for levels of accessibility, nor are there concrete guidelines for making this determination. Each organization must define for itself what ESI is considered reasonably accessible based on the circumstances of each case and the actual degree of difficulty in retrieving it. Likewise, with respect to cost, factors that may guide a determination of reasonability include the value of the case, the availability of resources, the volume of the data, or the time it might take to retrieve the ESI.

Generally, though, organizations may conclude that *active ESI*—email servers, file servers, PC workstations, or laptops currently in use—is going to be considered reasonably accessible and, provided that preserving and collecting them is not disproportionately costly, a party would likely be required to preserve these data assets. Conversely, sources such as backup tapes intended for disaster recovery; deleted, fragmented, or ephemeral data; off-line storage or archives; and data from legacy systems may be considered inaccessible. But, again, if the cost associated with accessing certain data sources is disproportionate to the amount at stake in the litigation, counsel may decide to resist discovery of this information.

The onus for demonstrating undue burden or cost falls on the party from whom the discovery is sought. At the same time, information that is "not reasonably accessible" could still be discoverable if the requesting party is able to show "good cause." Court decisions dealing with the issue of reasonably accessible ESI appear to turn most commonly on whether or not a party is able to provide sound information about the degree of difficulty and solid cost estimates. At the Rule 26(f) conference, parties should, therefore, be prepared to discuss and agree upon which sources of data will be preserved and collected. If there is a claim of inaccessible data, it will be necessary for the participants in the conference to also have a good understanding of the organization's technology infrastructure, as well as an accurate estimate of the costs necessary to retrieve, process, and review the ESI. The project manager's responsibilities are to advise the attorneys and the client on the practicality, cost, and time associated with identifying and preserving documents and ESI.

Documenting and Monitoring the Litigation Hold

As the litigation or investigation continues, an organization should monitor compliance with the litigation hold by periodically sending reminder notices and conferring with client personnel to ensure relevant documents and ESI are being retained. If additional custodians or sources of data are identified, it is necessary to reissue the litigation hold to include the new custodians.

A best practice regarding preservation and litigation holds is to prepare a memorandum documenting the efforts undertaken to identify and preserve documents and ESI. The memo should include:

- The date the duty to preserve arose;
- The date the litigation hold was initiated and by whom;
- The scope of the information, custodians, or systems to be preserved;
- Confirmation of compliance from custodians and handling of exceptions;
- A description of any preservation protocol, search, or limiting parameters.

Ideally, such a memorandum should be drafted by an attorney to protect the client's privileged and/or work product confidences. The memorandum should not reveal any strategy, legal analysis, or advice. Notwithstanding the confidential nature of this kind of memo, as it may be necessary to refer back to or share information from this document at a later date if the preservation effort is called into question. If the preservation effort is ever challenged, the memorandum should demonstrate that a reasonable, good-faith effort was made to identify and preserve information relevant to the case.

Conclusion

The identification and preservation phase is arguably the most important phase of a discovery project. ESI that is identified and preserved at this stage is the universe of data that is used throughout the remainder of the case. It is time consuming and costly to return to a client to identify and preserve additional ESI at a later stage of litigation. But doing it right the first time, with a proper litigation hold, custodian interviews, and communication and interaction with the client's IT personnel, will ensure the right ESI is preserved. Having identified and preserved the ESI, the project manager must now move into the collection stage of the project.

CHAPTER SEVEN SUMMARY

KEY POINTS

- The duty to identify and preserve documents and ESI arises once litigation is reasonably anticipated, threatened, or actually commenced.
- Identifying and preserving relevant documents and ESI is the primary planning stage of a discovery project.
- Identification of ESI involves identifying the custodians and locating the sources of potentially relevant documents and ESI.
- Preservation requires two steps: (1) implementing a litigation hold, and (2) physically preserving documents and ESI.
- A litigation hold is a formal notice not to alter or delete documents and ESI potentially relevant to a lawsuit.
- Interviews of custodians help to identify sources of ESI.
- Limiting the scope and volume of ESI should begin during identification and preservation phase of a project.

Key Identification and Preservation Tasks	Documentation
Identify custodians/departments/third parties in possession of potentially relevant documents/ESI.	Custodian list
Identify systems/data assets containing potentially relevant ESI.	Source log/data map/ system topology
Determine scope of duty to preserve (custodians, date range, systems).	Preliminary scope statement for collection
Determine whether ESI is reasonably accessible.	
Determine proportionality of preservation.	
Implement litigation hold.	Litigation hold notice
Suspend RIM disposition, auto-delete, and backup media rotation policies.	
Send preservation demand to opposing/ third parties.	Preservation letter
Interview custodians/IT staff regarding creation, storage, and management of documents and ESI.	Custodian interview form

CHAPTER SEVEN SUMMARY (cont'd)

Key Identification and Preservation Tasks	Documentation
Identify and mitigate any potential spoliation issues.	Memorandum to case file
Complete identification/preservation documentation.	Questionnaire
Assist to prepare for meet and confer/ preliminary conference.	Meet and Confer checklist
Monitor preservation and litigation hold.	Status report/ memorandum to case file

CHAPTER EIGHT

Collection of Electronically Stored Information

Electronic documents stored on an organization's computer systems are best collected by properly trained personnel. Trained technicians, computer examiners, and certified forensic examiners use industry-accepted software tools that track and verify the file collection process and that write-block individual files during the collection, thus preventing alteration of the ESI. Although, as noted previously, a full forensic collection is usually not required, experience proves that using personnel trained and certified in ESI collection techniques may be one of the most important decisions made during a discovery project. This is true for several reasons. First, if ESI is not properly collected using write-protection tools to preserve the metadata, the potential for problems later in the project—during processing, review, and production—will increase exponentially at each phase. If, for example, a case turns on whether or not a party took action or knew something on a specific date, and an electronic document that resolves the issue was collected in a way that altered or did not preserve the file and system dates, then the party advancing the argument is going to have difficulty making their point. Additionally, in most cases, it is necessary to produce certain fields of metadata. If ESI is collected improperly, some metadata may be impossible to produce.

A second reason for using trained examiners is to transfer some of the risk associated with a technical process to experts trained and accustomed to performing such work. Few corporations or law firms are staffed with computer forensics experts trained in electronic discovery, and fewer have the tools necessary to perform a proper collection. Engaging an outside expert or vendor for this purpose mitigates and transfers the risk to that vendor, and ensures the collection is performed properly.

Third, it is rarely a good idea to subject individuals at a client organization to scrutiny regarding how they collected their own ESI. Individual custodians or IT professionals may not recognize the relevance of certain electronic documents, and the process of self-selecting ESI may lead to errors and/or inadvertent spoliation of data. Trained examiners and others who regularly collect ESI, on the other hand, are accustomed to collecting ESI, providing expert testimony regarding their processes if necessary, and preparing chain of custody and other reports associated with collecting ESI.

This is not to say that, in appropriate circumstances, a client organization may not ever collect their own ESI. Indeed, it happens all the time. There are affordable software tools on the market that make the defensible collection of ESI fairly simple, although they do require some technical ability. The question for the organization and perhaps their outside counsel is how much risk they are willing to assume in connection with the collection. If the collection or discovery process becomes contentious, it may be necessary for whomever performed the collection to provide sworn testimony, and most lawyers prefer that their client or IT personnel not be required to testify. Once again, each case turns on its own unique circumstances and the collection method used should be based on the needs of the case.

Planning the Collection

The collection phase of a discovery project involves further iterative planning and requires the project manager to execute several tasks:

- Initiate the collection by working with the attorneys and client to outline in a written collection specification the scope of ESI to be collected, including the sources of ESI and custodians;

- Engage a collection examiner or other trained personnel, either internally or externally, and prepare a statement of work and cost estimate;
- Plan the collection in a team kick-off meeting that covers the scope, activities, schedule, and logistics of the collection;
- Establish clear lines of communication among the collection team and stakeholders;
- Assess and prepare for any risks associated with ESI collection;
- Ensure that quality controls are carried out to validate the proper collection of the ESI;
- Ensure proper chain of custody documentation is prepared;
- Prepare a status report at the conclusion of the collection to update stakeholders on the progress of the project.

During a collection project, the objectives are to perform a comprehensive—but not overinclusive—collection, maintain the integrity of the ESI collected, and provide for proper documentation to maintain the chain of custody and to establish the authenticity of the documents. At the same time, the collection must not disrupt the organization's business operations.

Adequate planning is critical to the success of the collection effort. Project managers are best suited to coordinate collections because of their knowledge of network and computer systems, experience with the processes involved, and familiarity in dealing with vendors who perform collections. The project manager is responsible for communicating with client's IT personnel and the individual performing the collection, and should coordinate, schedule, and monitor the actual collection process. During and after the collection, the project manager is responsible for reporting to the legal team the status of the collection.

A necessary starting point for any ESI collection effort is the data map of the organization's network systems. Together with information obtained during interviews conducted earlier, the project manager and the individual performing the collection will identify the specific data assets, network locations, workstations, or peripheral devices from which ESI is to be collected. IT personnel within the client organization should provide as much detail as possible about its systems, including file path information to individual user shares or departmental shares that will be collected, and computer names and passwords for user workstations. IT personnel will also need to provide administrative-level access to the organization's network servers.

Based on interviews of the client's personnel performed earlier, the legal team and the client should have developed a list of custodians and established the relevant date range of the documents. A list of keywords, concepts, or the general subject matter of documents may be formulated to facilitate a targeted search for relevant documents or to identify individual data stores, folders, directories, or entire machines. If, instead of targeted searching, forensic images of workstations or servers are to be taken, these assets should be clearly identified by the client organization's IT personnel.

The project manager also must coordinate with the case team and the client to determine exactly which types of data will be collected. Generally, there is active data (email and other documents and databases currently in use) and inactive data (offline storage, archives, and backups). The most typical sources of active ESI are:

- Computer workstation or laptop hard drives;
- Email systems (e.g., MS Outlook, Lotus Notes);
- Network, personal, or home directories for each user;
- Network group or departmental shared drives;
- Peripheral devices (e.g., network attached devices, personal storage devices, or other media);
- Smart phones or mobile devices (including text messages);
- Home computers or laptops (if used for business purposes);
- Company websites and/or social media sites;
- Instant messaging systems, Bloomberg messages;
- Voice messages (if retained).

It is also necessary to decide whether deleted data or unallocated space must be collected. As most people who use a computer already understand, pressing the Delete button on a keyboard or dragging a file to the Recycle Bin does not permanently delete a file. Computer hard drives and servers store deleted files in the unused space on the drives, called *unallocated space*. When a file is deleted, the file name and the associated metadata are deleted only from the file allocation table that stores information about the file. The data may remain on the drive until the system needs space to store additional files and that unused space is overwritten with the new files. Because data on most computers is fragmented into different sectors on a drive, even after new files overwrite deleted data, parts or fragments of files may still exist on the drive in the space (known as *slack space*) leftover after a new file partially overwrites a deleted file.[37]

Normally, deleted data need only be collected in cases involving computer fraud, intellectual property theft, or where the habits of a computer user are at issue. Because of the special attributes associated with the collection of deleted or fragmented ESI, a forensic expert should be engaged to collect and analyze data from the unallocated space of a drive.

When planning to collect ESI, it is always best to reach agreement with the other parties on the most important discovery issues. First, the parties should agree on the scope of the data to be collected, including custodian names, the date range of documents, file types, and the physical location of the ESI to be collected. Second, the importance of metadata to the case should be considered and the parties should agree whether or not it is necessary. Third, the use of search terms or other limiting or filtering criteria may be helpful, and the parties

---

37   These principles related to file deletion, unallocated space, and slack space are applicable to the magnetic media plates that make up the typical commercial hard drive today. A forensic examiner can usually recover deleted files from a magnetic hard drive. New solid state drives (SSDs) do not store data in the same way and do not have the unallocated space of magnetic drives. Instead, SSD storage devices use flash memory chips, most of which are immediately overwritten when a file is deleted. Some SSDs do provision a portion of the drive for better file management, but because this technology is relatively new it is not entirely clear how forensic examiners may attempt to recover deleted data from an SSD drive, or if it will be possible at all.

may want to agree upon the use of them. Finally, the format of the eventual production should be agreed upon as well. The FRCP and many state and local rules require the parties to meet and confer on these issues and to develop an electronic discovery plan and schedule, and it has become quite common throughout the legal industry for parties to enter into agreements or to sign stipulated discovery orders at the outset of litigation. Doing so is prudent because it signifies to the court and to the parties involved that there is an interest in the collection effort being orderly, efficient, and proportional.

Collecting ESI

When collecting ESI, the metadata associated with the electronic documents should not only be collected but it also should not be altered. Metadata is the hidden data or properties associated with electronic documents. The term most commonly refers to data elements, attributes, or properties of a document—such as the date it was created, the author, any Track Changes, and who last accessed or printed the document. When files are copied or moved on a computer using typical Windows functions (i.e., so-called "drag-and-drop" or "cut-and-paste" features), the operating system automatically updates the file creation data and other metadata. To preserve the metadata during a collection, write-blocking tools are used to prevent writing to the files as they are collected.

There are several ways to collect ESI, and the method used depends upon the circumstances of each case. The project manager and collection examiner should discuss with the legal team and the client which of the following methods for collecting ESI will be used:

Full Disk or Forensic Collection

Full disk acquisition is the process of using specialized software to make a bit-for-bit or forensic copy of an entire hard drive, server, or other media. This process copies all the resident data, including any recoverable deleted files—provided the data has not been overwritten—and captures any data in the slack space or unallocated space of a drive. This process is typically reserved for workstation or laptop hard drives when there is a reasonable possibility data was deleted, either inadvertently or intentionally, or when tracking user activity is an issue. It may also be used to collect an entire file server. When performing a full disk acquisition, it is best to use a certified computer forensic technician who is accustomed to large-scale data collections. A full disk acquisition generally takes longer to perform because it is copying the entire contents of a drive, but it provides a complete copy of the data asset, which allows the advantage of returning to the collected data at any time without having to return to the company's systems.

Directed or Targeted Collection

A directed or targeted collection involves the identification and collection of user-created files from specific locations on a hard drive, network server, or other media. Deleted data is generally not collected during a targeted collection, nor are files that are not recognized by the operating system. A directed collection can be designed to collect documents created by particular users or custodians, by file type, or in particular folders or directories that are identified in advance. Carefully designed keyword search terms may also be used to identify and collect documents, or documents within a certain date range. The advantage of a directed or targeted collection is that only ESI that is identified in advance or that is responsive to a search is collected. System files are normally excluded from a directed. Targeted collections normally result in a significantly reduced volume of documents.38

---

38   When considering the use of keyword searches during collection, it is vital to carefully design search parameters, particularly keyword search terms. The results of a search are only as good as the search itself. For example, searching for the word "insurance" in a case involving insurance is going to yield too many documents. Any keyword searching is also limited by the vagaries of language, spelling errors, the quality of the text contained in documents that have been scanned or faxed or copied multiple times, and of course the search tool employed.

Server-Based Email Collection

Unlike other user-generated electronic documents, such as Microsoft Word or Excel files, most email communications are not stored as stand-alone documents. Rather, email systems are actually sophisticated databases. Each piece of information relating to a particular email is stored in a table and what the user sees in the interface of the email application is a rendering of that data in an organized, memorandum-like format that makes it easy to read. Email is generally stored in a database and is exported from that database in a container-like file, called a .PST file for Microsoft Outlook Exchange, or an .NSF file for Lotus Notes application. The administrative features in email applications permit an email or network administrator to export a user's mailbox as a PST or NSF file, or to export certain folders within the mailbox. It is also possible to export a PST file using Windows PowerShell, a command line and scripting tool available in Microsoft Windows environments. Exporting email in these container files will not alter the metadata of individual email files. Searching emails, however, presents some challenges. It is ordinarily not recommended that searches be conducted in Outlook itself, for example, because the search features of Outlook are limited, and earlier versions of Outlook (prior to 2013) do not search email attachments. Later versions do a better job of indexing attachments.

Web-Based Email Collection

Email services administered by Internet Service Providers (also known as Application Service Providers or Cloud Service Providers) such as Google, Yahoo, or AOL, present unique challenges for collection. The email messages do not usually reside on a local PC or server, but on the service provider's servers—to which the average citizen does not have access. Unlike email stored on an organization's internal email server, information stored in these Web-based email systems is not easily exported from the ISP's servers. Of course, it is possible to make a request to or even serve a subpoena upon the service provider that maintains the email, but such efforts are usually resisted by the service provider on privacy grounds, or because releasing such information would violate the Stored Communications Act. One way to collect Web-based email is to set up an MS Outlook client on a local PC machine and use either the POP3 or IMAP features in the Outlook client to import the Web-based email into the local instance of Outlook, and then export the messages as a PST file from Outlook. This is not a recommended procedure for a novice, and it is important to understand that the process could result in the permanent alteration of the email messages and damage the integrity of the metadata. If it is necessary to collect Web-based email, it is advisable consult with an expert who has experience on proper procedures.39

Backup Media Collection

Collecting backup media presents unique challenges. First, it should be recognized that interrupting a company's backup processes may be disruptive to company operations. Second, backup tapes may contain huge volumes of data and are generally not readily accessible. In fact, backup tapes typically store data in a compressed format to maximize the storage space on the tape or other media. Backup media will usually need to be restored to a useable format before individual documents or data stores may be searched for or collected. Resorting to backup tapes should typically occur only if there is no other means to collect the requested ESI. It is important to remember, too, that in most organizations, backup tapes exist for disaster recovery purposes, not for litigation. It can be expensive and time consuming to restore, index, search, and retrieve documents from backup tapes. Still, most organizations will have backup policies and practices. There are likely to be instances where backup media is the only source of ESI, and a project manager should be prepared to collect and process data on backup media, if necessary.

---

39   Google has recently introduced a feature that enables a user to export the contents of their account, including Gmail, and download the content to a local machine. Facebook has long allowed this option for its users.

Manual Collection

Manual collection is the process of simply copying files from a hard drive or network location to some form of external media. This method of collecting ESI is ordinarily the least favored technique for collection because it alters the operating system metadata of the documents. Manual collection typically relies upon individual users or client IT personnel to copy the documents, which creates several potential problems. First, the collector tends to open each file when looking to determine whether documents must be collected. This may result in inadvertent alteration of the document. Second, if issues arise regarding the collection process, each user or IT person involved may be required to testify regarding how documents were collected. Third, many network systems are secured, and prevent users from accessing network drives or even their own hard drives. Such security interferes with the collection of necessary documents. Indeed, many users do not always know where they saved documents or if they saved them to multiple locations. Fourth, email systems such as Outlook and Lotus Notes generally do not permit users to copy a single email to an external location or to export their mailbox or folders. Collecting documents using the manual copy method should be reserved solely for cases where the parties have unequivocally agreed that formal collection procedures are not necessary in discovery. Even with such an agreement in place, the rules of evidence pertaining to foundation and authentication may still present obstacles to introducing manually copied documents into evidence.

Collecting Social Media and Mobile Device ESI

Electronically stored information created or stored on smartphones, tablet devices, and social media sites or webpages is frequently subject to collection in connection with litigation today. Given the ubiquity of mobile devices and their use by nearly everyone, it should come as no surprise that the data collected from these sources may be used for example to establish the timing of an event or the content of a text message. Likewise, social media sites like Facebook, Twitter and LinkedIn now have billions of users and these sites and others are fast becoming a means for communicating and sharing information. All of the data on these devices and websites is discoverable if relevant to a litigation. However, gaining access to this data and preserving it for collection may be limited for several reasons. First, call logs, text messages, calendars, and social media data is constantly changing. Second, in some instances the data is affected by the privacy settings imposed by individual users. Third, social media data may not even be controlled by the account holder, and absent the user's consent or a court order, collecting such data may violate the Stored Communications Act. Lastly, smartphone and social media data comes in many different formats, from very different platforms, and is stored in different ways. When genuinely necessary, it may be that the best way to collect this data is to obtain the user's consent and then use the appropriate tools to capture the information. There are several products on the commercial market capable of capturing web-based content and most service providers will have access to these tools. As for sites like Facebook and Google, the account holder has the ability to download data associated with her account. It is recommended, however, that someone other than the account holder actually perform the download.

ESI Stored in Databases

Almost all organizations use databases to store financial information, human resources data, customer relations, sales and marketing information, and more. The manner in which data is stored in these databases does not lend itself to typical ESI collection practices. Information in a database is most commonly stored in tables similar to large spreadsheets. There might be a table for customer addresses, a separate table for sales lead generation, or another for accounts receivable. The tables may or may not be related to each other, but either way, taken alone, such tables are just lists of information that are not very useful. What makes the information in databases useful to an organization are the search and reporting features in the application itself. These features are normally presented though a user or graphical interface or a web browser, and they enable a user to create a query that yields responsive information. Without the database application, however, the data in the table of the database may not be useful in discovery. So, while it is clearly advisable to preserve a copy of a database at a point in time that is appropriate to litigation, the most cost-effective and reasonable means of collecting the data may be to export reports that are responsive to specific document requests. One recommendation is to confer with opposing parties and agree on an efficient and affordable method for collecting information in databases.

Documenting the Collection of ESI

Regardless of the collection method employed, the collection examiner and project manager responsible for the collection effort should create an acquisition report or collection log. This report documents the sources and quantities of ESI collected. Each piece of media on which collected ESI is stored should be given a unique ID number. The collection log should contain this ID number, the source or custodian name, the date of the collection, and a description of the data. The log or report prepared by the collection examiner should also identify any problems or anomalies that occur during the collection.

The project manager should also ensure that a formal chain of custody form is initiated at the conclusion of the collection. A chain of custody form maintains the integrity of the collection effort. It includes the name of every person who touches the media on which collected ESI is stored, beginning with the person performing the collection. The chain of custody form should also contain the unique ID number for each piece of media, the name of the person handling the media, and the dates on which possession or custody was transferred. Should the integrity of the collection be called into question, the chain of custody will be one way of demonstrating a defensible collection was performed.[40]

Conclusion

The collection process is a critical stage of any discovery project because activities undertaken at this stage affect every subsequent stage. It is essential that a collection be performed in a defensible manner. Using trained personnel who are knowledgeable and skilled in the collection of ESI, in the planning and documenting the collection process, and in initiating a chain of custody are the critical elements of a sound, defensible collection process.

The project manager is responsible for working the attorneys and the client to plan and execute the collection effort, and for monitoring, controlling, and ensuring the quality of the collection. Having a sound, defensible collection strategy provides a strong foundation for later stages of work on the discovery project.

---

40   A sample chain of custody form is included in the Appendix.

CHAPTER EIGHT SUMMARY

KEY POINTS

- Collecting ESI is the most important aspect of the electronic discovery project because, if the collection is mishandled, it can lead to irreversible complications later in the project.
- Collections should be performed by trained personnel or forensic technicians using industry-acceptable tools.
- Using trained personnel avoids client self-collection, eliminates scrutiny of the client regarding the collection, and transfers risk to an expert accustomed to performing collections.
- Collections must be performed in a defensible manner that preserves the metadata associated with electronic documents.
- Metadata is largely hidden data elements, attributes, or properties associated with electronic documents, such as dates, author, Track Changes, etc.
- Planning in the collection phase includes gathering information, meeting with stakeholders, and preparing a collection specification.
- There are several procedures used for collecting ESI; the method used depends on the unique circumstances of each case.
- To demonstrate a sound, defensible ESI collection process, appropriate documentation is prepared during collection.

Key Collection Tasks	Documentation
Determine the scope of the collection.	Scope statement
Determine the collection type.	Collection specification
Determine resources, tools, and techniques.	Vendor documents (conflicts, NDA, SOW)
Engage resources to perform collection.	
Compile all pre-collection documentation	Custodian list, data map, machine names, etc.
Determine collection workflow, tools, and techniques.	

CHAPTER EIGHT SUMMARY (cont'd)

Confirm and schedule collection with client.	
Perform collection and validation.	
Prepare/obtain acquisition report or collection log.	Acquisition report/collection log
Initiate/obtain chain of custody documentation.	Chain of custody
Close collection/prepare status report for case team.	Status report

CHAPTER NINE

Processing Electronically Stored Information

After ESI has been collected, the data is usually copied to a network file server in preparation for processing. As an initial matter, when staging ESI from a client for processing, it is important to store the data in a consistent and systematic manner. Client data should be organized on the server in folders or file directories that are named for the client-matter or case to which the data is related.[41] Processing software is then pointed to the appropriate file server location to process the data that has been collected.

The overall objective during the processing phase of a discovery project is to prepare electronic documents for review and eventual production to other parties. Once a client's ESI is collected, it must be processed and converted to a format suitable for attorney review and analysis. This involves taking electronic documents—typically collected in a wide variety of native file formats—ingesting them into an industry-accepted processing software tool, extracting and indexing the metadata and text of each file, and creating data and image load files.

The processing software ingests the files and extracts the metadata and text of each document, storing this information in a fielded table in a database. The pages of each file are then either converted

---

41   Depending upon a number of variables it is advisable when staging client data to perform and initial scan of the client data for viruses and malware so as not to introduce infected data to the server environment.

to static TIFF images or maintained in their native or near-native format. Processing of ESI results in a deliverable that consists of the TIFF images and/or native files; a data file containing the extracted metadata; an image load file for loading images to a document review platform; and the text extracted from documents or, for documents from which text could not be extracted, the OCR-generated text. Any paper documents are typically scanned to TIFF, undergo OCR, and are delivered with an image load file and searchable text.

One thing to keep in mind at the outset of the processing phase is the importance of proper chain of custody documentation. Remember, the documents that have been collected may be evidence in a court proceeding. There should be a process for the intake and cataloging of ESI and documents following collection. In the very least, the project manager should log the intake of any media received from a client or vendor. If a project manager hands over the data to a third party vendor for processing, she should be sure to record that transmission, preferably on a standardized chain of custody form. It may be necessary to the eventual authentication and possible admission into evidence of these documents that a party be able to demonstrate a defensible argument for the integrity of the data. Thus, where data is sent to a vendor or otherwise changes hands, an entry in the chain of custody should be made.

At this stage in the project, the project manager will be coordinating technical processes and the staff and service providers performing the processing. Like each previous stage, the project manager will plan, execute, monitor, and control the processing phase, including the following objectives:

- Meet with the legal team to discuss their processing and review requirements, including filtering, searching and de-duplication;
- Work with the attorneys to prepare a written processing specification identifying how documents will be processed;
- Give direction to the technician or vendor performing the processing;
- Monitor project performance during the processing;

- Quality check the output upon the completion of processing;
- Record processing metrics and report on project performance.

Processing is performed on ESI for two basic reasons: (1) to reduce the volume of the data and (2) to facilitate more efficient document review.

Processing to Reduce the Volume of Documents

Processing seems much simpler than it actually is. One goal in the processing phase is to reduce the volume of documents that need to be reviewed by attorneys. The easiest way to reduce the volume of data to process and review is to limit the collection in the first case by source, custodian, and/or date range. Collecting only the documents that are required or agreeing with other parties to collect only from a select number of custodians or sources of documents limited to a defined time period eliminates unnecessary documents from the outset.

During the processing phase, several tools may be employed to further reduce the size of a data set. The project manager must confer with the legal team to determine precisely which tools will be used, and then prepare the processing specification that memorializes the process.

File Filtering and Exclusion

Filtering documents by date range, file type, or other limiting characteristics often occurs during processing to eliminate documents that could not contain potentially responsive material. Date filtering is a simple and efficient way to reduce the volume of documents to be processed and reviewed. Most cases will have a period of time in which relevant events or actions by the parties to the lawsuit took place. All of the metadata will be extracted and indexed during the processing phase, including the dates documents were created and modified so it is easy to filter documents by date.42 When filtering by

---

42   The importance of proper collection protocols is highlighted here. If, during the collection process, the system or file dates of documents are altered, either by failing to use write-protecting tools or by simply copying files, then

date, be sure to consider all of the date fields upon which the filter will be applied; overlooking a date field may result in missing documents within the time period.

Removing certain types of files from a population of electronic documents is another of the easiest and fastest filtering tools available during processing. One effective tool for doing this is a process known as *de-NISTing*, named after the National Institute of Standards and Technology (NIST), an agency of the U.S. Department of Commerce. The NIST agency has compiled a list of computer system files and their file extensions, which may be used by most processing software to exclude known system files. This culling method removes system files—those necessary to the operation of a computer or software application but not created by computer users—from the data set prior to processing. It is highly unlikely that system files will contain information that is relevant to the litigation. In some cases, however— namely some intellectual property litigations involving computer programming code—even system files or programming code itself may be relevant and discoverable. Industry-accepted ESI processing applications will have the ability to filter out the long list of file types on the NIST list of system and application files.

Electronic documents may also be filtered by file type. Typical computer users only really create a handful of file types, the vast majority of them with applications such as Microsoft Word, Excel, or PowerPoint. While text-based documents may not always be created in Adobe Acrobat, the ubiquity of documents in the Adobe Portable Document Format or PDF suggests this is another popular user-created file. Given that there are limited ways for users to create content, it may be sensible in a given case to filter by file type. But this decision must be made by the parties to the litigation, hopefully during a meet and confer session.

A word of caution is appropriate here: File extensions alone are not the best means for filtering documents because file extensions may be changed. Rather, it is best to search the header information

---

filtering or searching by some date fields may yield faulty results.

of documents to determine the actual file type, and most advanced processing tools have this capability.

Deduplication

Processing software can identify and remove duplicate documents and further reduce the collected ESI to a more manageable size. There is no more frustrating aspect of attorney document review than coming across the same document multiple times. It is inefficient and costly to look at the same document twice. If an email is sent to multiple recipients, that email will exist in each recipient's Inbox, plus the sender's Sent Items. Left untouched, that email will likely be reviewed and produced multiple times. There is no value in reviewing multiple times the same email sent to five different people. Worse yet is realizing that two different attorneys have reviewed and considered the same document in very different ways. For this reason, it is customary to deduplicate documents.

Deduplication is an automated process applied to a defined set of electronic documents to identify identical documents. The most common deduplication programs use an algorithm that is run against documents in a data set. Each document is assigned a numerical value, called a *hash value*, based on the unique properties, attributes, text, and characteristics of the document. The hash value is considered the digital fingerprint of an electronic document. It is virtually impossible for two documents to have an identical hash value—unless they are duplicates. Depending upon the processing software in use, other properties of a document may also help identify duplicate documents. During deduplication, the processing software compares the hash values of documents and identifies any that are identical. The duplicates are then set aside and not processed, thus reducing the number of documents that need to be processed and reviewed.

Deduplication of documents may take place (1) across all data sources and custodians, known as global or horizontal deduplication, or (2) within custodian, known as vertical deduplication. The former will usually result in a larger reduction of documents, but there is a chance, depending upon whether all of the data is processed at once and in a particular order, that the best original document may be deduplicated and set aside if a copy of it is encountered first during processing.

Keyword Search

During processing, searches may be performed to locate documents that will then be processed and prepared for attorney review. Most commonly, keyword search terms can be used to effectively search across a universe of documents and identify files containing certain words or phrases and thereby limit the processing to just those documents.

The use of keyword search terms is a widely accepted and fairly simple means for identifying potentially relevant documents. However, traditional keyword searching has been criticized as overly simplistic, naively incomplete, and likely to overlook relevant documents. Critics argue that selecting, for example, ten key words that relate to a case and searching for those terms across a document population will, given the vagaries of language and the written word, result in a less-than-ideal set of potentially relevant documents.

Still, keyword search remains the most popular method for identifying relevant ESI in discovery because, if performed correctly, it satisfies the needs of most litigants, it is cost-effective, and fairly simple to perform. But it is important to have transparency in the process. Parties should meet and confer to discuss search terms.

One often-overlooked fact is that a party and its attorneys are undoubtedly in a better position to know the contents of their own documents than the opposing party, and are therefore able to develop and recommend better search terms for identifying relevant ESI. A good practice, then, is to confer with opposing counsel and agree upon a list of keyword search terms. In this way, both parties are getting what they want, and the chance of adversarial motion practice or distracting satellite litigation on discovery issues is significantly reduced.

At the same time, not all documents responsive to a keyword search should be promoted to the document review stage. Rather, it is necessary to test the search terms and ensure they are hitting on the right, relevant documents. It is important to ensure that the search is not too broad, returning more documents than necessary. It is equally as important to ensure that the search is not too narrow and missing relevant documents. If a search term is used that should logically yield results but does not, the project team must investigate further to determine why; it is possible that relevant documents were not collected or that the search syntax is incorrect. Finally, consider spelling; less-than-perfect OCR generated from aged, paper documents and the limits of language itself may result in inaccurate search outcomes. The use of search terms to reduce the volume of discovery materials may be simplistic but, in many cases, it proves an acceptable and cost-effective alternative to complex and expensive analytical or concept-based tools.

Processing to Facilitate Efficient Document Review

Eventually, attorneys must review the processed documents to determine their relevance to the issues in the case. Sophisticated tools may be used to render the review process more efficient. These tools are not processing tools, per se, but they may be used during the processing phase to organize the extracted data and text of documents in such a way that, once loaded to a review platform, the documents may be reviewed more efficiently.

Near Deduplication

Near deduplication is not the same as deduplication, although it relies on similar technology. It can be an effective tool during document review, particularly in grouping similar documents together. Near deduplication examines the contents of files—usually the text or body of the document—and compares that content to other documents in a data set. The results identify documents that are similar, but not identical. Most software allows for the setting of a threshold level of similarity, or ranks documents based on their percentage of similarity. And some programs can highlight the minor differences in documents, making it easier to see why they are near-duplicates. Near deduplication is useful for grouping together documents such as drafts or slightly revised versions of documents, thereby allowing them to be reviewed together, reducing the time to review each document separately, and avoiding the possibility of different reviewers inconsistently coding similar documents.

Email Threading

Email threading is also useful during document review and may be used to reduce the number of emails and attachments that need to be reviewed. This process compares the message ID or other metadata in an email and determines whether the emails are part of the same conversation or email string. If they are, the email threading application groups the related email strings together and may highlight the last and most complete email in the chain. This enables review of related emails together or, if circumstances permit, review of just that last, most inclusive email, and can result in considerable time and cost savings.

Data Analytics

Recently, analytics software has emerged in the legal field as a result of the need to sift through large volumes of ESI collected and prepared for production in discovery. Analytics technologies may be used to find, group, or cluster documents together based on concepts, phrases, domain locations, author, and recipient in an email string or other content.43 Conceptual search, one of the more common forms of analytics, involves identifying key documents and then, using the text or data within those key documents, performing a search that effectively says, "find more like these." Documents may then be categorized or coded based on their conceptual similarity, as opposed to reviewing all documents and categorizing them one at a time as the

---

43   Not all analytics tools are deployed during the processing stage of a project. Depending upon the processing software in use and the document review platform to be used later, these tools may be activated in the review stage of the project as well.

review proceeds. Clustering is another form of analytics, and it is able to automatically categorize documents without human intervention based on the conceptual content of the documents. This may be useful if there is a need to review only certain categories of documents. Most analytics software can also score or rank documents based on their conceptual similarity to a key document, which enables review teams to make faster, more accurate judgments regarding the relevance of the documents. These tools are useful both when preparing to review a client's documents and when analyzing incoming document productions from other parties.

Analytics software uses algorithms that combine the disciplines of linguistics and math. There are several different applications and theories about which algorithm and which commercial product yields the most precise results but, at its core, what makes analytics software useful in the legal industry and in discovery projects in particular, is the ability to understand the relationship between words and phrases and to identify conceptual content. For example, at its most basic level, when searching for "pet," the results of an analytics search will include things such as "dog" and "cat," because it understands these are pets. This relationship and the use and frequency of terms, as well as their relationship to other terms, make analytics a powerful, time-saving tool that increases the speed and accuracy of document review.

Whatever tools are used in the processing phase, it is critical that the workflow developed is followed consistently throughout the lifecycle of a project or case. In addition, it is recommended that the methodology be memorialized in writing for future reference in the event it becomes necessary to defend the process. Consistency combined with proper documentation are the cornerstones of a defensible ESI processing strategy.

Developing an ESI Processing Plan

Preplanning is critical to a successful ESI processing project. Because the processing phase can be costly and time consuming, attorneys and the client should be involved in the decision-making process, and processing decisions should be made in consultation with the project manager. The project manager must work with a case team to develop detailed processing specifications. These specifications, together with the volume of data and the time frame for conducting the document review, will drive the nature, scope, and cost of the processing phase, the document review, and the eventual production.

One of the first things to consider is the review platform or database application that will be used to perform the document review. The project manager and the case team should review the specifications and capabilities of the review platform to ensure there is no misunderstanding regarding the documents that will be loaded to the database.

Will de-NISTing take place? Will the documents be deduplicated within custodian (horizontally) or across custodians (vertically)? Will search terms or other filtering take place at the processing stage? Will any form of analytics be used to cull and prepare the documents for review? What will be the format of the deliverable following processing – native, near-native or TIFF images? These are just some of the questions the project manager and case team must answer prior to processing.

It is also important to decide not only what data to process and how it will be processed, but also whether the data will be processed in any particular order, what format will best facilitate attorney review, and how and by whom the documents are to be reviewed. The project manager and attorneys should also consider the schedule and timing of the review, and the timing of productions. Deadlines and any specific production requirements must be known to the project manager.

Format of the Deliverable

Following the extraction of metadata and text, electronic documents are then either converted into a format such as a TIFF images, or they may be delivered in native or near-native form. Either way, a processing deliverable is prepared that includes the file itself or a converted TIFF of the file, a data file that contains the extracted metadata, and a load file that facilitates the proper loading of the documents to a database review platform. The text or body of the documents will also be delivered. The deliverable must be formatted to facilitate proper and efficient loading of the documents to the document review platform. Below are typical deliverable formats once processing is complete.

TIFF or Native Format

There are essentially two formats into which ESI may be processed: TIFF image or native format.44 It is common to have native files rendered as and delivered in the single-page TIFF image format. This is because TIFFs are static, difficult to alter, and are viewable using a single software application. TIFFs are easily endorsed with sequential Bates numbers for later reference, and redactions are easily applied to them. TIFFs also utilize less storage space than native file formats. When rendering a native file to TIFF, it is standard practice to unhide all data associated with a document. Thus, hidden comments or columns in a Word or Excel document are visible on the TIFF images.45

Most document review platforms today are also capable of accepting and displaying a rendering of the native file, or they have the ability to open the native file itself. Native file delivery has some advantages, not the least of which is the cost and time to prepare them for delivery during processing. Generally, it takes

---

44   As discussed previously, there is also near-native format. However, for purposes of discussion of the deliverable during the processing phase, the distinction between near-native and native is somewhat immaterial since the formatting decision would have been made earlier. Whether the deliverable following processing is near-native or native, the file itself is still delivered, together with a data file and extracted text for loading to a document review platform.

45   One caveat here is that certain files usually present problems when converting to TIFF. Spreadsheet files, for example, are frequently created with column and row features that were never intended to be printed. For these and other types of files, it is common practice to deliver only the native file, without ever converting it to a TIFF.

less time and is less costly to process and deliver native files, and therefore it is becoming a more common occurrence. And why not? The native file format is the original, unaltered, and arguably the best version of the document and it includes all the relevant metadata. But native file deliverables are not without issue. Native files are not static, and can be more difficult to review because, as live documents, attorneys may need to review them in a number of different applications, each of which must open within the review platform. Although many review applications now have native file viewers that accommodate most file types, there may still be issues reviewing native files. Additionally, some native files are subject to odd formatting requirements, which also makes them difficult to view. For example, some Excel files may contain hidden comments, formulas, or columns that, when viewed in native form, may be overlooked. Lastly, and perhaps most importantly, while a native file may be renamed with a Bates number or confidential legend, there is no way to Bates number, redact, or apply confidentiality designations to the individual pages of a native file—at least, not without altering the file itself. And altering a native file effectively makes it a near-native. These limitations makes orderly and organized production of native files difficult and impedes future reference to the documents on a page-level in depositions and at trial.

Nonetheless, case teams frequently decide to review documents in native format, but then later produce them in TIFF image form. When this is the case, a native file deliverable from a processing vendor must be converted to TIFF following review by the attorneys, a process that takes time and may impact production deadlines. Care must also be taken when printing native files to TIFF image because large or oddly formatted files such as Excel spreadsheets may not print to TIFF image well. Regardless of whether documents are processed to TIFF or native format, the metadata and the text is still extracted from the documents and prepared as part of the deliverable following processing.

Image Load Files

Load files may be prepared in several different formats, depending upon the platform used to review the documents. An image load file is a file that links the images of a particular document to the data associated with that document and the other pages of that document. It must be delivered in a format that is compatible with the specifications of the document review platform. The load file is typically delivered in a delimited text file or comma separated value (CSV) file, meaning the pieces of data for each page of a document are separated by commas or some other delimiting character.

One common load file format is the Opticon format (.OPT), which originates from one of the early document review tools. Others include .LFP or .DII formatted load files, which are common to other document review platforms and their viewers. Load files may be delivered in a flat text file and then manipulated for use by most any document review platform.

In Figure 6, a sample image load file is displayed showing the discreet parts of the file. This sample file is a CSV file, as indicated by the commas separating each column of data. The first piece of data in the far left column is the *image key*—the unique number assigned by the processing software to each image or page of a document. The image key enables a review software to quickly retrieve and display a page or pages based on input from a user, such as a search, or by simply selecting a document from a list. The second column of data in the image load file is the volume number. The next piece of data in the image load file is the file path, which includes the name of the actual TIFF image file, as indicated by the *.TIF* file extension. This data lets the review software know where the image is located on the file server that stores images.

Lastly, there may be other delimiters used in an image load file that give the review platform additional information about an image or document. In Figure 6, the load file uses the "Y" character to indicate the document breaks for each document. In other words, each time the review platform sees the *Y*, it knows it is the first page of a new document. If there is no *Y*, the review platform knows that image is associated with

158 ◀ MICHAEL I. QUARTARARO

Figure 6: Sample Image Load File

```
00010002,VOL001,C:\VOL001\Images\001\00010002.TIF,Y,,,
00010003,VOL001,C:\VOL001\Images\001\00010003.TIF,Y,,,
00010004,VOL001,C:\VOL001\Images\001\00010004.TIF,Y,,,
00010005,VOL001,C:\VOL001\Images\001\00010005.TIF,,,,
00010006,VOL001,C:\VOL001\Images\001\00010006.TIF,,,,
00010007,VOL001,C:\VOL001\Images\001\00010007.TIF,Y,,,
00010008,VOL001,C:\VOL001\Images\001\00010008.TIF,Y,,,
00010009,VOL001,C:\VOL001\Images\001\00010009.TIF,Y,,,
00010010,VOL001,C:\VOL001\Images\001\00010010.TIF,,,,
00010011,VOL001,C:\VOL001\Images\001\00010011.TIF,,,,
00010012,VOL001,C:\VOL001\Images\001\00010012.TIF,Y,,,
00010013,VOL001,C:\VOL001\Images\001\00010013.TIF,Y,,,
00010014,VOL001,C:\VOL001\Images\001\00010014.TIF,Y,,,
00010015,VOL001,C:\VOL001\Images\001\00010015.TIF,,,,
00010016,VOL001,C:\VOL001\Images\001\00010016.TIF,Y,,,
00010017,VOL001,C:\VOL001\Images\001\00010017.TIF,,,,
00010018,VOL001,C:\VOL001\Images\001\00010018.TIF,Y,,,
00010019,VOL001,C:\VOL001\Images\001\00010019.TIF,Y,,,
00010020,VOL001,C:\VOL001\Images\001\00010020.TIF,,,,
00010021,VOL001,C:\VOL001\Images\001\00010021.TIF,Y,,,
00010022,VOL001,C:\VOL001\Images\001\00010022.TIF,Y,,,
00010023,VOL001,C:\VOL001\Images\001\00010023.TIF,Y,,,
00010024,VOL001,C:\VOL001\Images\001\00010024.TIF,,,,
00010025,VOL001,C:\VOL001\Images\001\00010025.TIF,Y,,,
00010026,VOL001,C:\VOL001\Images\001\00010026.TIF,Y,,,
00010027,VOL001,C:\VOL001\Images\001\00010027.TIF,Y,,,
00010028,VOL001,C:\VOL001\Images\001\00010028.TIF,Y,,,
```

the image immediately preceding it as part of a document.

If documents are delivered in native format, an image load file is not necessary. A link to the file path of the native file is most commonly provided in the data file that accompanies a native file deliverable.

Data Deliverables

A data file deliverable contains the metadata of electronic documents extracted during processing. The most common format for a data file deliverable is a delimited file, such as a .DAT file or .CSV-type file. It is not, however, unusual to receive data files in any number of formats. The processing specification should clearly identify the desired format of the data file deliverable and specify the fields of data and format of the extracted text. The best practice for the project manager is to prepare the written processing specification and, if necessary, review the specification or confer with the individual analyst or vendor performing the processing to discuss the format of the data file.

While there are many metadata fields associated with the variety of electronic documents that users may create, certain fields of data are normally extracted during processing, mostly because only some of them are useful. The project manager, in consultation with the legal team, will decide which metadata fields are to be included in the data deliverable. Table 2 illustrates the data fields that are typically extracted from documents during processing.

Table 2: Metadata Fields Extracted During Processing

AUTHOR	The name (last, first, or username) of the author or creator of an application file
TO	The names (last name, first name) of the recipients of an email from the To field
FROM	The name (last name, first name) of the sender of an email from the From field
CC	The names (last name, first name) of the persons to whom a copy of an email was sent
BCC	The names (last name, first name) of the persons blind copied on an email
DATECREATED	The date an application file was created
DATELASTMOD	The date an application file was last modified
DATESENT	The date an email was sent
DATERCVD	The date an email was received
TIMESENT	The time an email was sent
TIMERCVD	The time an email was received
TIMECREATED	The time an email or application file was created
SUBJECT	The text in the Subject or Re line of an email or application file
TITLE	The text in the Title field of an application file
LASTAUTHOR	The name in the Last Author field of an application file
LASTSAVED	The date in the Last Saved field of an application file
LASTPRINTED	The date in the Last Printed field of an application file
FILESIZE	The size of a document in bytes

FILENAME	The name of the application file, including the file extension, at the time of collection
FILEPATH	The full folder and UNC path information for email, attachments, and application files beginning with the original source name at the time of collection
FILEEXT	The file name extension for each email, attachment, or application file
CONVERSATION/ MESSAGE ID	The conversation index number generated by an email application such as Microsoft Outlook used to identify related email conversations
TEXT	The extracted text or OCR text of a document (if not delivered as separate text files)

In addition to the actual metadata and text that is extracted from each document, processing software is able to generate fields of additional data during processing that aid in the review of ESI and help track and organize the documents once they are loaded to a document review platform. For example, all processing software generates and assigns to each document a unique control number or document identification number. It is common to refer to these additional fields as metadata fields, but these fields are not part of the internal data or properties associated with individual electronic documents. Instead, these data fields are created during processing. Table 3 illustrates some of the most common fields of data created during processing.

Table 3: Other Data Fields

BEGDOC	The beginning document prefix and control number assigned to a document
ENDDOC	The ending document prefix and control number assigned to a document
BEGATTACH	The beginning control number of a range of attached documents

ENDATTACH	The ending control number of a range of attached documents
ATTRANGE	The beginning and ending control number of a document family
PARENTDOC	The control number assigned to a document to indicate the document is a "parent" (only populated for parent documents)
ATTACHMENTS	The control number assigned to a document to indicate the document is a "child," or attachment to another document (only populated for attachments)
CUSTODIAN	The name (last name, first name) of the person, department, or business unit from which a document originates
NATIVEFILE	The file path or hyperlink to the native file
HASHVALUE	The output of an algorithm-generated hash value for each individual file

Assigning control numbers using a Bates-like prefix, and consistently formatting sequential numbers to each page of a document allows for the fast identification and tracking of a document or range of documents. Documents loaded to the document review database are given a unique Document ID, typically referred to as the BEGDOC number. A good practice is to have the control number prefix consist of the custodian name and then a number zero-filled to at least seven digits (e.g., SMITH-0000001). The custodian name provides context for the document, which allows users to see at a glance the source of the document. The custodian does not necessarily have to refer to a person; it can refer to a department or other entity from which the document originated (e.g., SALES-0000001). This control numbering and naming convention helps keep documents organized, and is a required element of the processing specification developed by the project manager. Vendors who perform any processing should be required to deliver documents in this manner.

The BEGDOC and ENDDOC fields contain these Bates-like control numbers. These numbers are not endorsed on the documents, but instead serve as a unique document identifier within a database. Similarly, the BEGATTACH and ENDATTACH fields contain data that enable users to easily identify the range of documents that are attached to one another, enabling reviewers to see an entire "family" of documents together in context.

A document family consists of a parent document and any child documents that may be attached to the parent. For example, if the creator of an email attaches two documents, the email is the parent document, the attachments are the child documents, and together the three documents are the document family. A data deliverable following processing may represent this relationship in a number of different ways, including the use of an additional Group ID field, but the most common form is to deliver data fields as illustrated in Tables 2 and 3, which use the control numbering scheme to represent the relationship between the documents.

Extracted and OCR Text

It is essential to a properly functioning document review database that the text of each document is searchable. Without the ability to search text, the legal team will not be able to perform searches of the content or body of the documents in the database. Advanced analytics features also rely upon the extracted or OCR text for the ability to index and search text documents.

The text extracted from electronic documents during processing and the OCR generated from documents that do not have any extractable text may be delivered in several ways. Text may be delivered in document or page-level text files containing the alpha-numeric characters appearing in each document or on each page. The file path location of the text files are mapped in the load file using the control or BEGDOC number to link the text file to the document. This enables the database to reach and search the text of each document when a search is performed in the database. Searchable text may also be delivered in the data file itself, usually in a field called "TEXT," or some variation thereof. Caution is necessary here because, for very large documents, the text delivered in a data file can become unwieldy and cause complications when loading the data.

Once processing is complete and the deliverables have been received, the project manager is responsible for quality checking each part of the data deliverable prior to and after having the data loaded to the document review platform. Once quality checked, the project manager may release the documents to the case team for review and coding.

It is also important that the project manager ensure the chain of custody form for the client's ESI is updated at the conclusion of processing if the data has changed hands.

Analysis and Reporting

During and following processing, several points of analysis should be undertaken to ensure the quality and completeness of the processing project. Personnel who perform processing and vendors engaged to perform ESI processing are able to analyze the data and generate helpful reports. Most processing software can produce such reports. Analysis and reporting serves two valuable purposes. First, it forces the examination of the processing process and the output to ensure that project specifications are being met. Second, reports can provide valuable information to attorneys who are managing the timing and costs of discovery, particularly attorney review time. For example, reports listing all the file types or the number of documents a search yields may help inform the size of the project and the resources necessary to complete the review phase of a project. Reports are also helpful to the project manager because they aid him in gauging the progress of the project, provide the necessary documentation, and provide valuable project metrics for future use.

The first and most common report is a simple *output report*. This report is usually prepared after ingesting all the ESI into a processing tool. It contains the data that has been collected and that is being staged for further processing, as well as the number of files per custodian, the overall size of the data set, the types of files, and the file names. Legal teams and project managers appreciate this report because it provides the first clear indication of the universe of data involved in the case. More importantly, this report will identify if an unpredicted or unusually high number of documents may be involved, thus suggesting the need for additional culling or filtering of the data.

Another useful report is a post-processing report, called a *data culling* or *search hit report*. This report—prepared after all searching, filtering, and deduplicating is completed—provides narrower information regarding the number of documents that hit on a particular search term, which can be useful in determining the value of the search terms. This report may also show the number of duplicate documents excluded from processing.

Lastly, and most importantly, is the *exception report*. This report provides details about any documents that could not be processed. There are numerous reasons why an electronic document cannot be processed, including file corruption, password protection, or unrecognized file format. During processing, an exception report must be prepared to memorialize the reason the processing software could not process a file. It is quite common that parties know a document exists, but cannot be processed. The project manager and the legal team must review this report and familiarize themselves with documents that are unable to be processed. If and when questions arise about a missing email attachment, the exception report should be among the first places a project manager looks for an answer.

It is also the project manager's responsibility to provide status reports to the legal team throughout the processing phase, and to involve the attorneys in substantive decisions or any issues that may arise during processing. Certainly, any legal issues should be brought to the attention of the legal team immediately.

Creating and Maintaining a Document Review Database

At the conclusion of the processing stage, processed ESI—including native files, TIFF images, data, and text, together with any scanned images of paper documents—need to be loaded into a document review platform that will become the principal workspace for attorneys and paralegals throughout the case. It is therefore important that databases are created with some care and forethought regarding the mechanics of discovery and document review.

There are several document review platforms available on the market that are used to manage documents and ESI in discovery. Regardless of which product is used, they all serve a similar purpose and have similar features. First, they all have a document viewer for TIFF images, or the ability to render documents in a native file viewer or open documents in their native application so that users may examine documents and decide whether they are relevant to the case. Second, they all have a coding or tagging feature that enables the legal team to mark documents in various ways, such as "responsive," "nonresponsive," or "privileged." And lastly, they all incorporate searching and sorting, and have various features that enable the project manager and case teams to find, organize and track their work product throughout the course of a case.

Some document review platforms are very complex and costly to license and install. Other programs are geared toward smaller firms and solo practitioners with smaller budgets. Some applications are hosted or web-based, and some are installed behind an organization's firewall. Most of the review tools on the market today may also be licensed through resellers or vendors who provide managed services contracts. Some review tools feature advanced technologies such as analytics and technology assisted review; others are more basic in their features. In the end, the selected document review platform should be geared toward the needs of an organization and its individual cases. It is less important which review platform is used; the key is that, in today's world, where nearly all documents are created and stored electronically, a database or document review application with even the most minimal features must be used to perform document review.

Prior to creating a new document review database, the project manager should confer with the legal team to discuss the following:

- The scope of the review and anticipated volume of documents;

- Any deadlines for review and production;
- Guidelines for the document review—the mechanics of the review;
- The attorney coding designations that may be used during review;
- Any particular manner in which documents will be organized or prioritized;
- The use of analytics or other specialized features;
- The names of attorneys on the review team;
- In what format the documents will be produced.

When documents are loaded to the review database, it is important to ensure that document boundaries are accurate, particularly with respect to paper documents that have been scanned to image format. Electronic documents created by commercially available software—such as email, word processing, or spreadsheet applications—usually have clear document boundaries. Paper documents, however, typically present challenges because not all people within an organization keep their paper files pristinely organized. For this reason, paper documents should be examined prior to being imaged to ensure that their document boundaries are clear to the individual scanning the documents. If documents are not properly unitized, it may impact the ability to code or tag individual documents, which will slow the pace of the document review.

Once a deliverable is received from a processing vendor—or, if processed internally, from the technician who performed the processing—it is important to ensure documents are properly loaded to the database prior to the start of the review. The project manager is ultimately responsible for performing quality checks on the loaded data and images or native files, although the reviewing attorneys, paralegals, and any other users of the database are also responsible for noting any anomalies. Once the processed data and TIFF images or native files are loaded to a database, the project manager must ensure compliance with the project specifications. This involves reviewing documents either one by one for small collections, or by spot-checking larger loads. Quality checking ensures, among other things, that the following objectives are met:

- The number of documents that were processed are loaded;
- All data fields are populated that should be populated;
- Parent and child documents are properly related and unitized;
- Images are legible and not cut off or crooked;
- Searchable text (extracted or OCR-generated) is present and matches the documents;
- There are no missing or oversized images.

Any anomalies should be reported to the case team, and the project manager must follow up with the vendor or technical analyst who performed the processing to ensure all loading issues are resolved as quickly as possible.

The project manager should consider creating and maintaining a tracking log of all documents loaded to a database, and should record certain metrics, including custodian names, the number of documents, and overall volume of data. Throughout the document review and production, this log should serve as a comprehensive history of all the documents received, loaded, and reviewed. Some review platforms have incorporated reporting features into the application itself but, generally, a simple log created in MS Excel will suffice.

Conclusion

The focus in the processing phase of discovery is to index, cull and filter, and analyze the ESI in ways that are designed to reduce the volume of documents to be reviewed and thereby minimize the time and cost associated with not only processing the documents, but also with attorney review. The project manager is responsible for planning and executing the processing plan, monitoring the progress of the project, and ensuring that the deliverables meet the processing specifications of the case.

CHAPTER NINE SUMMARY

KEY POINTS

- During processing, electronic documents collected in various formats are prepared for review and production in a uniform format.
- One objective during processing is to reduce the volume of the ESI through filtering by date or file type, deduplication, or keyword searching.
- A second objective is to prepare documents for efficient document review using tools like clustering, email threading, and near-duplication.
- Processing, like any other phase of discovery, requires careful planning and consultation between the project manager, attorneys, paralegals, and vendors.
- During processing, the metadata and text are extracted from electronic documents.
- Load files are the delimited files that accompany TIFF image deliverables and enable loading of TIFFs to a document review platform.
- Data files are delimited files, like a .DAT file, that contain the metadata fields extracted from the documents during processing.
- Extracted text or OCR-generated text may be delivered either as (1) text files linked to images or native files or (2) as part of the data file.

Key Processing Tasks	Documentation
Intake and catalog collected ESI.	Media intake form
Update chain of custody.	Chain of custody form
Plan for and determine resources, tools, and techniques.	
Identify ESI filtering processes (date, keyword, de-NIST, etc.), confirm deduplication process and delivery format.	Processing specification
Engage resources to perform processing.	Vendor documentation (conflicts, NDA, SOW)

CHAPTER NINE SUMMARY (cont'd)

Key Processing Tasks	Documentation
Ingest ESI, filter ESI, and generate reports.	Ingestion/EDA report/ search hit report
Perform processing of ESI.	
Image, code and OCR paper documents.	Imaging/coding specification
Monitor and quality check processing output.	
Review exceptions/anomalies in processing.	Processing exception report
Record ESI processed data metrics (custodians, data assets, volume of documents).	
Load data/images to document review platform.	
Perform quality check of loaded data/ images.	
Record ESI loaded data metrics.	
Update chain of custody/disposition of client data.	Chain of custody
Utilize analytics (clustering, near-duplicate, email threading, foreign language).	Analytics reports
Close processing/prepare status report.	Status report

CHAPTER TEN

Document Review

There are several objectives during document review in the context of litigation. First, attorneys must review and determine whether any documents are relevant to the case and responsive to requests for production. Second, attorneys must identify any documents that are privileged, or that contain attorney work product or other protected information, and ensure those documents are not produced. Third, for documents that are responsive, but which also contain protected information, attorneys must redact the privileged or confidential information prior to producing such documents. Fourth, documents that are crucial to the defense or prosecution of the case need to be identified. Lastly, documents produced by other parties will need to be reviewed and perhaps categorized in ways that are useful to the case team.

A document review may be conducted in several different ways. The process chosen depends on the needs of the case, the resources that are available, and the format of the documents to be reviewed. Most client organizations do not have sufficient resources to perform document review in-house. They need a document review platform and an adequate number of attorneys to review the documents. More commonly, corporate clients rely on outside counsel or service providers to help them review documents and manage the review process. In either event, document review is the most time-intensive and costly aspect of litigation. To be efficient and effective, review must be conducted in a systematic and organized manner. This chapter explores the mechanics of document review, the roles and responsibilities of the members of the document review team, and the best practices that enable a case team and project manager to most efficiently manage and review documents and ESI.

Roles and Responsibilities

As with each preceding stage of a discovery project, document review requires careful planning by the project manager. The project manager must be prepared to:

- Work with the legal team to define the scope and mechanics of the review;
- Identify activities, their dependencies, and the sequence of their execution;
- Prepare a schedule and time estimate for completing the review;
- Coordinate staffing and training for attorneys, including outsourcing to staffing agencies, if necessary;
- Develop with the legal team procedures for quality checking the document review;
- Establish clear lines of communication to ensure the timely and effective distribution of information to the review team;
- Monitor and control identifiable risks to scope, time, cost, and quality of the review;
- Coordinate outsourcing, including management of vendors and vendor processes.

The project manager will also be a central figure during execution and in monitoring the review. In this regard, the project manager must:

- Direct and manage the batching and distribution of documents to the review team;
- Assist in performing quality checks and ensure consistency in the coding of documents;
- Maintain the review database, manage technical processes relating to the review, and distribute information related to the use and maintenance of the database;

- Monitor and report on the progress of the review, working with the legal team to adjust staffing, tasks, and schedules as necessary to meet project deadlines.

The roles of the other key stakeholders associated with a document review project will vary from case to case and within an organization based on the availability of resources and the particular circumstances of each case. First, there will most certainly be a lead attorney—typically a senior associate or partner—who will direct and supervise the review effort; establish the overall scope, objectives, and deadlines; and develop guidelines for the review. The lead attorney will oversee daily progress, answer substantive questions from reviewing attorneys, and ensure documents are reviewed and coded accurately and consistently. Communication during a document review is critical, and the lead attorney is responsible for sharing information with the review team and encouraging the team to communicate regularly.

Second, most document reviews involving ESI require attorneys, possibly a large team of attorneys, who will review the documents in the first instance. Reviewing attorneys are primarily responsible for examining and coding documents pursuant to the guidelines established by the lead attorney. More often than not, junior associates perform the bulk of the document review at law firms. Corporations and law firms may also outsource document review to a service provider, or they may engage a staffing agency to employ temporary or contract attorneys.

Lastly, paralegals may also play a role in a document review project. In some instances, depending on her experience, the paralegal may oversee certain aspects of the review, assist the attorney or project manager to monitor the progress of the review, create and maintain a document review log that identifies which review attorney examined which documents, or coordinate other supporting tasks as needed.

As might be expected, communication during a document review is a common thread across the different roles of the review team, and it is crucial to the success of any document review project. Questions concerning substantive legal issues, the relevance of a document, or privileged documents should be raised with the lead attorney. Issues, questions, and answers should be memorialized and shared with the entire team. Any questions or concerns about the use of technology during the review should be raised with the project manager.

Defining the Scope of the Review

Before beginning a document review, the legal team should first develop clear guidelines for determining document relevance and responsiveness to discovery requests. Depending on the size of the document review and the complexity of the issues involved, it may be necessary to reduce these guidelines to writing in a document review protocol or memorandum.

To maximize team understanding of the document review process, the entire review team—including the attorneys, paralegal, and project manager—should meet prior to commencing the review to examine and discuss the facts of the case, the nature of the claims and defenses, the scope of the review, and any guidelines that govern the review. The more team members who know about the facts and issues of the case and the legal strategies of the parties, the better they will be able to understand and implement effective document review procedures.

To ensure a high level of understanding, members of the document review team should also familiarize themselves with the pleadings, requests for production of documents, and any confidentiality orders or stipulations in place. Names of key individuals, significant events, and types of important documents should also be discussed.

A firm understanding of the key issues and case strategy will strengthen the review team's ability to discern relevant and responsive documents. It will also help identify documents that may not be responsive to a document request but which, nonetheless, should be marked important for the purposes of building the case or responding to an adversary's arguments. During the team meeting, the lead attorney should also explain the types of documents that the review team can expect to encounter and how the team should treat each type when being reviewed.

Document review is a collaborative, iterative effort. It is imperative that everyone on the review team have the same understanding of and approach to the review. Some best practices for maintaining organization and the orderly flow of information during a document review are:

- Hold regular brief conference calls or meetings (i.e., daily, weekly) with the review team to address questions or concerns, or to provide additional instructions;
- Create an email distribution group list for the entire review team to use for efficient communication during the review;
- Communicate regarding issues that have arisen so that all reviewers are aware (e.g., how certain documents are to be handled during the review).

Document review—whether the client's or another party's documents—is not a rote activity, but a crucial, fact-gathering and case-building opportunity. Often, the information found in documents will shape and guide development of legal strategies in the case. Document reviewers usually begin to possess facts and information about the case that nonreviewing attorneys do not have, and it is important that the reviewers are able to communicate these facts and information to the senior attorneys on a case. Overall, consistency and quality control are critical during document review.

The Mechanics of Document Review

Databases used to review documents and ESI in discovery not only provide for a fast and relatively inexpensive way to house and retrieve documents, but they also streamline the review process and enable attorneys to easily code or tag documents in a variety of different ways. Using a database also enables project managers to quickly and easily batch, search for and sort documents for distribution to the review team, which enhances his ability to monitor the review.

Prior to starting a review, the project manager should first divide the universe of documents into batches and distribute them to each member of the review team. In this way, each member of the review team is assigned a group of documents to review and code. By performing queries in the database on how many documents have been reviewed and how they have been coded, it is easy to gather and report statistics on the status or progress of the review. The project manager may also create a document review log that lists the name of the reviewing team member and the range of documents assigned to that team member.

Responsiveness Coding

Once the database is organized, the documents are ready for review and coding. The project manager, in consultation with the legal team, must create a document review coding form or layout in the database which reviewers will initially use to mark documents responsive or non-responsive to the requests for document.

During responsiveness coding, documents should be coded in the database on the document level. For consistency across cases, one good practice is to have a standard set of fixed primary designations, codes, or tags in the document review database for use in every case. This way, the review team and attorneys become accustomed to a systematized process.

The most common primary designations are: Responsive, Non-Responsive, Privileged, Redact–Non Responsive, Redact–Privileged, and Further Review. These primary tags are mutually exclusive, meaning that each document can only be coded with one such tag. The primary tags are defined and should be used as follows:

- *Responsive.* These documents will be produced because they are relevant, responsive to a document request, and not privileged;
- *Non-Responsive.* These documents will not be produced because they are not relevant, not responsive to a document request, fall outside the date range, or have some other exclusionary criteria;
- *Redact–Non Responsive.* These are responsive documents that will be produced, but they need to be redacted because they contain information that is non-responsive. The reviewing

attorney will redact the non-responsive material and these documents will be produced in redacted form;

- *Privileged.* These are responsive documents that will be withheld from production entirely because they contain privileged information, attorney work product, or other protected information. These documents will later be itemized on a privilege log. It is a best practice when documents are coded Privileged to then prompt the reviewing attorney to enter the basis for the privilege (e.g., attorney-client or work product), and to enter a privilege log description;[46]
- *Redact–Privileged.* These are responsive documents that will be produced, but they need to be redacted because they contain privileged or work product information. The reviewing attorney will redact the privileged material from these documents, and they will be produced in redacted form. The redacted or privileged portion of the documents must be itemized on a privilege log or redaction log. When this tag is chosen, the reviewing attorney should be prompted to enter the basis for the privilege (e.g., attorney-client or work product) and a privilege or redaction log description;
- *Further Review.* Documents are coded with this tag when the reviewing attorney is uncertain as to the appropriate tag. It is helpful to include a Comments field on the coding form so that the reviewer may enter an explanation. This way, a senior attorney can review the comments in the database and code the document accordingly.

Legal teams and litigation support professionals may differ on the use of the names, types and nature of designations or tags used to code documents during review, and of course, the names of the designations may be changed. The key is to use the chosen review designations consistently.

---

46   Entering the basis for the privilege and a description, while it may slow document review, will facilitate the efficient and orderly creation of a privilege log at a later date.

There are logical practices applicable to all document reviews that should be followed when coding documents and the coding designations outlined above facilitate compliance with these best practices. For example, if a document is determined to be Responsive to a document request, it must then be determined if the document contains any privileged, work product, or non-responsive information that should not be produced. If it does, has the privilege been waived? If so, the document should be produced. If not waived, can the privileged information be redacted? If it can be redacted, the coded tag should be changed to Redact–Privileged, and the privilege fields should then be coded. If it cannot be redacted, then the Responsive tag should be changed to Privileged and the privilege fields should be coded because the document will be withheld. If a document is entirely privileged, the privileged fields should be coded.

These coding practices are not usually written down anywhere; rather, they are a common-sense approach to preserving the attorney-client privilege and they reasonably ensure that privileged materials are not produced in discovery. Another practice is to have senior attorneys review any documents marked by the review team for Further Review. Use of this tag generally means that the reviewing attorney was unable to determine the responsiveness or privileged status of a document.

It is also a best practice to code families of documents consistently during document review. If, for example, an email (the "parent" document) is coded Responsive, then any attachments to the email (the "child" documents) should also be coded Responsive in the first instance, and vice versa. The reasoning behind this rule is simple: When the author of an email attaches a document to the email and sends the email and attachment, it is the intent of that author for the two documents to be viewed together as a single communication. This, combined with the general notion of producing documents in the manner in which they are maintained, support the practice of consistent coding within document families.

This is not to say that there are not reasons to break up document families. It can and does happen, depending on the nature and circumstances of a given case. In either event, when document families are inconsistently coded or tagged, the project manager must ensure that the reviewing attorney is later prompted to resolve or provide an explanation for the inconsistency. For clarity, it is important that instructions regarding the treatment of document families are clear at the outset of the review.

Additionally, during a document review, the project manager should monitor the review by regularly examining the documents to ensure they are in fact being coded, that redactions are being applied to documents marked for redaction, and that documents that have been coded for Further Review are being promoted for review by a more senior or the lead attorney.

Confidentiality Designations

Another form of coding that may occur during document review is to apply confidentiality designations to individual documents. Depending upon the needs of the case, once it is determined that a document will be produced, the document may be endorsed with the words "Confidential," "Highly Confidential" or "Attorneys Eyes Only."

Confidentiality designations are almost always very case-specific. In most circumstances, the designation of documents as confidential or otherwise are governed by a protective or confidentiality order to which the parties of the case have agreed. Prior to the review, the project manager must create appropriate confidentiality designations on the coding form. When the documents with these tags are eventually produced, the selected confidentiality value will normally be endorsed on the images or printed pages, or appended to the file name for native files. If no value is chosen, no confidentiality designation will appear on the page.

Review team members must have a thorough understanding of confidentiality criteria to ensure consistency in the application of confidentiality designations. The review team should be given screening criteria, such as categories of documents or specific topics that will assist them in making such decisions.

Issue Coding

Issue coding involves categorizing documents in ways that may be helpful to the legal team. It may be necessary to categorize documents as relating to certain issues, subjects, or events in the case. Issue coding is helpful, organizes documents based on the issues in the case, and makes locating documents related to a particular topic faster and easier in later stages of the case. Issue tags are generally not mutually exclusive. Because a document may pertain to more than one issue or subject in a particular case, the document may require multiple issue tags.

The attorneys and review team must develop a list of the issues, subjects, or events for which documents are to be categorized. Each issue on the list should be very brief—no more than a word or two. The project manager must then create a series of tags in the database and add them to the document review coding layout so the review team may apply the tags to documents. It is important to keep in mind that issue coding can be time consuming and may add significantly to the time and cost of a document review.

Phases of Document Review

Depending upon the nature of the review, the volume of the documents, whether document production must be expedited, and the availability of resources, it is sometimes necessary to break a document review into phases—typically referred to as first pass review, second pass review, or privilege review. Each phase generally serves a different purpose. For example, a first pass review may be performed by junior associates, contract attorneys, or paralegals. A first pass may involve looking at documents for responsiveness to document requests or to simply weed out clearly irrelevant material. A second pass review may involve a more focused review to determine substantive or privileged documents, to perform issue coding, or to categorize the documents. Second pass review is typically performed by more skilled or senior attorneys. Another round of review may involve quality checking previous rounds. It may also be necessary to review documents produced by other parties to determine their relevance or to categorize them for use in the case.

The review of privileged documents is of particular significance. The attorney-client privilege in the legal world is a sacrosanct cornerstone of legal practice. It is undergirded by the notion that, in order for an attorney to best represent a client, the client must be 100% honest, and fully and candidly disclose facts and information about the case to her attorney without worrying that the attorney will report the information to the government, to law enforcement, or even to the opposing party. The attorney-client privilege fosters and preserves the secret or confidential nature of communications and advice between the attorney and the client and, for these reasons, a heightened level of scrutiny is necessary during a privilege review. Attorneys must focus on identifying, coding, and redacting documents that will be withheld on the basis of privilege, attorney work product, or other legal reasons for nondisclosure. During a privilege review, attorneys are making determinations on whether a document meets the legal definition of "privileged" or "work product," and coding the documents accordingly using review tags. It is best during a privilege review for the attorneys to also code the additional fields that will form the basis of the privilege log that will later be generated and exported directly from the document review platform. These practices are discussed in greater detail toward the end of this chapter.

Technology-Assisted Review

Entire books will likely be written about the value, mechanics, and appropriate workflows associated with technology-assisted review (TAR), sometimes referred to as "predictive coding," "machine learning," or "computer assisted review."[47] TAR relies on powerful

---

47   This book does not attempt to discuss TAR in more than cursory detail; instead, it introduces the basics of TAR in the context of the broader subject of document review because, ultimately, the function of most any TAR software or protocol is to categorize large volumes of documents and thereby

analytics software to analyze and categorize documents in ways that are useful to a case team and which are more efficient and cost-effective than human linear review of each document.

The technology behind TAR has been available for some time, but only recently has it entered the legal services industry as a result of the need to churn through and quickly understand the nature and substance of vast collections of ESI. Using algorithms designed by linguists, mathematicians, and software developers, TAR programs are able to categorize large collections of documents based on the coding by an attorney applied to just a small sampling of the documents. TAR can be an efficient way to parse through large volumes of ESI. For example, using TAR it is possible to categorize or code one-million documents by having an attorney actually review just a statistically significant sample of those documents. And case studies have shown that TAR and machine learning programs and protocols are more consistent and can be as accurate, if not more accurate, than teams of human document reviewers[48]—and it is almost certainly less costly, because large teams of lawyers are not needed to conduct the review. Theoretically, at least, TAR programs could limit the need for human linear document review—that is, eyes-on-each-document review by an attorney. TAR, however, may never replace the human reasoning of an attorney. TAR programs should simply be viewed as another tool in the litigator's arsenal. If nothing else, the TAR process may reveal the most relevant documents most efficiently.

The typical workflow in a TAR project might be for the project manager to index all documents in preparation for the project. A project manager and/or attorney may do some initial sifting through the documents to identify and eliminate graphical files with no text, very large or small documents, or documents with purely numerical

---

reduce the volume of documents to be reviewed, as well as the time and cost associated with document review.

48   Maura R. Grossman & Gordon V. Cormack, *Technology-Assisted Review in E-Discovery Can Be More Effective and More Efficient Than Exhaustive Manual Review*, XVII RICH. J.L. & TECH. 11 (2011), http://jolt.richmond.edu/v17i3/article11.pdf.

data. This process is necessary to build an optimized concept-based or analytics index. Documents with little or no text or with numbers only are not ideal when creating an analytics index because such documents do not contain conceptually rich content –namely, the necessary words and phrases from which concepts are derived and then used to categorize the documents. Likewise, very large documents may contain lots of text and many concepts, which is equally problematic because it is difficult to categorize a document that contains multiple concepts.

Next, it is preferable that a senior attorney with full understanding of the facts of the case review a seed set of documents that represent a statistically significant sample of the overall universe of documents. During *seed set review* the attorney reviews and codes the seed set documents as Responsive or Non-Responsive. These two designations will then be used to effectively teach the TAR program which documents contain conceptually relevant material and which do not.

Once the seed set or training review is complete, the project manager prompts the TAR application to categorize the other documents in the database based on what the attorney taught the system during seed set review. During categorization, the software analyzes the content of the documents in the seed set as reviewed by the attorney, and codes other conceptually similar documents in the database in the same way. In this way, very large collections of ESI can be efficiently categorized, and documents that are completely irrelevant to the subject matter of a case may be set aside.

Following the seed set review and the machine coding or categorization of the documents, the project manager and legal team must examine the categorization results. Additional rounds of seed set review may take place, and there must be one or more quality check or validation rounds to ensure that a statistically sound level of coding accuracy is achieved. In the end, only a small fraction of the documents are seed-set reviewed, and the legal team is left with a conceptually rich, likely relevant, and much smaller sub-set of documents that should then undergo attorney review for responsiveness and privilege before being produced. In theory, an attorney may not need to review documents categorized Non-Responsive and those determined to be of marginal relevance by the TAR application.

There are several TAR applications on the market, and each of them uses different technology to categorize documents. But make no mistake about these tools—none are yet sophisticated enough to eliminate human intervention with a set of documents or ESI. Indeed, some legal ethicists may likely argue that it is borderline malpractice for an attorney to review and produce documents using technology alone. Conservative commentators maintain that a document may not be produced unless a human being has reviewed the content of that document for relevance and privilege. The debate will be ongoing as the technology continues to develop.

Contract Attorneys and Document Review

Not all organizations, law firms, or departments—particularly corporate legal departments—have the resources to take on large-scale document review projects. Devoting more than a handful of attorneys to reviewing documents can quickly tap much-needed resources of even moderately sized organizations. Most corporations rely on outside counsel to provide attorneys for document review. It is common for corporations and law firms to employ temporary or contract attorneys to perform document review—at least as a first level review, to whittle the collection down to the more responsive documents.

When a document review involves the use of contract attorneys, the attorney leading the review project and the project manager need to monitor and quality check the contract attorneys' work. It is important to give clear instructions to the contract attorneys for determining document relevance and responsiveness. The hours worked should be controlled as well; contract attorneys who spend too much time reviewing can become fatigued and lose focus.

The productivity of contract attorneys should also be monitored during the review. Here, the project manager can help by gathering and reporting to the legal team on review metrics demonstrating how many documents are being reviewed by each contract attorney in a given time period. For example, depending upon the types of documents involved, a productive contract attorney may be able to review 500 or 600 documents during a 10-hour period. Regular reports to the lead or supervising attorney should confirm that the contract attorneys are meeting expectations.

Review of Privileged and Work-Product Documents

There are two main grounds for withholding otherwise responsive information from production: the attorney-client privilege and the work-product doctrine. One of the most important responsibilities during document review is to identify privileged and work product information within documents for the purpose of segregating those documents from the universe of material to be produced. It is essential that safeguards be in place to protect a client's privileged and work product information.[49]

Documents and information are generally *privileged* when they consist of communication between a client and his attorney, and that communication is transmitted for purposes of giving the client legal advice. The attorney-client privilege belongs to the client and, unless waived by the client, an attorney must not disclose the client's privileged communications. It is important to note, however, that the attorney-client privilege may be waived when the client or attorney shares the privileged communication with a non-attorney.

The *work-product doctrine* protects from discovery materials that might reveal the legal team's strategy. It applies to documents, materials, and information prepared by attorneys in anticipation of litigation.

---

49   FED. R. CIV. P. 26(b)(3)(B). A party may withhold documents and information from production on other legal grounds. For example, there are certain business-related grounds, such as proprietary information, trade secrets, or bank privileges. If multiple parties are defending a lawsuit, a joint-defense privilege may apply. The facts and circumstances of each case will determine whether documents may be withheld. Non-attorney project managers should consult with and defer to attorneys for full and complete definitions and understanding of these legal principles.

Any documents, communications, files, or other information that contain attorney thought processes, strategic thinking, or tactics to be used by the attorney in litigation is considered work product. Unlike privileged material, disclosure of work product may be required upon a showing of substantial need and an inability to obtain equivalent materials without undue hardship. But documents that might reveal an attorney's mental processes receive a higher degree of protection under the work-product doctrine. Even if another party obtains work product materials on a showing of need, the courts must still "protect against the disclosure of the mental impressions, conclusions, opinions, or legal theories of a party's attorney or other representative concerning the litigation."

Determining whether a document is privileged requires that a document reviewer analyze the document, its contents, and the people mentioned or referenced in the document. Members of the document review team should have not only a thorough understanding of the rules of privilege and other protections applicable to the case, but also a list of attorneys' names and other information provided to them by the lead attorney at the outset of a document review that will guide them in making privilege determinations. Indeed, determinations of privilege in document review can sometimes be difficult and may ultimately require the review and judgment of more senior attorneys. Therefore, it is the responsibility of the lead attorney to educate the review team on the basis upon which to withhold privileged documents.

Likewise, the review team must decide whether to code and withhold a document on work-product grounds. The reviewing attorney must determine whether the document was prepared in anticipation of litigation. At the outset of a document review, the lead attorney should discuss with the review team the parameters for claiming work-product protection (e.g., the date that litigation was reasonably anticipated), and provide guidance on how to apply the work product doctrine.

During privilege review, attorneys identify the nature of the privilege being asserted and determine whether documents should be produced in redacted form or entirely withheld. The project manager will have created a coding form in the database that will assist attorneys in coding documents as Privileged. Documents that are found to contain privileged information should be coded as Privileged or Redact–Privileged. A Privileged document is withheld in its entirety; a document coded Redact-Privileged is produced in redacted form. Documents requiring redactions will be redacted electronically by the reviewing attorney using the redaction tool in the document review platform. Nearly every review platform has a redaction feature, and the project manager should ensure that all reviewing attorneys are trained on the use of the redaction tool.

It is best during the privilege review to begin building a privilege log while the documents are being reviewed and coded. After the reviewer codes a document Privileged or Redact–Privileged, she should be prompted and enter the basis for withholding the document (e.g., attorney-client or work product). She should also enter a brief description of the document for inclusion on the privilege log. This practice, while requiring the investment of more time up front to code and describe privileged documents, proves efficient because, by entering the privilege log information into the database, the legal team may more easily generate the actual privilege log later by exporting the coded data from the database instead of manually creating and entering the information in log.

If possible, at the initial review kick-off meeting, it is best to provide to the review team a list of the names of the client's outside counsel, in-house attorneys, and paralegals, including all email domain names of the law firms. The list should be updated frequently and kept handy throughout the document review. It is important to note that not all in-house attorneys act in a legal capacity, and reviewers should be reminded of the difference between attorneys who act in a legal capacity and those who perform a business function.

Once the privilege review is complete, it is good practice to perform quality checks to ensure that privileged documents are accurately coded and properly withheld or redacted prior to production. These quality checks should be performed by an attorney, and may include searching for attorney names, law firms, or other privileged terms known to exist within documents in the database to ensure that privilege coding has been consistently applied and that redactions are consistent among the same or similar documents.

Before the final production is prepared, the project manager must run a variety of quality checks to ensure that emails and attachments are consistently coded across document families, that documents coded Privileged are not included, and that documents coded Redact–Privileged actually have redactions.

When documents are withheld based on a claim of privilege or work-product, it is necessary to create a privilege log. The preparation and production of privilege logs can be quite contentious, and opposing parties occasionally challenge each other's logs, claiming important information has been withheld. Rule 26(b)(5)(A) of the FRCP requires a party to "describe the nature of the documents, communications, or tangible things not produced or disclosed—and do so in a manner that, without revealing information itself privileged or protected, will enable other parties to assess the claim."[50] A *privilege log*, then, is a list of documents that contain privileged information that is either being withheld from disclosure to other parties or that has been redacted. The log typically contains the nature of the privilege asserted, a brief description of each document, the date of the document, and its author and recipients. The objective is to create a facially sufficient privilege log that limits or avoids challenges by opposing counsel or the court.

Once the document review is complete and, assuming that the review team has coded privileged documents during the review, the privilege log can be exported directly from the database. Prior to the review, the project manager should create several data fields in the database that will facilitate the creation and export of the privilege log. The most common fields appearing on a privilege log are Date Created, To, From, CC, Title, Author, Basis of Privilege, and Document

---

50 The procedural rules and actual practice for creating a privilege log and the level of detail required in the privilege log descriptions varies from one jurisdiction to the next. State practice, for instance, differs as to how complete a description must be. Practitioners should be sure to consult state and local rules.

Description. It is also helpful for internal tracking purposes to export the database control number—or, for redacted documents, the Bates number of the document—in the event a document must be quickly located later. Many of these fields may already exist based on the fields of data extracted during processing.

Once all the privileged documents have been identified in the database and the necessary fields in the database have been coded, the log may be exported from the database into an Excel file or other delimited file type for final editing. If the privilege log has not been coded during the review, it will be necessary to code the documents in the database in order to export the log, a task that paralegals frequently complete.

Privileged documents and documents containing work product information are occasionally overlooked during document review, and may be inadvertently produced to other parties in the case. In such circumstances, Fed. R. Evid. 502(e) and Fed. R. Civ. P. 26(b)(5) (B) govern a party's rights and obligations once it is discovered, or a party is notified by its adversary, that privileged information may have been inadvertently produced.

A claw-back agreement is the most efficient means to ensure the return of inadvertently produced privileged documents. To ensure preservation of the attorney-client privilege and to safeguard attorney work-product, it is advisable for attorneys on both sides to reach agreement, or seek an order of the court, on what is referred to as a *claw-back agreement*. A claw-back agreement typically provides that in the event a party inadvertently produces privileged or work product materials the receiving party should return the documents to the producing party and such disclosure does not constitute a waiver of the attorney-client privilege or other protection. Such agreements are typically incorporated into confidentiality agreements or ESI protocols in the early stages of the case.

Conclusion

Document review is often regarded as a mindless and boring

task. It is, perhaps, the most dreaded task that attorneys may perform, and it is usually relegated to junior attorneys. Nonetheless, legal disputes are largely driven by the facts of the case, and those facts are usually uncovered during discovery—specifically during document review. Identifying the facts from the documents in a case often enables attorneys to strategize and offer the best possible advice to their clients. For these reasons, document review should be viewed as one of the most important aspects of a discovery project.

CHAPTER TEN SUMMARY

KEY POINTS

- The objectives of document review are to determine which responsive, nonprivileged documents will be produced to other parties and to identify documents that are important to defending or prosecuting the case.
- Planning, defining the scope, and maintaining good communication are critical to a successful document review.
- A project manager helps plan a review, batches documents, prepares a coding form, and monitors and reports on the review, while maintaining the review database.
- During document review attorneys code documents as Responsive, Non-Responsive, Privileged, or otherwise, and may code for confidentiality or issues
- Technology Assisted Review (TAR) is a document review methodology that leverages advanced analytics tools to quickly and efficiently categorize large sets of documents.
- Privileged and work-product documents should be coded in detail in a database to facilitate later export of a privilege log.
- Claw-back agreements are used to retrieve privileged documents inadvertently produced to opposing parties.

Key Document Review Tasks	Documentation
Meet and plan document review process.	Document review protocol
Determine resources, tools and techniques, and mechanics of review.	
Engage resources required for review.	Vendor documentation (NDA, SOW, agency agreement)
Prepare review attorney/contract attorney roster.	Review roster
Batch/prioritize documents for review.	

CHAPTER TEN SUMMARY (cont'd)

Key Document Review Tasks	Documentation
Train/instruct review attorneys.	Pleadings, document requests, etc.
Perform linear document review.	Document review log
Perform first/second pass responsiveness review.	
Perform privilege review.	
Redact documents.	
Perform quality control on documents reviewed.	
Perform technology assisted review (if applicable).	TAR protocol
Build and optimize analytics index.	
Review and code seed set documents.	
Perform categorization/machine coding.	Statistical reports
Review, analyze, and QC coding.	
Monitor review and report review metrics.	Document review progress report
Assist to prepare privilege/redaction log.	Privilege/redaction log
Close document review/prepare status report.	Status report

CHAPTER ELEVEN

Document Production

O nce the review of documents is complete, all responsive nonprivileged documents will be prepared for production to the requesting parties. While a project manager does not choose the documents that will be produced, he is responsible to prepare the documents for production. Whether it is a large electronic production from a database or a small collection of paper documents, a great deal of care and focus on details is required when preparing documents for production.

It should be understood that, while some cases are more complex than others, the single most important consideration when producing documents is consistency in the process. There are significant risks associated with providing a client's documents to other parties but, if handled in a deliberate, consistent manner and quality checked throughout the process, the risks are significantly reduced.

Many law firms and some legal departments have technical staff who prepare the actual production at the direction of the project manager. Paralegals may also be involved in overseeing a document production. Either way, it is the project manager's responsibility to manage the staff and ensure that necessary activities are carried out in accordance with standardized procedures. This includes:

- Define the necessary tasks based on the production specification;
- Establish lines of communication with the legal team;

- Give assignments to appropriate staff and properly sequencing the tasks;
- Perform conflict checks for inconsistent or improper coding;
- Establish and adhere to a schedule for completion of the production;
- Perform quality checks throughout the process;
- Manage change during the production process;
- Assess and mitigate risks associated with the production;
- Manage the expectations of stakeholders, particularly the legal team.

Communication with the legal team is critical during the production phase. It is common for last-minute changes to be made to a production, and the project manager must be accessible and responsive during the final stages of the production process.

Planning a Document Production

As with each previous phase of a discovery project, the production stage requires careful planning. The scope, timing, and requirements for the production must be clear and documented. The legal team should communicate to the project manager the scope and requirements for the production. A best practice is to have the production requirements prepared in writing through use of a production specification form.51 Many law firms, organizations, and service providers use a standard form that includes at least the following details necessary to complete the production:

- Name of the requesting attorney/paralegal;
- Client/matter or case information;
- Due date and time;
- The source or name of the database from which documents will be produced;
- The criteria for identifying documents to be produced;
- Any specifics about documents that are to be excluded;

---

51   A sample production specification form is included in the Appendix.

- The starting Bates number and location on image;
- Whether confidentiality stamps will be endorsed and the location on image;
- Whether redacted documents are to be included;
- Load file requirements (i.e., database system of opposing counsel);
- Whether and which data fields will be produced (e.g., author, recipient, date);
- Whether searchable text will be produced;
- The image format in which documents will be produced (e.g., TIFF, JPEG, PDF);
- Whether native files will be produced;
- The media to be used for delivery (e.g., CD, DVD, hard drive or SFTP transmission);
- Label information for the CD or hard drive media;
- Number of copies of media.

With these production requirements, a project manager will be able to prepare the production; export the images, native files, text, and any metadata; and burn the production and load files to CD, DVD, or an external hard drive. The production may also be transmitted to other parties via secure FTP site.

Forms of Production

Documents must be produced in a reasonably useable format for discovery. It is preferable to know the format of the document production before the production is requested. A party requesting documents may specify the form of the production; but if that does not occur or if the responding party objects to the requested form, the responding party should let the other parties know its intended form of production. Ideally, the parties will have agreed to the format of the production earlier in the case or during the Rule 26(f) meet and confer conference but, frequently, there is no agreement until the time of production. When this is the case, the project manager must then review the production format options with the case team. There are essentially three formats in which to produce documents: TIFF, native file, or printed paper.

TIFF Image Files

The most common practice when using a commercial document review platform is to produce documents as single-page TIFF images with appropriate image load files. They are common because TIFF images are static images that cannot easily be altered; they are easily endorsed with Bates numbers, redactions, or confidentiality legends; and they are compact and easily transmitted on CDs, DVDs, or via FTP site. TIFF images have various formats and resolutions. They may be black and white or color. The common format is group IV, 2-bit compression, and 300 DPI. The project manager should confirm the appropriate format with the party receiving the documents.52

Native Files

Entire document productions in native or near-native file format are still somewhat rare. Providing other parties with a live Word, Excel, or PowerPoint file could result in the production of hidden privileged or work-product information that is embedded in the metadata of the files. In addition, the recipient of a native file production must have each software application in order open each type of native file, although most modern document review platforms do now incorporate a native file viewer that will render a native file to, for example, an HTML format. Still, it is difficult to produce some files natively. An Access database file, for example, would not be useful if the recipient of the file does not have the MS Access application and the skills required to load and open the file in Access. Similarly, PST, NSF, and other types of database files, or files unique to proprietary applications, also present challenges when attempting to view them

---

52   Another form of image file is Adobe PDF. In smaller cases with fewer documents—when there is no need for searching, sorting, or filtering through metadata—it is common to produce documents in simple PDF format. This is particularly true when smaller firms or solo practitioners with limited resources are involved.

natively. In the end, native files cannot be Bates numbered, redacted, or endorsed with confidential stamps. This is usually an obstacle to legal teams because they need to refer to documents by Bates number and, for documents that are privileged or confidential, attorneys need to apply redactions prior to producing the documents. Ultimately, before producing native files, a thorough discussion should be held with the case team regarding the limitations of this format.

At the same time, some electronic documents do not lend themselves well to TIFF conversion. For example, Excel spreadsheets can contain many, many columns and tens of thousands of rows of data. Documents of this size are never intended to be printed or converted to TIFF, and attempting to do so may result in virtually unusable documents. For this reason, it has become a common practice to produce Excel spreadsheet files in their native format. Still, the same cautions for producing native files should be discussed with the case team prior to producing any native files, including Excel files.

When documents are produced in native format, the usual procedure is either to rename the file with a production Bates number and any confidential designation, or to append the production Bates number to the name of the native file. If TIFFs are being produced for other documents, it is common to include a slip sheet or tiff image placeholder to indicate that the file is being produced in native format.

Paper Documents

A production in paper form is just that—documents in a database printed to paper with Bates numbers or other endorsements. In very small cases, it may be that the documents are not imaged and loaded to a database at all, with the Bates numbers being affixed manually or to paper copies during duplication. The project manager should still be consulted to coordinate a paper document production, and a copy of the final production should be provided to the project manager for scanning and addition to a database. This will provide a permanent electronic record of the production.

Producing Metadata and Searchable Text

Metadata is data about data, and is most commonly found in the properties and attributes of a given electronic document. Metadata shows how the software and its user interact during the life of an electronic document. The question of whether to produce metadata must be addressed in each case involving ESI. Court decisions have held that metadata is part of the document and is therefore discoverable. This can vary from one jurisdiction to the next, so it is important for the attorneys to be familiar with controlling authorities, court rules, and customary practice in a given jurisdiction to determine whether it is necessary to produce metadata.

There are also some misconceptions about metadata. Some fields of data that accompany document productions are technically not metadata fields. The Custodian field, for example, is not a data field that any software application or operating system creates in the course of creating or storing a document; rather, it is a data field created during processing and added to the database to help keep ESI organized. Similarly, the hash value of a file is not metadata, as it is generated during collection or processing to verify that a file has not changed, to facilitate deduplication, and to provide a digital fingerprint for the file. Bates numbers are not metadata either; they are assigned to each document while preparing the production.

When producing scanned images from hard copy documents, keep in mind that there will be no metadata to produce. Scanning a document and storing it in a file system generates only minimal metadata for a document, such as the file name and the date it was created. Scanned documents may be manually coded for data fields such as Author, Date, or Subject; but, unlike electronic documents, such data is not considered metadata because it was added to the database after the documents were scanned, not extracted from the document itself. It may be important to distinguish between true electronic documents and documents that have been scanned, and it is the project manager's responsibility to do so.

Normally when producing electronic documents, it is customary to produce fields of metadata such as Author, Recipient, Subject,

Date, etc. This facilitates searching and sorting and the building of timelines or chronologies later in the case. Metadata extracted from electronic documents is most commonly produced in a delimited data file that contains a header row that lists the data fields being produced and, as illustrated in Figure 7, the delimited columns of the data.

Figure 7: Excerpt from a DAT File

```
þSTARTBATESþ◊þENDBATESþ◊þDATECREATEDþ◊þDOCTYPEþ◊þDOCTITLEþ◊þTOþ◊þFROMþ◊þFILESIZEþ
þPM00010002þ◊þPM00010002þ◊þ00/00/0000þ◊þFile Noteþ◊þWriting Attendance Noteþ◊þGandolfi;JA, Elmer, Chris,þ◊26
þPM00010003þ◊þPM00010003þ◊þ12/19/2011þ◊þCorrespondenceþ◊þUntitledþ◊þMcCorman;SLþ◊þSimmons;RCþ◊25
þPM00010004þ◊þPM00010006þ◊þ12/20/2011þ◊þCorrespondenceþ◊þAgreement Confirmationþ◊þMcCorman;SLþ◊þMcMurrian;HPþ◊30
þPM00010007þ◊þPM00010007þ◊þ12/23/2011þ◊þCorrespondenceþ◊þData Programþ◊þþ◊þSimmons;RCþ◊10
þPM00010008þ◊þPM00010008þ◊þ11/23/2011þ◊þAccountsþ◊þAudit of Trust Company £000,000sþ◊þþ◊þþ◊19
þPM00010009þ◊þPM00010011þ◊þ02/03/2014þ◊þCorrespondenceþ◊þIn Bankruptcyþ◊þSandoz;WCþ◊þSaer;EHþ◊38
þPM00010012þ◊þPM00010012þ◊þ10/21/2011þ◊þCorrespondenceþ◊þLoan Agreement Dated D19821104þ◊þGandolfi;JAþ◊þWeller;CEþ◊123
þPM00010013þ◊þPM00010013þ◊þ06/03/2011þ◊þCorrespondenceþ◊þUntitledþ◊þGandolfi;JAþ◊þBaum;HAþ◊19
þPM00010014þ◊þPM00010015þ◊þ06/06/2011þ◊þCorrespondenceþ◊þUntitledþ◊þGandolfi;JA, Fudd;EFþ◊þKoonz;Hþ◊27
þPM00010016þ◊þPM00010017þ◊þ05/25/2011þ◊þCorrespondenceþ◊þDatabaseþ◊þþ◊þKoonz;Hþ◊26
þPM00010018þ◊þPM00010018þ◊þ07/16/2013þ◊þCorrespondenceþ◊þUntitledþ◊þ þ◊þMcDonald;JEþ◊111
þPM00010019þ◊þPM00010020þ◊þ11/10/2011þ◊þCorrespondenceþ◊þData Programsþ◊þþ◊þKoonz;Hþ◊25
þPM00010021þ◊þPM00010021þ◊þ10/17/2011þ◊þCorrespondenceþ◊þData Programþ◊þþ◊þGandolfi;JAþ◊34
þPM00010022þ◊þPM00010022þ◊þ10/17/2011þ◊þCorrespondenceþ◊þData Programþ◊þþ◊þGandolfi;JAþ◊56
þPM00010023þ◊þPM00010024þ◊þ04/00/2011þ◊þFinancial Paperþ◊þTable of Data Concerning Loansþ◊þþ◊þþ◊98
þPM00010025þ◊þPM00010025þ◊þ01/04/2012þ◊þCorrespondenceþ◊þUntitledþ◊þDoumani;EMþ◊þNordgren;Rþ◊145
þPM00010026þ◊þPM00010026þ◊þ04/15/2012þ◊þMemorandumþ◊þGandolfi, 1st Southþ◊þHeiner;RTþ◊þHauser;MDþ◊210
þPM00010027þ◊þPM00010027þ◊þ04/15/2012þ◊þMemorandumþ◊þUntitledþ◊þHeiner;RTþ◊þHauser;MDþ◊19
þPM00010028þ◊þPM00010029þ◊þ04/09/2012þ◊þCorrespondenceþ◊þUntitledþ◊þMouse;MCþ◊þHarris;LAþ◊28
þPM00010030þ◊þPM00010030þ◊þ00/00/0000þ◊þCorrespondenceþ◊þUntitledþ◊þGandolfi;JA þ◊þWeller;CE, Hauser;MDþ◊167
þPM00010031þ◊þPM00010032þ◊þ00/00/0000þ◊þScheduleþ◊þSecurityþ◊þþ◊þþ◊220
þPM00010033þ◊þPM00010034þ◊þ00/00/0000þ◊þScheduleþ◊þReal Propertyþ◊þþ◊þþ◊210
þPM00010035þ◊þPM00010035þ◊þ06/16/2011þ◊þCorrespondenceþ◊þUntitledþ◊þWeller;CEþ◊þRigling;Nþ◊128
þPM00010036þ◊þPM00010064þ◊þ00/00/0000þ◊þFinancial Reportþ◊þUntitledþ◊þþ◊þþ◊290
þPM00010065þ◊þPM00010066þ◊þ00/00/2011þ◊þNoteþ◊þCash Flows for 1982-83þ◊þþ◊þþ◊28
þPM00010067þ◊þPM00010069þ◊þ00/00/2011þ◊þNoteþ◊þBalance Sheetþ◊þþ◊þþ◊37
þPM00010070þ◊þPM00010070þ◊þ06/13/2011þ◊þFile Noteþ◊þConversation Between Smith and Jonesþ◊þþ◊þHauser;MDþ◊15
þPM00010071þ◊þPM00010071þ◊þ09/15/2011þ◊þCorrespondenceþ◊þUntitledþ◊þGandolfi;JAþ◊þDarling;GHþ◊17
þPM00010072þ◊þPM00010072þ◊þ00/00/0000þ◊þContractþ◊þUntitledþ◊þþ◊þGandolfi;JAþ◊79
þPM00010073þ◊þPM00010073þ◊þ08/31/2011þ◊þCorrespondenceþ◊þUntitledþ◊þGandolfi;JAþ◊þDarling;GHþ◊111
```

As can be seen, the first line of text in this file contains the names of each field in the *.dat* or data file. The first two columns contain the STARTBATES and ENDBATES numbers, which should also be endorsed on each individual image file. The third delimited column of data contains the DATECREATED field. All of the data fields that are being produced will be contained in a data file like this.

Many productions also include the searchable text of documents. Searchable text is generated in two ways: First, during processing, the text or body of each document is extracted from the documents. Second, for documents that do not have searchable text, it is common to OCR them to generate searchable text. Text may be produced as individual text files linked to each document, or it may be produced as part of the data file in a field, called Text (see the earlier discussion on searchable text during Processing, chapter 9).

An image load file should accompany productions in TIFF format. This load file links the images to the appropriate data and sets the document boundaries for each document. The images are linked to the data through an image key or unique document identifier (see Sample Image Load File, Chapter 9).

There is some lack of standardization in production deliverables across the electronic discovery and litigation support industry. In many cases, confusion, wasted time and effort, and acrimonious discovery disputes could be avoided if all parties produced images, native files, and data in a standard, universal format. The best practice, as noted above, is to prepare a written document production specification and communicate the specifications to the parties in the case.

It is also useful if the production is organized in several folders or directories on the deliverable media. Figure 8 identifies one way to organize the production deliverable.

Figure 8: Standardized Production Directories

Name	Date modified	Type
DATA	1/14/2014 2:48 PM	File folder
IMAGES	1/14/2014 2:48 PM	File folder
NATIVES	1/14/2014 2:48 PM	File folder
TEXT	1/14/2014 2:48 PM	File folder

The Images directory should contain all of the images divided into subdirectories, with no more than a few thousand images in each directory. The Natives directory contains all native files produced. The Data directory should contain the DAT file and the image load file. The Text directory should contain all of the individual text files. The load files will point to these directories. This standard delivery format aids the project manager and the parties involved because it enables analysis and efficient loading of electronic documents once they are produced.

Quality Checking a Document Production

A request to prepare documents for production typically originates from an attorney or paralegal. The requestor should prepare a production specification or work with a project manager to identify the production requirements.

Once a request to produce documents is received, the project manager should review the specifications and the documents proposed for production and perform a series of quality checks. The project manager should check for inconsistent coding, ensure that parent documents and their attachments are included, and determine whether any other irregularities may require attorney attention or further review. The project manager should confirm that documents marked for redaction do in fact have redactions, and that the redacted documents have undergone re-OCR to ensure the text that has been redacted does not appear in the text files or in the DAT file that will be produced. These steps are usually referred to as a *conflict check*, and it is the first of the quality control steps in the production process. Documents that are coded inconsistently or that do not have redactions but are labeled as such must be referred to the legal team for resolutions prior to production. Once all issues or conflicts are resolved, the project manager or technician can begin to prepare the production.

After the production has been run—the TIFFs and load files have been generated and natives have been exported—there should be a second round of quality checks. The project manager is looking to ensure that the requirements in the productions specification have been adhered to and that the following criteria are met during this second round of quality checks:

- The correct documents have been prepared for production;
- The requested data and/or text have been exported;
- No documents coded privileged are included;
- Documents with redactions have undergone OCR to remove redacted text;
- The production conforms to the agreed upon technical requirements;

- Images are legible and have been endorsed with Bates stamps and confidentiality designations in the proper locations.

As noted above, the project manager is responsible for ensuring that documents with redactions undergo OCR to generate new searchable text. Failure to do this will result in production of the unredacted text or—more precisely—the production of the redacted, usually privileged, material. By regenerating the OCR text, the redacted material is removed from the searchable text.

Once the production is complete, the project manager should ask that the attorney for whom the production was prepared perform a final check of the documents to make sure the redactions have been properly endorsed on the appropriate documents and that the documents and data intended to be withheld are not included in the production. This involves looking at the production images in the database and performing test searches for privileged information, as well as confirming that the Bates numbers and confidential stamps are endorsed as they should be on each page. Quality control searches should be performed on attorney names or other known, privileged terms to ensure that privileged information does not appear in the production.

One more quality check should take place once the production is transferred to DVD or other external media or FTP to ensure that the correct images, native files and data are being transmitted.

Lastly, productions consisting of client documents should be encrypted and/or password protected before they leave a firm or service provider. In the event the external media is lost or misdirected, this will hopefully prevent anyone from viewing the documents. Encryption keys or passwords should likewise be delivered securely to the intended recipient of the media.

Throughout the entire production process, the project manager is responsible for communicating the status of the project to the legal team.

Maintaining a Production Log

The production log is a formal record of the documents produced in a case. It is a best practice to create and update a production log—a chart or other means to illustrate precisely which documents are produced. This responsibility may fall to a paralegal or a project manager. In either event, the log should include at least the following information:

- Date produced
- Production Bates prefixes and numbers
- General description of the documents
- Producing party
- Receiving party
- Type of media
- Means of delivery

It is important to keep the production log accurate and current. Contemporary document review platforms may provide a means for creating a production log or maintaining a production history, and the project manager is responsible for recording the details of each production made from the database.

Productions from Other Parties

Legal teams not only produce documents, they also receive document productions from other parties in the case. When an attorney, paralegal or project manager becomes aware that other parties to litigation are planning to produce documents in electronic format, they should coordinate to ensure that any other parties' production is prepared and delivered in the proper format. As emphasized earlier, the form of a production should be agreed upon by the parties prior to production. Even though the most common format of production is TIFF images, a load file, and a data file, the amount of time wasted sorting through poorly formatted or improperly created load files can be eliminated if the parties and their technologists agree upon the correct format in advance. While there are a number of acceptable formats for production deliverables, a common format will enable a project manager and technical staff to load the documents to a database with relative ease.

Project managers must be able to recognize various load file formats and evaluate not only the content and format of the production, but also the volume and completeness of the production to determine whether it can be loaded to a database. The project manager must alert the supervising attorney if the production does not conform to the agreed upon technical requirements. If issues arise concerning the format of a production from another party, the project manager must explain to the case team what is required to correct the production. It may be necessary for counsel to contact the producing party or their litigation support personnel to request the production in another format.

If paper production documents are received, the case team and project manager should coordinate to determine whether the documents should be scanned and loaded to a database. Paper documents should first be unitized, a process that involves identifying where each documents starts and stops prior to scanning. The case team should consider whether the documents need to be coded, and whether OCR will be required. The project manager is responsible for coordinating with any vendors and with the case team to unitize, scan, code, and OCR the documents.

Conclusion

The production stage is commonly the last step in a discovery project. There may be multiple productions in a given case or requests to add to or change a production. Parties frequently supplement productions later in the case as new information or additional documents and ESI are identified. For most project managers, nearly every task –from Identification through Review—culminates in a document production. There may also be depositions, or, as will be seen in the next chapter, a trial, during which documents and ESI may need to be presented as evidence by the case team. The attorneys may also pursue dispositive motions to dismiss or for summary judgment. But whether the project ends here or not, because this is the stage at which a client's documents are shared with other parties, it is critically important during the Production stage that the project manager pay attention to details, adhere to the production specifications and format, and quality check the production before it goes out.

CHAPTER ELEVEN SUMMARY

KEY POINTS

- In the production stage, the responsive, nonprivileged documents designated by the legal team are prepared for delivery in a format useful to other parties.
- The project manager oversees the preparation of a document production, including all technical processes, personnel, and quality control steps.
- A production specification provides written, detailed instructions regarding which documents are being produced, the format, and the timing of the production.
- Several quality control checkpoints should be established to ensure the right documents are being produced in the right format.
- A document production may include TIFF images, native files, a data file containing metadata, image load files, and searchable text.
- A production log should be maintained of not only documents that are prepared for production, but also documents received from other parties.

Key Document Production Tasks	Documentation
Meet with case team to plan and schedule production.	
Determine format, tools, and techniques for production.	
Determine Bates numbering and image endorsements.	
Prepare production specification documentation.	Production specification
Perform quality/conflict check of coding, document families and OCR.	
Generate TIFF images.	
Export data, images, or native files in required format.	

CHAPTER ELEVEN SUMMARY (cont'd)

Key Document Production Tasks	Documentation
Deliver production to case team for quality check.	
Perform final quality check of data, text, and images.	
Prepare deliverable media.	
Perform quality checks of deliverable.	
Prepare/update document production log.	Production log
Deliver production.	
Close production/prepare status report.	Status report

CHAPTER TWELVE

Presentation of Electronic Documents

S ome small percentage of the ESI and documents that are collected, reviewed, and produced may eventually be used as evidence
in court, arbitrations, hearings, or depositions. So much of what a
project manager does on a daily basis—indeed, nearly all responsibilities outlined in this book—is geared toward properly preparing
documents and ESI for presentation, usually during a trial.[53] Whether
that presentation is to a trial judge, a jury, an arbitration panel, or a
client, the desired outcome is the same: a sound, defensible process
that demonstrates the authenticity of a document and its significance
to the issues in the case.

During the presentation phase, it is the project manager's
responsibility to work with the attorneys, paralegals, and sometimes
the client, to prepare documents and ESI and other materials for
presentation during trial. Documents and ESI collected, processed,
reviewed and produced during the course of a litigation or
investigation may need to be displayed in court. Among the project
manager's responsibilities during the presentation phase are the
following tasks:

---

53   While trials and the presentation of ESI or other digital evidence
during trials or other proceedings are technically not part of the discovery
phase of a litigation, the presentation phase is covered here because it is part of
the EDRM framework and it is the culmination of so much of what a project
manager does during a discovery project.

- Assist in the creation of a list of exhibits to be used at trial;
- Assist to create or coordinate the creation of document designations and/or video deposition clips to be played at trial;
- Coordinate the engagement of service providers or the leasing of equipment needed in the trial war room or courtroom;
- Set up equipment for use at trial, including printers, copy machines, scanners, projectors, monitors, laptops or PCs, and possibly a small local area network;
- Prepare documents designated as exhibits for display in the courtroom;
- Work with attorneys to help prepare witnesses and opening and closing statements.

A Brief History of the Use of Technology in Trials

In the not-too-distant past, and certainly in some circumstances still today, attorneys would walk into a courtroom with notepads, pens, and possibly an easel to display demonstrative exhibits on giant foam boards. Entourages of associates or paralegals carried boxes and litigation bags containing more notepads and all of the documents that would be used during the course of a trial. Some cases were so large that a separate room at the courthouse or a hotel conference room nearby would be reserved to store trial materials. This practice gave birth to the term war room to describe the area in which trial attorneys store documents, meet with witnesses, and make critical decisions regarding the evidence to be presented during the trial. The smoking-gun document in the case would be blown up into a giant, poster-sized foam board, carried into the courtroom, and placed on the easel at the appropriate time and with appropriate dramatic effect. There could be dozens of these foam boards for a single case. Documents to be shown to a witness or circulated during trial would be printed and copied multiple times to ensure a sufficient number of copies for the parties, the witness, the jury, the judge, and even a copy for the court clerk. Then there were the binders. Any paralegal who has worked in the litigation practice of a law firm is familiar with the preparation of binders. There were trial books, witness binders, exhibit binders, "hot" document binders, and any other sort of binder that an attorney requested. Inside the binders were numbered or lettered, prepunched tabs that separated each document. In any given case, there could be dozens of binders and multiple copies of each. If the case were big enough, rolling carts with shelves would be brought in or rented to store and move the binders or boxes—always with the labels on the spines facing out for quick reference while preparing the case in the war room.

Every document to be used during trial had to be marked as an exhibit. A document could be marked for identification purposes only, or it could be assigned an exhibit number. The parties would usually agree upon the exhibit-numbering configuration. Some judges would insist that the parties premark their exhibits, a task that required someone to place an exhibit sticker on each document; in other cases, only the clerk could number an exhibit after it had been properly entered into evidence.

Deposition transcripts—used to cross-examine a witness or present the testimony of a witness who cannot physically be present at the trial—were needed as well. Transcripts that ran hundreds of pages long would typically be digested by a paralegal to capture the salient points but, in court, the actual transcript would be needed and, it too, might need to be marked as an exhibit. If a witness could not appear, then someone would be designated to read the paper deposition transcript of that witness to the jury. All of these materials and the witnesses were at the immediate disposal of the trial attorney. With a little luck, strong facts, and some persuasive argument by the lawyers, a party could win a favorable verdict.

As technology developed, it became clear that technology can and should play a larger role in trials. As advancements in data and image management, communication, and graphics became available, enterprising attorneys and paralegals began to find ways to more efficiently prepare and present evidence at trials. Paper documents became electronic documents; easels became projector screens or flat screen monitors; and foam boards became computer graphics and animated presentations. Laptops and tablet computers have even begun to replace the once-ubiquitous fourteen-inch yellow legal pad.

Modern Trial Preparation

Today, legal teams increasingly arrive in court carrying laptops or tablet devices on which they have loaded their documents. The entourage is gone, and the boxes and binders have been replaced by computers and a trial technician, who presents documents and evidence in the courtroom on a computer screen at the request of the attorney. Modern courtrooms are often wired for sound, and are equipped with flat screen monitors and projectors. The days of the ELMO projector have been replaced by digital cameras, elaborate and sometimes expensively crafted animations and devices that can display, move, manipulate, or change images, pictures, and videos in seconds. Presenting evidence has become much more efficient in the courtroom, in large part due to the increased demand for and use of technology.

Still, very few cases actually make it to trial, and there are several good reasons for this. First, trials are expensive. They are time consuming, require many resources, and can cost a great deal of money. Second, juries and judges are unpredictable. Before a client goes to trial, a risk vs. reward analysis must take place. Most cases settle because, after the parties have considered the risks, their financial stakes, and the potential outcomes, clients usually decide it is not worth risking an unfavorable verdict and the time and cost of a trial, let alone a possible appeal. At the same time, some litigants are adamant about acquiring vindication through the courts. Others have nothing to lose, and so they opt for a trial.

When a case is scheduled for trial, a great deal of preparation is necessary. As with any project or subproject, it necessary to plan for a trial. As soon as practicable, the trial team should be encouraged to meet with the project manager to discuss what role, if any, technology will play in the trial, the necessary resources, and to determine exactly how they would like to present evidence. At this planning meeting, the project manager should, at a minimum, inquire about:

- The number, timing and scheduling of witness testimony;
- Which documents, video, or other materials must be prepared for use at trial;
- The technology tools needed for presentation of the evidence;
- Equipment needed in the courtroom and war room.

As noted previously, everything a project manager does throughout the course of a discovery project—from identification, preservation, collection, review, and through production—is designed to lead to the presentation of evidence in a courtroom or hearing room. Defensible processes are required throughout the phases of a discovery project to ensure that, when it comes time to introduce an electronic document in evidence before a jury, an attorney may establish the authenticity of a document, lay the proper evidentiary foundation for the document, and use the document without objection from opposing parties. This can be difficult to do if, during the collection process, the metadata of the documents was altered, if there is not a chain of custody to demonstrate how a document moved from one location to another, or if the attorney cannot establish the origin of a document.

Project managers working in a litigation support role are responsible to assist attorneys in the preparation of a case for trial. This may involve preparing electronic documents for migration to a trial presentation application, setting up equipment for use at the trial, or actually presenting evidence on the screen in the courtroom.

It is initially important to distinguish between a project manager and a trial technician. Not all project managers make good trial technicians. The trial technician role is not for everyone; it is a very demanding and stressful role. Trial technicians are responsible to ensure that an exhibit—whether a document, video clip, or photograph—is presented quickly, seamlessly, and without interruption. When an attorney asks for an exhibit or the video clip of a witness, the trial technician must present the requested item in seconds. Judges, too, are generally impatient with technology that falters and delays the proceedings. A jury can be even more unforgiving—and jurors hold the client's fate in their hands.

The work of a trial technician also requires very long hours and frequent travel, sometimes to remote locations. Trial technicians work closely with demanding attorneys to help prepare witness testimony or to rehearse opening and closing statements, and work often goes late into the night as the attorneys strategize and plan the following day's presentation. A trial technician's job in the courtroom may seem appealing, in that they are in the thick of the adversarial process, playing a role in the outcome of court proceedings, but the courtroom work may actually be the easy part; the hard part is the preparation, and most of that work takes place after 6:00 PM every night during a trial.

Trial technicians come from various backgrounds. Most trial technicians have a technical background and have worked in either litigation support or paralegal roles. Occasionally, and depending upon the size of the case and the people and budget involved, the trial technician may simply be the paralegal or even an associate assigned to the case. Few law firms or corporations have permanent trial technicians on staff, though, and it is therefore common for large firms or clients to hire a trial consulting firm that can provide a range of services, including jury research, a dedicated trial technician, and equipment. But there are also service providers and independent trial technicians, who provide trial preparation and presentation services.

A project manager who is preparing a case for trial must work closely with the trial technician, assuming the project manager is not also filling the trial technician role. To prepare the case for trial, several things need to happen:

- Deposition transcripts and videos must be digitized and synchronized so they may be loaded to a trial presentation application;[54]

---

54 The process of synchronizing video and text files can be time consuming. Ideally, this process should be completed early in the case. In most cases, synchronized video can be ordered directly from the court reporting service

- Deposition designations that highlight the portions of testimony and/or video that may be played during the trial must be exchanged with other parties;
- Video clips of deposition designations need to be created in the trial presentation application;
- The actual exhibits to be used in the courtroom must be exported from the document review database in which they were initially reviewed and loaded to the trial presentation application;
- A final list of exhibits must be prepared and distributed to the parties;
- Laptops must be prepared and configured for use at the trial site;
- Any additional equipment (copy machines, scanners, monitors, projectors) must be ordered and prepared for delivery to the trial site.

In most cases, a pre-trial order (PTO), which outlines the course and conduct of the trial, is prepared by the parties or issued by the court. Usually, the parties work together to prepare the PTO and present it to the court for approval. A typical PTO contains the primary issues to be tried, a list of witnesses who will testify, exhibits that may be used, and possibly guidance on other logistical issues relating to the trial. The project manager should obtain a copy of the PTO.

The project manager may also be responsible to coordinate the use of technology in the courtroom. The most common equipment will likely be laptops, projectors, screens, or flat panel monitors. This may require contacting the court's administrative or IT staff to determine what equipment is available in the courtroom and what equipment may be permitted by the court. Many modern courthouses have policies and procedures for the use of technology during a trial, and these should be consulted well in advance of any scheduled trial date.

---

at the time of a deposition.

Some jurisdictions require parties to obtain the judge's permission to bring technology equipment into the courtroom.

Trial attorneys who will examine witnesses in court typically prepare an outline for each witness, which includes questions they will ask and the exhibits or video clips they will play during each witness's testimony. The project manager and/or trial technician should have copies of these outlines and review them prior to the witness testimony so that the documents to be presented during that witness' testimony may be identified and prepared in advance. Exhibits that need to be presented during the testimony of a witness should be organized and filed in a way that makes them easily accessible during presentation in the courtroom.

It may also be necessary to prepare witnesses prior to their testimony. The project manager or trial technician may need to set up a laptop, projector, and screen in a small room so that the attorneys may walk through the testimony with the witness in advance of the trial and preview any exhibits or videos.

Similarly, it may be necessary to rehearse opening or closing statements. Again, most attorneys typically have an outline or notes from which they deliver their opening or closing, and they have in mind the exhibits and video clips they may want to play during the course of their argument. The project manager or trial technician will need to work closely with the attorney to prepare for and deliver the most effective presentation possible.

All of the pre-trial preparation will take place while the attorneys and other parties are making motions and arguments *in limine* (Latin for "at the start") to include or exclude evidence, while at the same time preparing witnesses or negotiating a possible settlement of the case. The point is that, preparing for and being a part of a trial can be a very frenetic and stressful time, and the project manager assigned to a trial must be prepared to manage the typical requests for assistance while remaining flexible and amenable to changes in strategy or direction.

It may be challenging for a project manager to persuade attorneys to focus on technology and equipment issues in the run-up to a trial.

Lawyers will be focused on their case, their witnesses, the evidence, and their client. A good project manager will delicately prod and remind the legal team that technology and equipment are a necessary component of modern trial practice.

Trial Presentation Applications

Several commercially available trial presentation applications may be used to present documents, graphics, and video during trial. These applications function as databases—much like document review platforms—but they also have video viewing and editing features, tools, and utilities for manipulating images and graphics, numbering exhibits, and reporting features that provide for exporting exhibit lists or deposition designation reports.

Commonly, documents and video files are exported from other file management platforms and are imported into the trial presentation software. With such software, the project manager or trial technician can create video clips of depositions using the synchronized transcripts and video files, which she may then organize into numbered exhibits to be played during trial. Likewise, documents may be assigned exhibit numbers and organized in a manner that makes them easy to display when a witness takes the stand or when opening and closings arguments are made.

One of the most important things to consider in preparing for a trial using technology is that any equipment or data source must be backed up or duplicated. Courts—and perhaps, more importantly, juries—have little patience for delays caused by faulty equipment or clumsy equipment operators. Delays also take away from the story the attorney is trying to tell and from the continuity of the presentation of the evidence. If a laptop contains the trial presentation database, a second identical laptop should be available in the event anything goes wrong with the first one. Likewise, all of the data related to the trial must be stored on an external hard drive, and there should be a duplicate or backup copy of the hard drive as well.

Trial Equipment

The project manager assigned to a trial should be prepared to secure the equipment needed at trial and to help set up equipment as it arrives at the trial location or in the war room. The equipment necessary for a trial will vary from case to case. If a firm does not own the equipment, it will be necessary to lease or rent the equipment. In some circumstances, it may make sense to share the rental of the courtroom equipment with other parties.

In the courtroom, the equipment needed is likely to consist of laptops, a projector, and either a portable screen or flat panel monitors to display documents and video. There may be one large screen for everyone to view, or there may be several monitors on counsel's table, for the judge, and for the jury. Other equipment may be used as well, including modern digital display equipment. Today, there are even applications designed for iPad users to connect to a projector or other display device wirelessly. In most modern courtrooms, the judge is likely to determine what is displayed on screen, so it is wise to inquire whether the assigned judge requires a kill switch or emergency stop that will turn off a display on demand.

The war room requires equipment that is more extensive. Remember, the attorneys are looking to have the full resources and functionality of their office available during the trial, including PCs and/or laptop computers, a copy machine, a scanner, and any equipment that will be used in the courtroom. It may also be necessary to construct a local network within the war room to enable the case team to connect to a single data source to access and share documents, video, or transcripts. Technology today makes this a relatively simple and cost-effective task. Small, portable servers more than adequately meet small networking needs, or a single PC may be set up as the host PC of a small network. Alternatively, the case team may choose to use the law firm's existing infrastructure and connect to the firm's network remotely, or they may use a secure, cloud-based solution to store documents. In either event, if the war room is at a hotel, the project manager should reach out to hotel IT personnel to inquire about dedicated Internet bandwidth. If this is not possible, contact should be made with service providers who can drop wired or wireless services into the war room.

In the end, participation in a trial—particularly if the result is a verdict favorable to a project team's client—can be one of the most rewarding aspects of work as a project manager or trial technician. The hours are long and hard work is required, but few things in the world of litigation are as fulfilling as having worked on a case from start to finish, with all of the bumps and hiccups along the way, and having a favorable result.

Conclusion

Quite apart from the drama and sound bites seen in legal programs on television, trials in the actual legal system involve a great deal of preparation time and little or no excitement. Technology is one of the many tools that attorneys may use to prepare and present evidence. The project manager involved in a trial or an arbitration hearing plays an integral role in the preparation of the evidence, and it is through adherence to the best practices outlined in this book that the project manager fulfills the obligation to client and indeed the legal system itself.

CHAPTER TWELVE SUMMARY

KEY POINTS

- Nearly all of a project manager's responsibilities to this point are geared toward properly preparing to present documents and ESI at trial, at arbitration, or at a deposition.
- It is during the presentation phase that documents and ESI may be used as evidence, and it is when authenticity of documents and ESI may be challenged by opposing parties or the court.
- *Authenticity* refers to the ability to demonstrate the genuineness of a document, its origin, and chain of custody.
- Technology plays a larger role in modern-day trials than it has in the past; courtrooms are equipped with projectors and screens and wired for Internet and audio/visual presentation.
- Trial technicians or specialists are often employed to present electronic evidence during trials.
- Trial preparation includes setting up equipment for use by the legal team to make access to and the presentation of evidence more efficient.

Key Presentation and Trial Preparation Tasks	Documentation
Meet and plan for deposition, hearing, or trial.	Pretrial order; deposition notice
Determine resources, tools, and techniques for trial.	Vendor documentation (NDA, SOW)
Engage resources to prepare for trial.	
Coordinate war room/court room technology.	Lease/rental agreements
Prepare exhibits.	Exhibit list
Prepare deposition designations/video clips.	Text excerpt reports
Assist with pretrial motions.	
Assist to prepare witness testimony/opening statement.	Examination outlines
Coordinate trial graphics.	
Perform trial presentation.	
Close presentation.	Status report

Conclusion

D iscovery of the truth is the foundational principle of our civil and criminal justice systems. When judgment is rendered in a legal proceeding we want to believe that truth has lit the path to justice. The judicial truth-seeking process, however, is only as good as the information presented as evidence. The pursuit of truth is more complicated today because we live in an electronic ecosphere in which almost everyone is surrounded by an increasingly vast amount of information. Ubiquitous computer devices transmit and store information, up-to-the-minute news, sound bites, video, and social media feeds. Some of this information may play a pivotal role in the truth-seeking process, helping litigants to investigate events and tell their stories in court. And every indication suggests that there will only be more information, more documents, and more digital content.

Nearly everything we do today is somehow dependent upon computer-related or electronic devices that store information. These machines are integral to daily life and they supplement the shortages of mere mortal memories. Indeed, computers are now being programmed to think like humans. There is more information created in the last few years than existed in all of humankind in the thousands of years prior. It should surprise no one that electronic discovery is a growing and thriving industry. Along with the continued data explosion comes a generation of lawyers and paralegals entering the legal business today who simply do not know a time without the internet and smartphones. This new generation will surely become more accepting of new and emerging technologies that supplement legal practice. But, in the meantime, there is work to be done.

The tsunami of information that has washed over the litigation practices of the world's largest firms and corporations is not going to recede. The Federal Rules of Civil Procedure, first adopted in 1934 and in the ensuing 70 years amended just a handful of times, have been amended twice in the past ten years specifically to deal with electronically stored information. The number of reported cases relating to e-discovery has skyrocketed in recent years and continues to grow. There are now professional organizations devoted to e-discovery and a multi-billion dollar software and service provider industry has risen up to capitalize on the changes in legal practice and new technologies brought about by the deluge of data. Recruiters and headhunters now specialize in placing project managers, technical analysts, e-discovery specialists, and yes, e-discovery attorneys.

Software development over the past decade has been an exciting phenomenon to witness, particularly in the litigation support and electronic discovery industry. Companies and their tools have come and gone, and today we have excellent tools needed to collect, process, review and produce the ESI associated with litigations and investigations. E-discovery tools have become more user-friendly, more affordable, and they offer welcoming interfaces. But software alone cannot not supply the solution.

What is needed is a consistently structured process for getting at the truth more quickly, more efficiently, and more reliably. Project management and the principles and practices outlined in this book provide the solution.

The use of project management in electronic discovery ends the self-inflicted misery that the legal industry has imposed upon itself. It makes practical and, more importantly, good economic sense to learn and adhere to the practices outlined in this book. Most human beings have an inherent if not instinctive desire to be organized and efficient, particularly in business and in the professions. It is why we categorize almost everything; it is how the human mind works. Some people do it better than others, for sure, but in the end we all want to get from point A to point B by the most direct route and complete a task in the most efficient manner possible. So, it is no surprise that the legal industry inundated by ESI in discovery seeks more efficient and cost-effective ways to manage and understand the vast amounts of information involved in litigation. And as the e-discovery and litigation support field continues to grow and thrive, there will continue to be a need for skilled, talented, polished and competent project managers and other litigation support professionals who are able to assist attorneys, paralegals, and their clients in the practice of law –particularly as it relates to discovery. Great talent in this industry is difficult to find, but dozens of smart, capable and incredibly over-worked leaders and managers have emerged who are preparing the next generation of project leaders in the field. Still, the "secret sauce" to success is project management. With this book you now possess the knowledge and information needed to succeed.

Finally, to the vast majority of people in the world –even to many in the legal business—the words "electronic discovery" have little or no meaning. At the same time, it is difficult for litigation support and e-discovery project professionals to provide a short answer when asked the question "What do you do?" Project management, on the other hand, is a more intuitively understood profession. People understand it to mean that you lead people, marshal resources, and manage processes that lead to a desired outcome. But to truly comprehend the scope and impact of the work of litigation support and e-discovery project professionals in the legal industry, it is necessary to focus, first, on the body of work in the legal industry – what lawyers and paralegals do. Second, attention should be paid to fundamental project management methodologies. And lastly, a clear understanding of the e-discovery process must be obtained. This book comprehensively exposes the basic principles of traditional project management and the best practices of electronic discovery. For the seasoned practitioner or the novice, this book will hopefully contribute to the truth-seeking process.

Best of luck.

APPENDIX A

Project Management Process Groups and Sample Project Management Forms

A.1 Project Management Process Groups and Knowledge Areas[55]

	INITIATING	PLANNING	EXECUTING	MONITORING & CONTROLLING	CLOSING
INTEGRATION MANAGEMENT	**Develop Project Charter** Inputs: Statement of work Business need Agreements Enterprise environmental factors Organizational process assets Tools & Techniques: Expert judgment Facilitation techniques Outputs: Project charter	**Develop Project Management Plan** Inputs: Project charter Output from other processes Enterprise environmental factors Organizational process assets Tools & Techniques: Expert judgment Facilitation techniques Outputs: Project management plan	**Direct and Manage Project Work** Inputs: Project management plan Approved change requests Enterprise environmental factors Organizational process assets Tools & Techniques: Expert judgment Project management information system Meetings Outputs: Deliverables Work performance information Change requests Project management plan updates Project document updates	**Monitor and Control Project Work** Inputs: Project management plan Schedule forecasts Cost forecasts Validated changes Work performance information Enterprise environmental factors Organizational process assets Tools & Techniques: Expert judgment Analytical techniques Project management information system Meetings Outputs: Change requests Work performance reports Project management plan updates Project document updates **Perform Change Control** Inputs: Project management plan Work performance information Change requests Enterprise environmental factors Organizational process assets Tools & Techniques: Expert judgment Meetings Change control tools Outputs: Approved change requests Change log Project management plan updates Project document updates	**Close Project** Inputs: Project management plan Accepted deliverables Organizational process assets Tools & Techniques: Expert judgment Analytics techniques Meetings Outputs: Final product, service, result transition Organizational process assets updates

55   Project Management Institute, *A Guide to the Project Management Body of Knowledge*, 5th Ed. (2013). Copyright and all rights reserved. This table has been reproduced with the permission of PMI.

	INITIATING	PLANNING	EXECUTING	MONITORING & CONTROLLING	CLOSING
SCOPE MANAGEMENT		**Plan Scope Management** Inputs: Project management plan Project charter Enterprise environmental factors Organizational process assets Tools & Techniques: Expert judgment Meetings Outputs: Scope management plan Requirements management plan **Collect Requirements** Inputs: Scope management plan Requirements management plan Project charter Stakeholder register Tools & Techniques: Interviews Focus groups Facilitated workshops Group creativity techniques Group decision-making techniques Questionnaires and surveys Observations Prototypes Benchmarks Context diagrams Document analysis Outputs: Requirements documentation Requirements traceability matrix **Define Scope** Inputs: Scope management plan Project charter Requirements documentation Organizational process assets Tools & Techniques: Expert judgment Product analysis Alternatives generation Facilitated workshops Outputs: Project scope statement Project document updates **Create Work Breakdown** Structure Inputs: Scope management plan Project scope statement Requirements documentation Enterprise environmental factors Organizational process assets Tools & Techniques: Decomposition Expert judgment Outputs: Scope baseline Project document updates		**Validate Scope** Inputs: Project management plan Requirements documentation Requirements traceability matrix Verified deliverables Work performance data Tools & Techniques: Inspection Group decision-making techniques Outputs: Accepted deliverables Change requests Work performance information Project document updates **Control Scope** Inputs: Project management plan Requirements documentation Requirements traceability matrix Work performance data Organizational process assets Tools & Techniques: Variance analysis Outputs: Work performance information Change requests Project management plan updates Project document updates Organizational process asset updates	

	INITIATING	PLANNING	EXECUTING	MONITORING & CONTROLLING	CLOSING
TIME MANAGEMENT		**Plan Schedule Management** Inputs: Project management plan Project charter Enterprise environmental factors Organizational process assets Tools & Techniques: Expert judgment Analytical techniques Meetings Outputs: Schedule management plan Define Activities Inputs: Schedule management plan Scope baseline Enterprise environmental factors Organizational process assets Tools & Techniques: Decomposition Rolling wave planning Expert judgment Outputs: Activity list Activity attributes Milestone list **Sequence Activities** Inputs: Schedule management plan Activity list Activity attributes Milestone list Project scope statement Enterprise environmental factors Organizational process assets Tools & Techniques: Precedence diagramming method Dependency determination Leads and lags Outputs: Project schedule network diagrams Project document updates **Estimate Activity Resources** Inputs: Schedule management plan Activity list Activity attributes Resource calendars Risk register Activity cost estimates Enterprise environmental factors Organizational process assets Tools & Techniques: Expert judgment Alternatives analysis Published estimating data Bottom-up estimating Project management software Outputs: Activity resource requirements Resource breakdown structure Project document updates **Estimate Activity Durations** Inputs: Schedule management		**Control Schedule** Inputs: Project management plan Project schedule Work performance data Project calendars Schedule data Organizational process assets Tools & Techniques: Performance reviews Project management software Resource optimization techniques Modeling techniques Leads and lags Schedule compression Scheduling tool Outputs: Work performance information Schedule forecasts Change requests Project management plan updates Project document updates Organizational process asset updates	

	INITIATING	PLANNING	EXECUTING	MONITORING & CONTROLLING	CLOSING
QUALITY MANAGEMENT		**Plan Cost Management** Inputs: Project management plan Project charter Enterprise environmental factors Organizational process assets Tools & Techniques: Expert judgment Analytical techniques Meetings Outputs: Cost management plan **Estimate Costs** Inputs: Cost management plan Human resource management plan Scope baseline Project schedule Risk register Enterprise environmental factors Organizational process assets Tools & Techniques: Expert judgment Analogous estimating Parametric estimating Bottom-up estimating Three-point estimating Reserve analysis Cost of quality Project management software Vendor bid analysis Group decision-making techniques Outputs: Activity cost estimates Basis of estimates Project document updates **Determine Budget** Inputs: Cost management plan Scope baseline Activity cost estimates Basis of estimates Project schedule Resource calendars Risk register Agreements Organizational process assets Tools & Techniques: Cost aggregation Reserve analysis Expert judgment Historical relationships Funding limit reconciliation Outputs: Cost baseline Project funding requirements Project document updates		**Control Costs** Inputs: Project management plan Project funding requirements Work performance data Organizational process assets Tools & Techniques: Earned value management Forecasting To-complete performance index Performance reviews Project management software Reserve analysis Outputs: Work performance information Cost forecasts Change requests Project management plan updates Project document updates Organizational process asset updates	

	INITIATING	PLANNING	EXECUTING	MONITORING & CONTROLLING	CLOSING
QUALITY MANAGEMENT		**Plan Quality Management** <u>Inputs</u>: Project management plan Stakeholder register Risk register Requirements documentation Enterprise environmental factors Organizational process assets <u>Tools & Techniques</u>: Cost-benefit analysis Cost of quality Seven basic quality tools Benchmarking Design of experiments Statistical sampling Additional quality planning tools Meetings <u>Outputs</u>: Quality management plan Quality metrics Quality checklists Project document updates	**Perform Quality Assurance** <u>Inputs</u>: Quality management plan Process improvement plan Quality metrics Quality control measurements Project documents <u>Tools & Techniques</u>: Quality management and control tools Quality audits Process analysis <u>Outputs</u>: Change requests Project management plan updates Project document updates Organizational process asset updates	**Control Quality** <u>Inputs</u>: Project management plan Quality metrics Quality checklists Work performance data Approved change requests Deliverables Project documents Organizational process assets <u>Tools & Techniques</u>: Seven basic quality tools Statistical sampling Inspection Approved change requests review <u>Outputs</u>: Quality control measurements Validated changes Verified deliverables Work performance information Change requests Project management plan updates Project document updates Organizational process asset updates	

	INITIATING	PLANNING	EXECUTING	MONITORING & CONTROLLING	CLOSING
HUMAN RESOURCE MANAGEMENT		**Plan Human Resource Management** Inputs: Project management plan Activity resource requirements Enterprise environmental factors Organizational process assets Tools & Techniques: Organization charts and job descriptions Networking Organizational theory Expert judgment Meetings Outputs: Human resource management plan	**Acquire Project Team** Inputs: Human resource management plan Project management plan Enterprise environmental factors Organizational process assets Tools & Techniques: Pre-assignment Negotiation Acquisition Virtual teams Multi-criteria decision analysis Outputs: Project staff assignments Resource calendars Project management plan updates **Develop Project Team** Inputs: Human resource management plan Project staff assignments Resource calendars Tools & Techniques: Interpersonal skills Training Team-building activities Ground rules Co-location Recognition and rewards Personnel assessment tools Outputs: Team performance assessments Enterprise environmental factor updates **Manage Project Team** Inputs: Human resource management plan Project staff assignments Team performance assessments Work performance reports Organizational process assets Tools & Techniques: Observation and conversation Project performance appraisals Conflict management Interpersonal skills Outputs: Change requests Project management plan updates Project document updates Enterprise environmental factor updates Organizational process asset updates		

	INITIATING	PLANNING	EXECUTING	MONITORING & CONTROLLING	CLOSING
COMMUNICATION MANAGEMENT		**Plan Communications Management** Inputs: Project management plan Stakeholder register Stakeholder management strategy Enterprise environmental factors Organizational process assets Tools & Techniques: Communication requirements analysis Communication technology Communication models Communication methods Meetings Outputs: Communications management plan Project document updates	**Manage Communications** Inputs: Communications management plan Work performance reports Enterprise environmental factors Organizational process assets Tools & Techniques: Communication technology Communication models Communication methods Information management systems Performance reporting Outputs: Project communications Project management plan Project document updates Organizational process asset updates	**Control Communications** Inputs: Project management plan Project communications Issue log Work performance data Organizational process assets Tools & Techniques: Information management systems Expert judgment Meetings Outputs: Work performance information Change requests Project management plan updates Project document updates Organizational process asset updates	

	INITIATING	PLANNING	EXECUTING	MONITORING & CONTROLLING	CLOSING
RISK MANAGEMENT		**Plan Risk Management** Inputs: Project management plan Project charter Stakeholder register Enterprise environmental factors Organizational process assets Tools & Techniques: Analytical techniques Expert judgment Meetings Outputs: Risk management plan **Identify Risks** Inputs: Risk management plan Cost management plan Schedule management plan Quality management plan Human resource management plan Scope baseline Activity cost estimates Activity duration estimates Stakeholder register Project documents Procurement documents Enterprise environmental factors Organizational process assets Tools & Techniques: Documentation reviews Information gathering techniques Checklist analysis Assumption analysis Diagramming techniques SWOT analysis Expert judgment Outputs: Risk register **Perform Qualitative Risk Analysis** Inputs: Risk management plan Scope baseline Risk register Enterprise environmental factors Organizational process assets Tools & Techniques: Risk probability and impact assessment Probability and impact matrix Risk data quality assessment Risk categorization Risk urgency assessment Expert judgment Outputs: Project document updates **Perform Quantitative Risk Analysis** Inputs: Risk management plan Cost management plan Schedule management plan Risk register Enterprise environmental factors Organizational process assets Tools & Techniques: Data gathering and representation techniques Quantitative risk analysis and modeling techniques	**Control Risks** Inputs: Project management plan Risk register Work performance data Work performance reports Tools & Techniques: Risk reassessment Risk audits Variance and trend analysis Technical performance measurement Reserve analysis Meetings Outputs: Work performance information Change requests Project management plan updates Project document updates Organizational process asset updates		

	INITIATING	PLANNING	EXECUTING	MONITORING & CONTROLLING	CLOSING
PROCUREMENT MANAGEMENT		**Plan Procurement Management** Inputs: Project management plan Requirements documentation Risk register Activity resource requirements Project schedule Activity cost estimates Stakeholder register Enterprise environmental factors Organizational process assets Tools & Techniques: Make-or-buy analysis Expert judgment Market research Meetings Outputs: Procurement management plan Procurement statement of work Procurement documents Source selection criteria Make-or-buy decision Change requests Project document updates	**Conduct Procurements** Inputs: Procurement management plan Procurement documents Source selection criteria Seller proposals Project documents Make-or-buy decisions Procurement statement of work Organizational process assets Tools & Techniques: Bidder conference Proposal evaluation techniques Independent estimates Expert judgment Advertising Analytical techniques Procurement negotiations Outputs: Selected sellers Agreements Resource calendars Change requests Project management plan updates Project document updates	**Control Procurements** Inputs: Project management plan Procurement documents Agreements Approved change requests Work performance reports Work performance data Tools & Techniques: Contract change control system Procurement performance reviews Inspections and audits Performance reporting Payment systems Claims administration Records management system Outputs: Work performance information Change requests Project management plan updates Project document updates Organizational process asset updates	**Close Procurements** Inputs: Project management plan Procurement documents Tools & Techniques: Procurement audits Procurement negotiations Records management system Outputs: Closed procurements Organizational process asset updates

	INITIATING	PLANNING	EXECUTING	MONITORING & CONTROLLING	CLOSING
STAKE-HOLDER MANAGEMENT	**Identify Stakeholders** Inputs: Project charter Procurement documents Enterprise environmental factors Organizational process assets Tools & Techniques: Stakeholder analysis Expert judgment Meetings Outputs: Stakeholder register	**Plan Stakeholder Management** Inputs: Project management plan Stakeholder register Enterprise environmental factors Organizational process assets Tools & Techniques: Expert judgment Meetings Analytical techniques Outputs: Stakeholder management plan Project document updates	**Manage Stakeholder Engagement** Inputs: Stakeholder management plan Communications management plan Change log Organizational process assets Tools & Techniques: Communication methods Interpersonal skills Management skills Outputs: Issue log Change requests Project management plan updates Project document updates Organizational process assets updates	**Control Stakeholder Engagement** Inputs: Project management plan Issue log Work performance data Project documents Tools & Techniques: Information management systems Expert judgment Meetings Outputs: Work performance information Change requests Project management plan updates Project document updates Organizational process asset updates	

A.2 Sample Project Charter

Project Title:	
Prepared by:	
Proposed Start:	
Duration:	
Stakeholders:	
Project Scope:	
Assumptions:	
Milestones:	
Resources:	
Roles and responsibilities:	
Constraints:	
Budget:	

Signatures:	
Date:	

A.3 Sample Project Management Plan

Project Name:			
Project Manager:			
Date Initiated:		**Version:**	

I. INITIATING PROCESSES

Stakeholders

Name	Title	Email / Phone

II. PLANNING PROCESSES

Project Scope Statement		

Milestones	Deliverables	Date

Schedule

	Duration/Dates

Costs

	Budget	Actual	Variance

Resources

Resource	Constraints (if any)
Project Budget:	$
Personnel:	
Equipment:	
Vendors:	

Project Risks

Risk	Mitigation Strategy

Quality Management

Communications Management

III. EXECUTING PROCESSES

Quality Assurance

Policies:	Checkpoints:

Project Team/Vendors

Name	Responsibility	Email / Phone

IV. MONITORING AND CONTROLLING PROCESSES

Quality Assurance

Standards:	Measurements:

Change Requests

V. CLOSING PROCESSES

Validate Deliverables:	Lessons Learned:

Signatures

Name	Signature	Date
Sponsor		
Project Manager		

APPENDIX B

Federal Rules of Civil Procedure and Rule 502 of the Federal Rules of Evidence

B.1 Federal Rules of Civil Procedure, Rule 1, 16, 26, 30-31, 33-34,-36-37

FRCP Rule 1. Scope and Purpose

These rules govern the procedures in all civil actions and proceedings in the United States District courts, except as stated in Rule 81. They should be construed, administered, *and employed by the courts and the parties* to secure the just, speedy, and inexpensive determination of every action and proceeding.

(Author Commentary: This rule was amended in December of 2015 to place emphasis on the responsibility of the parties, not just the courts, to be cooperative and proportional in the use of procedural discovery tools).

FRCP Rule 16. Pretrial Conferences; Scheduling; Management

(a) **Purposes of a Pretrial Conference.** In any action, the court may order the attorneys and any unrepresented parties to appear for one or more pretrial conferences for such purposes as:

(1) expediting disposition of the action;

(2) establishing early and continuing control so that the case will not be protracted because of lack of management;

(3) discouraging wasteful pretrial activities;

(4) improving the quality of the trial through more thorough preparation; and

(5) facilitating settlement.

(b) Scheduling

(1) *Scheduling Order.* Except in categories of actions exempted by local rule, the district judge – or a magistrate judge when authorized by local rule – must issue a scheduling order:

(A) after receiving the parties' report under Rule 26(f); or

(B) after consulting with the parties' attorneys and any unrepresented parties at a scheduling conference.

(2) *Time to Issue.* The judge must issue the scheduling order as soon as practicable, but *unless the judge finds good cause for delay, the judge must issue it* within the earlier of *90* days after any defendant has been served with the complaint or *60* days after any defendant has appeared.

(3) *Contents of the Order.*

(A) *Required Contents.* The scheduling order must limit the time to join other parties, amend the pleadings, complete discovery, and file motions.

(B) *Permitted Contents.* The scheduling order may:

(i) modify the timing of disclosures under Rules 26(a) and 26(e)(1);

(ii) modify the extent of discovery;

(iii) provide for disclosure *or preservation* of electronically stored information;

(iv) include any agreements the parties reach for asserting claims of privilege or of protection as trial-preparation material after information is produced, *including agreements reached under Federal Rule of Evidence 502*;

(v) *direct that before moving for an order relating to discovery, the movant must request a conference with the court;*

(vi) set dates for pretrial conferences and for trial; and

(vii) include other appropriate matters.

(Author Commentary: In 2015, the time to issue a scheduling order was reduced in order to reduce delays in the beginning of litigation and possibly to get parties talking about discovery issues earlier in the case. Additional

provisions were added to Rule 16(b)(3)(B) to permit the court to provide in a scheduling order for the preservation of electronically stored information (ESI), to incorporate agreements of the parties under FRE 502, and to require parties to request a conference with the court before making a motion related to discovery issues).

FRCP Rule 26. Duty to Disclose; General Provisions Governing Discovery

(a) Required Disclosures.

(1) *Initial Disclosure.*

(A) *In General.* Except as exempted by Rule 26(a)(1)(B) or as otherwise stipulated or ordered by the court, a party must, without awaiting a discovery request, provide to the other parties:

(i) the name and, if known, the address and telephone number of each individual likely to have discoverable information--along with the subjects of that information--that the disclosing party may use to support its claims or defenses, unless the use would be solely for impeachment;

(ii) a copy--or a description by category and location--of all documents, electronically stored information, and tangible things that the disclosing party has in its possession, custody, or control and may use to support its claims or defenses, unless the use would be solely for impeachment;

(iii) a computation of each category of damages claimed by the disclosing party--who must also make available for inspection and copying as under Rule 34 the documents or other evidentiary material, unless privileged or protected from disclosure, on which each computation is based, including materials bearing on the nature and extent of injuries suffered; and

(iv) for inspection and copying as under Rule 34, any insurance agreement under which an insurance business may be liable to satisfy all or part of a possible judgment in the action or to indemnify or reimburse for payments made to satisfy the judgment.

(B) *Proceedings Exempt from Initial Disclosure.* The following proceedings are exempt from initial disclosure:

(i) an action for review on an administrative record;

(ii) a forfeiture action in rem arising from a federal statute;

(iii) a petition for habeas corpus or any other proceeding to challenge a criminal conviction or sentence;

(iv) an action brought without an attorney by a person in the custody of the United States, a state, or a state subdivision;

(v) an action to enforce or quash an administrative summons or subpoena;

(vi) an action by the United States to recover benefit payments;

(vii) an action by the United States to collect on a student loan guaranteed by the United States;

(viii) a proceeding ancillary to a proceeding in another court; and

(ix) an action to enforce an arbitration award.

(C) *Time for Initial Disclosures--In General.* A party must make the initial disclosures at or within 14 days after the parties' Rule 26(f) conference unless a different time is set by stipulation or court order, or unless a party objects during the conference that initial disclosures are not appropriate in this action and states the objection in the proposed discovery plan. In ruling on the objection, the court must determine what disclosures, if any, are to be made and must set the time for disclosure.

(D) *Time for Initial Disclosures--For Parties Served or Joined Later.* A party that is first served or otherwise joined after the Rule 26(f) conference must make the initial disclosures within 30 days after being served or joined, unless a different time is set by stipulation or court order.

(E) *Basis for Initial Disclosure; Unacceptable Excuses.* A party must make its initial disclosures based on the information then reasonably available to it. A party is not excused from making its disclosures because it has not fully investigated the case or because it challenges the sufficiency of another party's disclosures or because another party has not made its disclosures.

(2) *Disclosure of Expert Testimony.*

(A) *In General.* In addition to the disclosures required by Rule 26(a)(1), a party must disclose to the other parties the identity of any witness it may use at trial to present evidence under Federal Rule of Evidence 702, 703, or 705.

(B) *Witnesses Who Must Provide a Written Report.* Unless otherwise stipulated or ordered by the court, this disclosure must be accompanied by a written report--prepared and signed by the witness--if the witness is one retained or specially employed to provide expert testimony in the case or one whose duties as the party's employee regularly involve giving expert testimony. The report must contain:

(i) a complete statement of all opinions the witness will express and the basis and reasons for them;

(ii) the facts or data considered by the witness in forming them;

(iii) any exhibits that will be used to summarize or support them;

(iv) the witness's qualifications, including a list of all publications authored in the previous 10 years;

(v) a list of all other cases in which, during the previous 4 years, the witness testified as an expert at trial or by deposition; and

(vi) a statement of the compensation to be paid for the study and testimony in the case.

(C) *Witnesses Who Do Not Provide a Written Report.* Unless otherwise stipulated or ordered by the court, if the witness is not required to provide a written report, this disclosure must state:

(i) the subject matter on which the witness is expected to present evidence under Federal Rule of Evidence 702, 703, or 705; and

(ii) a summary of the facts and opinions to which the witness is expected to testify.

(D) *Time to Disclose Expert Testimony.* A party must make these disclosures at the times and in the sequence that the court orders.

Absent a stipulation or a court order, the disclosures must be made:

(i) at least 90 days before the date set for trial or for the case to be ready for trial; or

(ii) if the evidence is intended solely to contradict or rebut evidence on the same subject matter identified by another party under Rule 26(a)(2)(B) or (C), within 30 days after the other party's disclosure.

(E) *Supplementing the Disclosure.* The parties must supplement these disclosures when required under Rule 26(e).

(3) ***Pretrial Disclosures.***

(A) *In General.* In addition to the disclosures required by Rule 26(a)(1) and (2), a party must provide to the other parties and promptly file the following information about the evidence that it may present at trial other than solely for impeachment:

(i) the name and, if not previously provided, the address and telephone number of each witness--separately identifying those the party expects to present and those it may call if the need arises;

(ii) the designation of those witnesses whose testimony the party expects to present by deposition and, if not taken stenographically, a transcript of the pertinent parts of the deposition; and

(iii) an identification of each document or other exhibit, including summaries of other evidence--separately identifying those items the party expects to offer and those it may offer if the need arises.

(B) *Time for Pretrial Disclosures; Objections.* Unless the court orders otherwise, these disclosures must be made at least 30 days before trial. Within 14 days after they are made, unless the court sets a different time, a party may serve and promptly file a list of the following objections: any objections to the use under Rule 32(a) of a deposition designated by another party under Rule 26(a)(3)(A)(ii); and any objection, together with the grounds for it, that may be made to the admissibility of materials identified under Rule 26(a)(3)(A)(iii). An objection not so made--except for one under Federal Rule of Evidence 402 or 403--is waived unless excused by the court for good cause.

(4) *Form of Disclosures.* Unless the court orders otherwise, all disclosures under Rule 26(a) must be in writing, signed, and served.

(b) Discovery Scope and Limits.

(1) *Scope in General.* Unless otherwise limited by court order, the scope of discovery is as follows: Parties may obtain discovery regarding any nonprivileged matter that is relevant to any party's claim or *defense and proportional to the needs of the case, considering the importance of the issues at stake in the action, the amount in controversy, the parties' relative access to relevant information, the parties' resources, the importance of the discovery in resolving the issues, and whether the burden or expense of the proposed discovery outweighs its likely benefit. Information within this scope of discovery need not be admissible in evidence to be discoverable.*

(2) *Limitations on Frequency and Extent.*

(A) *When Permitted.* By order, the court may alter the limits in these rules on the number of depositions and interrogatories or on the length of depositions under Rule 30. By order or local rule, the court may also limit the number of requests under Rule 36.

(B) *Specific Limitations on Electronically Stored Information.* A party need not provide discovery of electronically stored information from sources that the party identifies as not reasonably accessible because of undue burden or cost. On motion to compel discovery or for a protective order, the party from whom discovery is sought must show that the information is not reasonably accessible because of undue burden or cost. If that showing is made, the court may nonetheless order discovery from such sources if the requesting party shows good cause, considering the limitations of Rule 26(b)(2)(C). The court may specify conditions for the discovery.

(C) *When Required.* On motion or on its own, the court must limit the frequency or extent of discovery otherwise allowed by these rules or by local rule if it determines that:

(i) the discovery sought is unreasonably cumulative or duplicative, or can be obtained from some other source that is more convenient, less burdensome, or less expensive;

(ii) the party seeking discovery has had ample opportunity to obtain the information by discovery in the action; or

(iii) the proposed discovery is *outside the scope permitted by Rule 26(b)(1)*.

(3) *Trial Preparation: Materials.*

(A) *Documents and Tangible Things.* Ordinarily, a party may not discover documents and tangible things that are prepared in anticipation of litigation or for trial by or for another party or its representative (including the other party's attorney, consultant, surety, indemnitor, insurer, or agent). But, subject to Rule 26(b)(4), those materials may be discovered if:

(i) they are otherwise discoverable under Rule 26(b)(1); and

(ii) the party shows that it has substantial need for the materials to prepare its case and cannot, without undue hardship, obtain their substantial equivalent by other means.

(B) *Protection Against Disclosure.* If the court orders discovery of those materials, it must protect against disclosure of the mental impressions, conclusions, opinions, or legal theories of a party's attorney or other representative concerning the litigation.

(C) *Previous Statement.* Any party or other person may, on request and without the required showing, obtain the person's own previous statement about the action or its subject matter. If the request is refused, the person may move for a court order, and Rule 37(a)(5) applies to the award of expenses. A previous statement is either:

(i) a written statement that the person has signed or otherwise adopted or approved; or

(ii) a contemporaneous stenographic, mechanical, electrical, or other recording--or a transcription of it--that recites substantially verbatim the person's oral statement.

(4) *Trial Preparation: Experts.*

(A) *Deposition of an Expert Who May Testify.* A party may depose any person who has been identified as an expert whose opinions may be presented at trial. If Rule 26(a)(2)(B) requires a report from the expert, the deposition may be conducted only after the report is provided.

(B) *Trial-Preparation Protection for Draft Reports or Disclosures.* Rules 26(b)(3)(A) and (B) protect drafts of any report or disclosure required under Rule 26(a)(2), regardless of the form in which the draft is recorded.

(C) *Trial-Preparation Protection for Communications Between a Party's Attorney and Expert Witnesses.* Rules 26(b)(3)(A) and (B) protect communications between the party's attorney and any witness required to provide a report under Rule 26(a)(2)(B), regardless of the form of the communications, except to the extent that the communications:

> (i) relate to compensation for the expert's study or testimony;

> (ii) identify facts or data that the party's attorney provided and that the expert considered in forming the opinions to be expressed; or

> (iii) identify assumptions that the party's attorney provided and that the expert relied on in forming the opinions to be expressed.

(D) *Expert Employed Only for Trial Preparation.* Ordinarily, a party may not, by interrogatories or deposition, discover facts known or opinions held by an expert who has been retained or specially employed by another party in anticipation of litigation or to prepare for trial and who is not expected to be called as a witness at trial. But a party may do so only:

> (i) as provided in Rule 35(b); or

> (ii) on showing exceptional circumstances under which it is impracticable for the party to obtain facts or opinions on the same subject by other means.

(E) *Payment.* Unless manifest injustice would result, the court must require that the party seeking discovery:

> (i) pay the expert a reasonable fee for time spent in responding to discovery under Rule 26(b)(4)(A) or (D); and

> (ii) for discovery under (D), also pay the other party a fair portion of the fees and expenses it reasonably incurred in obtaining the expert's facts and opinions.

(5) ***Claiming Privilege or Protecting Trial-Preparation Materials.***

(A) *Information Withheld.* When a party withholds information otherwise discoverable by claiming that the information is privileged or subject to protection as trial-preparation material, the party must:

(i) expressly make the claim; and

(ii) describe the nature of the documents, communications, or tangible things not produced or disclosed--and do so in a manner that, without revealing information itself privileged or protected, will enable other parties to assess the claim.

(B) *Information Produced.* If information produced in discovery is subject to a claim of privilege or of protection as trial-preparation material, the party making the claim may notify any party that received the information of the claim and the basis for it. After being notified, a party must promptly return, sequester, or destroy the specified information and any copies it has; must not use or disclose the information until the claim is resolved; must take reasonable steps to retrieve the information if the party disclosed it before being notified; and may promptly present the information to the court under seal for a determination of the claim. The producing party must preserve the information until the claim is resolved.

(c) Protective Orders.

(1) ***In General.*** A party or any person from whom discovery is sought may move for a protective order in the court where the action is pending--or as an alternative on matters relating to a deposition, in the court for the district where the deposition will be taken. The motion must include a certification that the movant has in good faith conferred or attempted to confer with other affected parties in an effort to resolve the dispute without court action. The court may, for good cause, issue an order to protect a party or person from annoyance, embarrassment, oppression, or undue burden or expense, including one or more of the following:

(A) forbidding the disclosure or discovery;

(B) specifying terms, including time and place *or the allocation of expenses*, for the disclosure or discovery;

(C) prescribing a discovery method other than the one selected by the party seeking discovery;

(D) forbidding inquiry into certain matters, or limiting the scope of disclosure or discovery to certain matters;

(E) designating the persons who may be present while the discovery is conducted;

(F) requiring that a deposition be sealed and opened only on court order;

(G) requiring that a trade secret or other confidential research, development, or commercial information not be revealed or be revealed only in a specified way; and

(H) requiring that the parties simultaneously file specified documents or information in sealed envelopes, to be opened as the court directs.

(2) **Ordering Discovery.** If a motion for a protective order is wholly or partly denied, the court may, on just terms, order that any party or person provide or permit discovery.

(3) **Awarding Expenses.** Rule 37(a)(5) applies to the award of expenses.

(d) **Timing and Sequence of Discovery.**

(1) Timing. A party may not seek discovery from any source before the parties have conferred *as* required by Rule 26(f), except in a proceeding exempted from initial disclosure under Rule 26(a)(1)(B), or when authorized by these rules, by stipulation, or by court order.

(2) Early Rule 34 Requests.

(A) Time to Deliver. More than 21 days after the summons and complaint are served on a party, a request under Rule 34 may be delivered;

(i) to that party by any other party, and

(ii) by that party to any plaintiff or to any other party that has been served.

(B) When Considered Served. The request is considered to have been served at the first Rule 26(f) conference.

(1) Sequence. Unless *the parties stipulate* or the court orders otherwise for the parties' and witnesses' convenience and in the interests of justice:

(A) methods of discovery may be used in any sequence; and

(B) discovery by one party does not require any other party to delay its discovery.

(e) Supplementing Disclosures and Responses.

(1) *In General.* A party who has made a disclosure under Rule 26(a)--or who has responded to an interrogatory, request for production, or request for admission--must supplement or correct its disclosure or response:

(A) in a timely manner if the party learns that in some material respect the disclosure or response is incomplete or incorrect, and if the additional or corrective information has not otherwise been made known to the other parties during the discovery process or in writing; or

(B) as ordered by the court.

(2) *Expert Witness.* For an expert whose report must be disclosed under Rule 26(a)(2)(B), the party's duty to supplement extends both to information included in the report and to information given during the expert's deposition. Any additions or changes to this information must be disclosed by the time the party's pretrial disclosures under Rule 26(a)(3) are due.

(f) Conference of the Parties; Planning for Discovery.

(1) *Conference Timing.* Except in a proceeding exempted from initial disclosure under Rule 26(a)(1)(B) or when the court orders otherwise, the parties must confer as soon as practicable--and in any event at least 21 days before a scheduling conference is to be held or a scheduling order is due under Rule 16(b).

(2) *Conference Content; Parties' Responsibilities.* In conferring, the parties must consider the nature and basis of their claims and defenses and the possibilities for promptly settling or resolving the case; make or arrange for the disclosures required by Rule 26(a)(1); discuss any issues about preserving discoverable information; and develop a proposed discovery plan. The attorneys of record and all unrepresented parties that have appeared in the case are jointly responsible for arranging the conference, for attempting in good faith to agree on the proposed discovery plan, and for submitting to the court within 14

days after the conference a written report outlining the plan. The court may order the parties or attorneys to attend the conference in person.

(3) *Discovery Plan.* A discovery plan must state the parties' views and proposals on:

(A) what changes should be made in the timing, form, or requirement for disclosures under Rule 26(a), including a statement of when initial disclosures were made or will be made;

(B) the subjects on which discovery may be needed, when discovery should be completed, and whether discovery should be conducted in phases or be limited to or focused on particular issues;

(C) any issues about disclosure, discovery, *or preservation* of electronically stored information, including the form or forms in which it should be produced;

(D) any issues about claims of privilege or of protection as trial-preparation materials, including – if the parties agree on a procedure to assert these claims after production –whether to ask the court to include their agreement in an order *under Federal Rule of Evidence 502*;

(E) what changes should be made in the limitations on discovery imposed under these rules or by local rule, and what other limitations should be imposed; and

(F) any other orders that the court should issue under Rule 26(c) or under Rule 16(b) and (c).

(4) *Expedited Schedule.* If necessary to comply with its expedited schedule for Rule 16(b) conferences, a court may by local rule:

(A) require the parties' conference to occur less than 21 days before the scheduling conference is held or a scheduling order is due under Rule 16(b); and

(B) require the written report outlining the discovery plan to be filed less than 14 days after the parties' conference, or excuse the parties from submitting a written report and permit them to report orally on their discovery plan at the Rule 16(b) conference.

(g) Signing Disclosures and Discovery Requests, Responses, and Objections.

(1) *Signature Required; Effect of Signature.* Every disclosure under Rule 26(a)(1) or (a)(3) and every discovery request, response, or objection must be signed by at least one attorney of record in the attorney's own name--or by the party personally, if unrepresented--and must state the signer's address, e-mail address, and telephone number. By signing, an attorney or party certifies that to the best of the person's knowledge, information, and belief formed after a reasonable inquiry:

(A) with respect to a disclosure, it is complete and correct as of the time it is made; and

(B) with respect to a discovery request, response, or objection, it is:

(i) consistent with these rules and warranted by existing law or by a nonfrivolous argument for extending, modifying, or reversing existing law, or for establishing new law;

(ii) not interposed for any improper purpose, such as to harass, cause unnecessary delay, or needlessly increase the cost of litigation; and

(iii) neither unreasonable nor unduly burdensome or expensive, considering the needs of the case, prior discovery in the case, the amount in controversy, and the importance of the issues at stake in the action.

(2) *Failure to Sign.* Other parties have no duty to act on an unsigned disclosure, request, response, or objection until it is signed, and the court must strike it unless a signature is promptly supplied after the omission is called to the attorney's or party's attention.

(3) *Sanction for Improper Certification.* If a certification violates this rule without substantial justification, the court, on motion or on its own, must impose an appropriate sanction on the signer, the party on whose behalf the signer was acting, or both. The sanction may include an order to pay the reasonable expenses, including attorney's fees, caused by the violation.

(*Author Commentary*: *The 2015 amendments to Rule 26 redefined the scope of discovery and inserted provisions relating to proportionality that should limit discovery. Discovery may now be had of information that is relevant to a party's claims or defensed and that is proportional to the needs of the case. See Rule 26(b)(1). Added to Rule 26(c)(1)(B) is language allowing a court to specify how expenses may be allocated when a party seeks a protective order. Another significant change in 2015 is the addition of Rule 26(d), which allows for a party to deliver "early" Rule 34 document requests more than 21 days after the party is served and before the Rule 26(f) meet and confer. It appears that "delivery" prior to the 26(f) conference would cause a more substantive discussion of discovery issues at the 26(f) conference).*

FRCP Rule 30. Depositions by Oral Examination

(a) When a Deposition May Be Taken.

(1) Without Leave. A party may, by oral questions, depose any person, including a party, without leave of court except as provided in Rule 30(a)(2). The deponent's attendance may be compelled by subpoena under Rule 45.

(2) With Leave. A party must obtain leave of court, and the court must grant leave to the extent consistent with Rule 26(b)*(1) and* (2):

   (A) if the parties have not stipulated to the deposition and:

   (i) the deposition would result in more than 10 depositions being taken under this rule or Rule 31 by the plaintiffs, or by the defendants, or by the third-party defendants;

   (ii) the deponent has already been deposed in the case; or

   (iii) the party seeks to take the deposition before the time specified in Rule 26(d), unless the party certifies in the notice, with supporting facts, that the deponent is expected to leave the United States and be unavailable for examination in this country after that time; or

   (B) if the deponent is confined in prison.

(b) Notice of the Deposition; Other Formal Requirements.

(1) Notice in General. A party who wants to depose a person by oral questions must give reasonable written notice to every other party. The notice must state the time and place of the deposition and, if known, the deponent's name and address. If the name is unknown, the notice must provide a general description sufficient to identify the person or the particular class or group to which the person belongs.

(2) Producing Documents. If a subpoena duces tecum is to be served on the deponent, the materials designated for production, as set out

in the subpoena, must be listed in the notice or in an attachment. The notice to a party deponent may be accompanied by a request under Rule 34 to produce documents and tangible things at the deposition.

(3) Method of Recording.

(A) Method Stated in the Notice. The party who notices the deposition must state in the notice the method for recording the testimony. Unless the court orders otherwise, testimony may be recorded by audio, audiovisual, or stenographic means. The noticing party bears the recording costs. Any party may arrange to transcribe a deposition.

(B) Additional Method. With prior notice to the deponent and other parties, any party may designate another method for recording the testimony in addition to that specified in the original notice. That party bears the expense of the additional record or transcript unless the court orders otherwise.

(4) By Remote Means. The parties may stipulate--or the court may on motion order--that a deposition be taken by telephone or other remote means. For the purpose of this rule and Rules 28(a), 37(a)(2), and 37(b)(1), the deposition takes place where the deponent answers the questions.

(5) Officer's Duties.

(A) Before the Deposition. Unless the parties stipulate otherwise, a deposition must be conducted before an officer appointed or designated under Rule 28. The officer must begin the deposition with an on-the-record statement that includes:

(i) the officer's name and business address;

(ii) the date, time, and place of the deposition;

(iii) the deponent's name;

(iv) the officer's administration of the oath or affirmation to the deponent; and

(v) the identity of all persons present.

(B) Conducting the Deposition; Avoiding Distortion. If the deposition is recorded non-stenographically, the officer must repeat the items in Rule 30(b)(5)(A)(i)-(iii) at the beginning of each unit of the recording medium. The deponent's and attorneys' appearance or demeanor must not be distorted through recording techniques.

(C) After the Deposition. At the end of a deposition, the officer must state on the record that the deposition is complete and must set out any stipulations made by the attorneys about custody of the transcript or recording and of the exhibits, or about any other pertinent matters.

(6) Notice or Subpoena Directed to an Organization. In its notice or subpoena, a party may name as the deponent a public or private corporation, a partnership, an association, a governmental agency, or other entity and must describe with reasonable particularity the matters for examination. The named organization must then designate one or more officers, directors, or managing agents, or designate other persons who consent to testify on its behalf; and it may set out the matters on which each person designated will testify. A subpoena must advise a nonparty organization of its duty to make this designation. The persons designated must testify about information known or reasonably available to the organization. This paragraph (6) does not preclude a deposition by any other procedure allowed by these rules.

(c) Examination and Cross-Examination; Record of the Examination; Objections; Written Questions.

(1) Examination and Cross-Examination. The examination and cross-examination of a deponent proceed as they would at trial under the Federal Rules of Evidence, except Rules 103 and 615. After putting the deponent under oath or affirmation, the officer must record the testimony by the method designated under Rule 30(b)(3)(A). The testimony must be recorded by the officer personally or by a person acting in the presence and under the direction of the officer.

(2) Objections. An objection at the time of the examination--whether to evidence, to a party's conduct, to the officer's qualifications, to the manner of taking the deposition, or to any other aspect of the deposition--must be noted on the record, but the examination still proceeds; the testimony is taken subject to any objection. An objection must be stated concisely in a nonargumentative and nonsuggestive manner. A person may instruct a deponent not to answer only when necessary to

preserve a privilege, to enforce a limitation ordered by the court, or to present a motion under Rule 30(d)(3).

(3) Participating Through Written Questions. Instead of participating in the oral examination, a party may serve written questions in a sealed envelope on the party noticing the deposition, who must deliver them to the officer. The officer must ask the deponent those questions and record the answers verbatim.

(d) Duration; Sanction; Motion to Terminate or Limit.

(1) Duration. Unless otherwise stipulated or ordered by the court, a deposition is limited to 1 day of 7 hours. The court must allow additional time consistent with Rule 26(b)*(1) and* (2) if needed to fairly examine the deponent or if the deponent, another person, or any other circumstance impedes or delays the examination.

(2) Sanction. The court may impose an appropriate sanction--including the reasonable expenses and attorney's fees incurred by any party--on a person who impedes, delays, or frustrates the fair examination of the deponent.

(3) Motion to Terminate or Limit.

(A) Grounds. At any time during a deposition, the deponent or a party may move to terminate or limit it on the ground that it is being conducted in bad faith or in a manner that unreasonably annoys, embarrasses, or oppresses the deponent or party. The motion may be filed in the court where the action is pending or the deposition is being taken. If the objecting deponent or party so demands, the deposition must be suspended for the time necessary to obtain an order.

(B) Order. The court may order that the deposition be terminated or may limit its scope and manner as provided in Rule 26(c). If terminated, the deposition may be resumed only by order of the court where the action is pending.

(C) Award of Expenses. Rule 37(a)(5) applies to the award of expenses.

(e) Review by the Witness; Changes.

(1) Review; Statement of Changes. On request by the deponent or a party before the deposition is completed, the deponent must be

allowed 30 days after being notified by the officer that the transcript or recording is available in which:

(A) to review the transcript or recording; and

(B) if there are changes in form or substance, to sign a statement listing the changes and the reasons for making them.

(2) Changes Indicated in the Officer's Certificate. The officer must note in the certificate prescribed by Rule 30(f)(1) whether a review was requested and, if so, must attach any changes the deponent makes during the 30-day period.

(f) Certification and Delivery; Exhibits; Copies of the Transcript or Recording; Filing.

(1) Certification and Delivery. The officer must certify in writing that the witness was duly sworn and that the deposition accurately records the witness's testimony. The certificate must accompany the record of the deposition. Unless the court orders otherwise, the officer must seal the deposition in an envelope or package bearing the title of the action and marked "Deposition of [witness's name]" and must promptly send it to the attorney who arranged for the transcript or recording. The attorney must store it under conditions that will protect it against loss, destruction, tampering, or deterioration.

(2) Documents and Tangible Things.

(A) Originals and Copies. Documents and tangible things produced for inspection during a deposition must, on a party's request, be marked for identification and attached to the deposition. Any party may inspect and copy them. But if the person who produced them wants to keep the originals, the person may:

(i) offer copies to be marked, attached to the deposition, and then used as originals--after giving all parties a fair opportunity to verify the copies by comparing them with the originals; or

(ii) give all parties a fair opportunity to inspect and copy the originals after they are marked--in which event the originals may be used as if attached to the deposition.

(B) Order Regarding the Originals. Any party may move for an order that the originals be attached to the deposition pending final disposition of the case.

(3) Copies of the Transcript or Recording. Unless otherwise stipulated or ordered by the court, the officer must retain the stenographic notes of a deposition taken stenographically or a copy of the recording of a deposition taken by another method. When paid reasonable charges, the officer must furnish a copy of the transcript or recording to any party or the deponent.

(4) Notice of Filing. A party who files the deposition must promptly notify all other parties of the filing.

(g) Failure to Attend a Deposition or Serve a Subpoena; Expenses. A party who, expecting a deposition to be taken, attends in person or by an attorney may recover reasonable expenses for attending, including attorney's fees, if the noticing party failed to:

(1) attend and proceed with the deposition; or

(2) serve a subpoena on a nonparty deponent, who consequently did not attend.

FRCP Rule 31. Depositions by Written Questions

(a) When a Deposition May Be Taken.

(1) *Without Leave.* A party may, by written questions, depose any person, including a party, without leave of court except as provided in Rule 31(a)(2). The deponent's attendance may be compelled by subpoena under Rule 45.

(2) *With Leave.* A party must obtain leave of court, and the court must grant leave to the extent consistent with Rule 26(b)*(1) and* (2):

(A) if the parties have not stipulated to the deposition and:

(i) the deposition would result in more than 10 depositions being taken under this rule or Rule 30 by the plaintiffs, or by the defendants, or by the third-party defendants;

(ii) the deponent has already been deposed in the case; or

(iii) the party seeks to take a deposition before the time specified in Rule 26(d); or

(B) if the deponent is confined in prison.

(3) Service; Required Notice. A party who wants to depose a person by written questions must serve them on every other party, with a notice stating, if known, the deponent's name and address. If the name is unknown, the notice must provide a general description sufficient to identify the person or the particular class or group to which the person belongs. The notice must also state the name or descriptive title and the address of the officer before whom the deposition will be taken.

(4) Questions Directed to an Organization. A public or private corporation, a partnership, an association, or a governmental agency may be deposed by written questions in accordance with Rule 30(b)(6).

(5) Questions from Other Parties. Any questions to the deponent from other parties must be served on all parties as follows: cross-questions, within 14 days after being served with the notice and direct questions; redirect questions, within 7 days after being served with cross-questions; and recross-questions, within 7 days after being served with redirect questions. The court may, for good cause, extend or shorten these times.

(b) Delivery to the Officer; Officer's Duties. The party who noticed the deposition must deliver to the officer a copy of all the questions served and of the notice. The officer must promptly proceed in the manner provided in Rule 30(c), (e), and (f) to:

(1) take the deponent's testimony in response to the questions;

(2) prepare and certify the deposition; and

(3) send it to the party, attaching a copy of the questions and of the notice.

(c) Notice of Completion or Filing.

(1) Completion. The party who noticed the deposition must notify all other parties when it is completed.

(2) Filing. A party who files the deposition must promptly notify all other parties of the filing.

FRCP Rule 33. Interrogatories to Parties

(a) In General.

(1) *Number.* Unless otherwise stipulated or ordered by the court, a party may serve on any other party no more than 25 written inter-

rogatories, including all discrete subparts. Leave to serve additional interrogatories may be granted to the extent consistent with Rule 26(b)*(1) and* (2).

(2) *Scope.* An interrogatory may relate to any matter that may be inquired into under Rule 26(b). An interrogatory is not objectionable merely because it asks for an opinion or contention that relates to fact or the application of law to fact, but the court may order that the interrogatory need not be answered until designated discovery is complete, or until a pretrial conference or some other time.

(b) Answers and Objections.

(1) *Responding Party.* The interrogatories must be answered:

(A) by the party to whom they are directed; or

(B) if that party is a public or private corporation, a partnership, an association, or a governmental agency, by any officer or agent, who must furnish the information available to the party.

(2) *Time to Respond.* The responding party must serve its answers and any objections within 30 days after being served with the interrogatories. A shorter or longer time may be stipulated to under Rule 29 or be ordered by the court.

(3) *Answering Each Interrogatory.* Each interrogatory must, to the extent it is not objected to, be answered separately and fully in writing under oath.

(4) *Objections.* The grounds for objecting to an interrogatory must be stated with specificity. Any ground not stated in a timely objection is waived unless the court, for good cause, excuses the failure.

(5) *Signature.* The person who makes the answers must sign them, and the attorney who objects must sign any objections.

(c) Use. An answer to an interrogatory may be used to the extent allowed by the Federal Rules of Evidence.

(d) Option to Produce Business Records. If the answer to an interrogatory may be determined by examining, auditing, compiling, abstracting, or summarizing a party's business records (including electronically stored information), and if the burden of deriving or ascertaining the answer will be substantially the same for either party, the responding party may answer by:

(1) specifying the records that must be reviewed, in sufficient detail to enable the interrogating party to locate and identify them as readily as the responding party could; and

(2) giving the interrogating party a reasonable opportunity to examine and audit the records and to make copies, compilations, abstracts, or summaries.

FRCP Rule 34. Producing Documents, Electronically Stored Information, and Tangible Things, or Entering onto Land, for Inspection and Other Purposes

(a) In General. A party may serve on any other party a request within the scope of Rule 26(b):

(1) to produce and permit the requesting party or its representative to inspect, copy, test, or sample the following items in the responding party's possession, custody, or control:

(A) any designated documents or electronically stored information--including writings, drawings, graphs, charts, photographs, sound recordings, images, and other data or data compilations--stored in any medium from which information can be obtained either directly or, if necessary, after translation by the responding party into a reasonably usable form; or

(B) any designated tangible things; or

(2) to permit entry onto designated land or other property possessed or controlled by the responding party, so that the requesting party may inspect, measure, survey, photograph, test, or sample the property or any designated object or operation on it.

(b) Procedure.

(1) *Contents of the Request.* The request:

(A) must describe with reasonable particularity each item or category of items to be inspected;

(B) must specify a reasonable time, place, and manner for the inspection and for performing the related acts; and

(C) may specify the form or forms in which electronically stored information is to be produced.

(2) *Responses and Objections.*

(A) *Time to Respond.* The party to whom the request is directed must respond in writing within 30 days after being served *or – if the request was delivered under Rule 26(d)(2)* – within 30 days after the parties first Rule 26(f) conference. A shorter or longer time may be stipulated to under Rule 29 or be ordered by the court.

(B) *Responding to Each Item.* For each item or category, the response must either state that inspection and related activities will be permitted as requested or *state with specificity the grounds for objecting to the request, including the reasons. The responding party may state that it will produce copies or documents or of electronically stored information instead of permitting inspection. The production must then be completed no later than the time for inspection specified in the request or another reasonable time specified in the response.*

(C) *Objections. An objection must state whether any responsive materials are being withheld on the basis of that objection.* An objection to part of a request must specify the part and permit inspection of the rest.

(D) *Responding to a Request for Production of Electronically Stored Information.* The response may state an objection to a requested form for producing electronically stored information. If the responding party objects to a requested form--or if no form was specified in the request--the party must state the form or forms it intends to use.

(E) *Producing the Documents or Electronically Stored Information.* Unless otherwise stipulated or ordered by the court, these procedures apply to producing documents or electronically stored information:

(i) A party must produce documents as they are kept in the usual course of business or must organize and label them to correspond to the categories in the request;

(ii) If a request does not specify a form for producing electronically stored information, a party must produce it in a form or forms in which it is ordinarily maintained or in a reasonably usable form or forms; and

(iii) A party need not produce the same electronically stored information in more than one form.

(c) Nonparties. As provided in Rule 45, a nonparty may be compelled to produce documents and tangible things or to permit an inspection.

(*Author Commentary*: *Amendments to Rule 34 in 2015 conform the rule to other amendments and require that a party objecting to a request for production state with greater specificity than previously required the grounds for the objection*).

FRCP Rule 36. Requests for Admission

(a) Scope and Procedure.

(1) *Scope.* A party may serve on any other party a written request to admit, for purposes of the pending action only, the truth of any matters within the scope of Rule 26(b)(1) relating to:

(A) facts, the application of law to fact, or opinions about either; and

(B) the genuineness of any described documents.

(2) *Form; Copy of a Document.* Each matter must be separately stated. A request to admit the genuineness of a document must be accompanied by a copy of the document unless it is, or has been, otherwise furnished or made available for inspection and copying.

(3) *Time to Respond; Effect of Not Responding.* A matter is admitted unless, within 30 days after being served, the party to whom the request is directed serves on the requesting party a written answer or objection addressed to the matter and signed by the party or its attorney. A shorter or longer time for responding may be stipulated to under Rule 29 or be ordered by the court.

(4) *Answer.* If a matter is not admitted, the answer must specifically deny it or state in detail why the answering party cannot truthfully admit or deny it. A denial must fairly respond to the substance of the matter; and when good faith requires that a party qualify an answer or deny only a part of a matter, the answer must specify the part admitted and qualify or deny the rest. The answering party may assert lack of knowledge or information as a reason for failing to admit or deny only if the party states that it has made reasonable inquiry and that

the information it knows or can readily obtain is insufficient to enable it to admit or deny.

(5) *Objections.* The grounds for objecting to a request must be stated. A party must not object solely on the ground that the request presents a genuine issue for trial.

(6) *Motion Regarding the Sufficiency of an Answer or Objection.* The requesting party may move to determine the sufficiency of an answer or objection. Unless the court finds an objection justified, it must order that an answer be served. On finding that an answer does not comply with this rule, the court may order either that the matter is admitted or that an amended answer be served. The court may defer its final decision until a pretrial conference or a specified time before trial. Rule 37(a)(5) applies to an award of expenses.

(b) Effect of an Admission; Withdrawing or Amending It. A matter admitted under this rule is conclusively established unless the court, on motion, permits the admission to be withdrawn or amended. Subject to Rule 16(e), the court may permit withdrawal or amendment if it would promote the presentation of the merits of the action and if the court is not persuaded that it would prejudice the requesting party in maintaining or defending the action on the merits. An admission under this rule is not an admission for any other purpose and cannot be used against the party in any other proceeding.

FRCP Rule 37. Failure to Make Disclosures or to Cooperate in Discovery; Sanctions

(a) Motion for an Order Compelling Disclosure or Discovery.

(1) *In General.* On notice to other parties and all affected persons, a party may move for an order compelling disclosure or discovery. The motion must include a certification that the movant has in good faith conferred or attempted to confer with the person or party failing to make disclosure or discovery in an effort to obtain it without court action.

(2) *Appropriate Court.* A motion for an order to a party must be made in the court where the action is pending. A motion for an order to a nonparty must be made in the court where the discovery is or will be taken.

(3) *Specific Motions.*

(A) *To Compel Disclosure.* If a party fails to make a disclosure required by Rule 26(a), any other party may move to compel disclosure and for appropriate sanctions.

(B) *To Compel a Discovery Response.* A party seeking discovery may move for an order compelling an answer, designation, production, or inspection. This motion may be made if:

(i) a deponent fails to answer a question asked under Rule 30 or 31;

(ii) a corporation or other entity fails to make a designation under Rule 30(b)(6) or 31(a)(4);

(iii) a party fails to answer an interrogatory submitted under Rule 33; or

(iv) a party *fails to produce documents or* fails to respond that inspection will be permitted--or fails to permit inspection--as requested under Rule 34.

(C) *Related to a Deposition.* When taking an oral deposition, the party asking a question may complete or adjourn the examination before moving for an order.

(4) *Evasive or Incomplete Disclosure, Answer, or Response.* For purposes of this subdivision (a), an evasive or incomplete disclosure, answer, or response must be treated as a failure to disclose, answer, or respond.

(5) *Payment of Expenses; Protective Orders.*

(A) *If the Motion Is Granted (or Disclosure or Discovery Is Provided After Filing).* If the motion is granted--or if the disclosure or requested discovery is provided after the motion was filed--the court must, after giving an opportunity to be heard, require the party or deponent whose conduct necessitated the motion, the party or attorney advising that conduct, or both to pay the movant's reasonable expenses incurred in making the motion, including attorney's fees. But the court must not order this payment if:

(i) the movant filed the motion before attempting in good faith to obtain the disclosure or discovery without court action;

(ii) the opposing party's nondisclosure, response, or objection was substantially justified; or

(iii) other circumstances make an award of expenses unjust.

(B) *If the Motion Is Denied.* If the motion is denied, the court may issue any protective order authorized under Rule 26(c) and must, after giving an opportunity to be heard, require the movant, the attorney filing the motion, or both to pay the party or deponent who opposed the motion its reasonable expenses incurred in opposing the motion, including attorney's fees. But the court must not order this payment if the motion was substantially justified or other circumstances make an award of expenses unjust.

(C) *If the Motion Is Granted in Part and Denied in Part.* If the motion is granted in part and denied in part, the court may issue any protective order authorized under Rule 26(c) and may, after giving an opportunity to be heard, apportion the reasonable expenses for the motion.

(b) Failure to Comply with a Court Order.

(1) *Sanctions in the District Where the Deposition Is Taken.* If the court where the discovery is taken orders a deponent to be sworn or to answer a question and the deponent fails to obey, the failure may be treated as contempt of court.

(2) *Sanctions in the District Where the Action Is Pending.*

(A) *For Not Obeying a Discovery Order.* If a party or a party's officer, director, or managing agent--or a witness designated under Rule 30(b)(6) or 31(a)(4)--fails to obey an order to provide or permit discovery, including an order under Rule 26(f), 35, or 37(a), the court where the action is pending may issue further just orders. They may include the following:

(i) directing that the matters embraced in the order or other designated facts be taken as established for purposes of the action, as the prevailing party claims;

(ii) prohibiting the disobedient party from supporting or opposing designated claims or defenses, or from introducing designated matters in evidence;

(iii) striking pleadings in whole or in part;

(iv) staying further proceedings until the order is obeyed;

(v) dismissing the action or proceeding in whole or in part;

(vi) rendering a default judgment against the disobedient party; or

(vii) treating as contempt of court the failure to obey any order except an order to submit to a physical or mental examination.

(B) *For Not Producing a Person for Examination.* If a party fails to comply with an order under Rule 35(a) requiring it to produce another person for examination, the court may issue any of the orders listed in Rule 37(b)(2)(A)(i)-(vi), unless the disobedient party shows that it cannot produce the other person.

(C) *Payment of Expenses.* Instead of or in addition to the orders above, the court must order the disobedient party, the attorney advising that party, or both to pay the reasonable expenses, including attorney's fees, caused by the failure, unless the failure was substantially justified or other circumstances make an award of expenses unjust.

(c) Failure to Disclose, to Supplement an Earlier Response, or to Admit.

(1) *Failure to Disclose or Supplement.* If a party fails to provide information or identify a witness as required by Rule 26(a) or (e), the party is not allowed to use that information or witness to supply evidence on a motion, at a hearing, or at a trial, unless the failure was substantially justified or is harmless. In addition to or instead of this sanction, the court, on motion and after giving an opportunity to be heard:

(A) may order payment of the reasonable expenses, including attorney's fees, caused by the failure;

(B) may inform the jury of the party's failure; and

(C) may impose other appropriate sanctions, including any of the orders listed in Rule 37(b)(2)(A)(i)-(vi).

(2) *Failure to Admit.* If a party fails to admit what is requested under Rule 36 and if the requesting party later proves a document to be genuine or the matter true, the requesting party may move that the party who failed to admit pay the reasonable expenses, including attorney's fees, incurred in making that proof. The court must so order unless:

(A) the request was held objectionable under Rule 36(a);

(B) the admission sought was of no substantial importance;

(C) the party failing to admit had a reasonable ground to believe that it might prevail on the matter; or

(D) there was other good reason for the failure to admit.

(d) Party's Failure to Attend Its Own Deposition, Serve Answers to Interrogatories, or Respond to a Request for Inspection.

(1) *In General.*

(A) *Motion; Grounds for Sanctions.* The court where the action is pending may, on motion, order sanctions if:

(i) a party or a party's officer, director, or managing agent--or a person designated under Rule 30(b)(6) or 31(a)(4)--fails, after being served with proper notice, to appear for that person's deposition; or

(ii) a party, after being properly served with interrogatories under Rule 33 or a request for inspection under Rule 34, fails to serve its answers, objections, or written response.

(B) *Certification.* A motion for sanctions for failing to answer or respond must include a certification that the movant has in good faith conferred or attempted to confer with the party failing to act in an effort to obtain the answer or response without court action.

(2) *Unacceptable Excuse for Failing to Act.* A failure described in Rule 37(d)(1)(A) is not excused on the ground that the discovery sought was objectionable, unless the party failing to act has a pending motion for a protective order under Rule 26(c).

(3) *Types of Sanctions.* Sanctions may include any of the orders listed in Rule 37(b)(2)(A)(i)-(vi). Instead of or in addition to these sanctions, the court must require the party failing to act, the attorney advising that party, or both to pay the reasonable expenses, including attorney's fees, caused by the failure, unless the failure was substantially justified or other circumstances make an award of expenses unjust.

(e) Failure to *Preserve* Electronically Stored Information. *If electronically stored information that should have been preserved in the anticipation or conduct of litigation is lost because a party failed to take reasonable steps to preserve it, and it cannot be restored or replaced through additional discovery, the court:*

> *(1) upon finding prejudice to another party from loss of the information, may order measures no greater than necessary to cure the prejudice; or*
>
> *(2) only upon a finding that the party acted with the intent to deprive another party of the information's use in the litigation may:*
>
> > *(A) presume that the lost information was unfavorable to the party;*
> >
> > *(B) instruct the jury that it may or must presume the information was unfavorable to the party; or*
> >
> > *(C) dismiss the action or enter a default judgment.*

(f) Failure to Participate in Framing a Discovery Plan. If a party or its attorney fails to participate in good faith in developing and submitting a proposed discovery plan as required by Rule 26(f), the court may, after giving an opportunity to be heard, require that party or attorney to pay to any other party the reasonable expenses, including attorney's fees, caused by the failure.

*(**Author Commentary**: The 2015 amendments to Rule 37 relate primarily to the consequences for failure to properly preserve ESI. The so-called "safe harbor provision," which previously protected a party from sanctions as a result of the loss or inadvertent destruction of ESI due to the good faith operation of a computer system, has been removed. Commentators had reached the conclusion that the safe harbor provision did very little to protect parties against sanctions anyway. A new paragraph (e), added in 2015, now speaks to the failure to preserve ESI. Parties must "take reasonable steps" to preserve ESI. The consequences for failure to do so are now "measures no greater than necessary to cure the prejudice." Only upon a finding that a party intentionally deprived another party of discoverable information may the court impose the most serious adverse inference or terminating sanctions.*

B.2 Federal Rules of Evidence Rule 502 (as amended in 2008)

Rule 502. Attorney-Client Privilege and Work Product; Limitations on Waiver

The following provisions apply, in the circumstances set out, to disclosure of a communication or information covered by the attorney-client privilege or work-product protection.

(a) Disclosure Made in a Federal Proceeding or to a Federal Office or Agency; Scope of a Waiver. When the disclosure is made in a federal proceeding or to a federal office or agency and waives the attorney-client privilege or work-product protection, the waiver extends to an undisclosed communication or information in a federal or state proceeding only if:

(1) the waiver is intentional;

(2) the disclosed and undisclosed communications or information concern the same subject matter; and

(3) they ought in fairness to be considered together.

(b) Inadvertent Disclosure. When made in a federal proceeding or to a federal office or agency, the disclosure does not operate as a waiver in a federal or state proceeding if:

(1) the disclosure is inadvertent;

(2) the holder of the privilege or protection took reasonable steps to prevent disclosure; and

(3) the holder promptly took reasonable steps to rectify the error, including (if applicable) following Federal Rule of Civil Procedure 26(b)(5)(B).

(c) Disclosure Made in a State Proceeding. When the disclosure is made in a state proceeding and is not the subject of a state-court order concerning waiver, the disclosure does not operate as a waiver in a federal proceeding if the disclosure:

(1) would not be a waiver under this rule if it had been made in a federal proceeding; or

(2) is not a waiver under the law of the state where the disclosure occurred.

(d) Controlling Effect of a Court Order. A federal court may order that the privilege or protection is not waived by disclosure connected with the litigation pending before the court — in which event the disclosure is also not a waiver in any other federal or state proceeding.

(e) Controlling Effect of a Party Agreement. An agreement on the effect of disclosure in a federal proceeding is binding only on the parties to the agreement, unless it is incorporated into a court order.

(f) Controlling Effect of this Rule. Notwithstanding Rules 101 and 1101, this rule applies to state proceedings and to federal court-annexed and federal court-mandated arbitration proceedings, in the circumstances set out in the rule. And notwithstanding Rule 501, this rule applies even if state law provides the rule of decision.

(g) Definitions. In this rule:

(1) "attorney-client privilege" means the protection that applicable law provides for confidential attorney-client communications; and

(2) "work-product protection" means the protection that applicable law provides for tangible material (or its intangible equivalent) prepared in anticipation of litigation or for trial.

Sample E-Discovery Forms

C.1 Sample Proposed Discovery Plan

UNITED STATES DISTRICT COURT
_____ DISTRICT OF _____

---x

ABC Corporation,

                        Plaintiff Docket No.:

            -against-

XYZ Company,

                        Defendant.

---x

[DRAFT] PROPOSED STIPULATION AND ORDER GOVERNING DISCOVERY

Plaintiff ABC Corporation and Defendant XYZ Company (hereafter "the Parties"), by and through the undersigned attorneys, hereby agree and stipulate to the following:

1. Electronically stored information ("ESI") will be part of the discoverable material in this case and the parties agree to cooperatively exchange discoverable ESI and use reasonable, good faith efforts to identify, preserve, collect, review and produce non-privileged ESI and other documents that are relevant to a party's claims or defenses and which are proportional to the needs of this case pursuant to Fed. R. Civ. Proc 26(b)(1).

2. The parties agree to plan for and meet and confer on discovery issues pursuant to Fed. R. Civ. Proc. 26(f), including discussion regarding preservation of discoverable ESI, the development of a joint proposed discovery plan, the subjects on which discovery may be needed, the timing of discovery and any issues about ESI and the form in which it should be produced.

Sources of and Limitations on ESI

3. Absent a showing of good cause by the requesting party, the parties shall not modify, on a going-forward basis, their internal procedures used by them in the ordinary course of business to backup, archive, store, or manage information systems and ESI, except that the parties will preserve non-duplicative discoverable ESI currently in their possession, custody or control and proportional to the needs of the case.

4. The parties recognize their mutual obligation to take reasonable and proportional steps to identify and preserve discoverable information within a party's possession, custody and control, and agree to identify and preserve ESI only from the following data sources: [*list examples below – e.g., email system, PC/laptop hard drives, file servers*].

5. Absent a showing of good cause the following categories of ESI need not be preserved or collected and are considered inaccessible due to undue burden and/or expense, or because the information is more reasonably available elsewhere:

   a. Unallocated, slack space, deleted data, file fragments or other data accessible by use of computer forensics;

   b. Random access memory (RAM), temporary files, or other difficult to preserve ephemeral data;

   c. Data relating to online access, such as temporary Internet files, browser history, file or memory caches and cookies;

   d. Data in metadata fields that are frequently updated automatically as part of the usual operation of a software application, operating system or network (e.g., date last accessed or printed);

   e. Backup or archived data that is substantially duplicative of data that is more reasonably accessible elsewhere;

f. Telephone or VOIP voice messages;

g. Instant messages, pin-to-pin and other electronic text messages sent to or from mobile devices, smartphones or Blackberry devices, that are not regularly stored or saved on a server dedicated to storing such data;

h. Other data stored on mobile or handheld devices, smartphones or Blackberry devices, such as calendars, tasks, call logs, photographs, contacts or notes, provided that copies of such information is routinely saved or stored elsewhere;

i. Operating system files, executable files, network, server or system logs;

j. Data from systems that are no longer in use ("Legacy Data") that is unreadable or unintelligible on current systems.

General Production Format

6. The parties will produce ESI in single-page TIFF image format provided that the documents do not become illegible or unusable when converted to TIFF image format. Documents that become illegible or unusable when converted to TIFF image format (e.g., Microsoft Excel files), will be produced in native format. The parties reserve the right to reasonably seek additional electronic documents in their native format for good cause shown.

7. Documents originating in paper form will be scanned to TIFF image format at 300 DPI and undergo Optical Character Recognition (OCR). These documents will be produced in single-page TIFF image format as indicated below together with document-level OCR text files. Paper documents will be logically unitized to reflect original document boundaries for each document.

8. All ESI and documents will be produced with image load files, the data fields provided in Table 1, below, and either extracted text or text generated using OCR that render documents searchable. In those instances where redaction is used, OCR text will be provided in lieu of the extracted text to allow for removal of the redacted text from production. For documents produced in native format, in addition to producing extracted text and the data fields in Table 1 below, the producing party will provide TIFF-image slip sheets endorsed with the

production number and level of confidentiality pursuant to any applicable protective order in this case.

9. ESI will be processed and produced with all hidden text (e.g., track changes, speaker's notes, hidden rows or columns, comments, markups, notes, etc.) and formulas exposed, expanded and extracted and rendered in the TIFF image.

10. ESI and documents originally in paper form shall be produced as kept in the usual course of business. A producing party need not include in its production any indication of the document request(s) to which a document may be responsive.

11. Images, native files, metadata and text files to be produced will be delivered on appropriate media (CD/DVD or portable external drive) and will be organized in separate folders named "IMAGES," "NATIVE," "DATA" and "TEXT."

Image Format

12. Documents that are converted to TIFF image format will be produced in accordance with the following technical specifications:

a. Single-page, 1-bit, group IV TIFF image files at 300 dpi; color images will be single-page JPEG format;

b. TIFF file names cannot contain embedded spaces;

c. Bates numbers should be endorsed on the lower right corner of all TIFF images and will be a unique, consistently formatted identifier, i.e. alpha prefix along with a fixed length number (e.g., ABC0000001). The number of digits in the numeric portion of the bates number will be zero-filled to seven digits and the format of the Bates numbering convention should not change in subsequent productions;

d. Confidential designations, if any, will be endorsed on the lower left corner of all TIFF images;

e. Presentations, including PowerPoint slides, should be rendered to TIFF in "notes" format to include the full slide image together with any speaker notes following the appropriate slide image;

f. Drawings, photographs and any other graphical files, including 2-D and 3-D drawings, engineering drawings, AutoCAD and SoldWorks, should be rendered to single-page TIFF image format or rendered to JPEG format with color in the original maintained.

g. Excel spreadsheets will only be rendered to TIFF image format if (1) the file can be fully viewed, meaning that all hidden information in the Excel file (e.g., rows, columns and comments) will be rendered to TIFF; or (2) the Excel file has undergone redaction.

h. TIFF images will be delivered with a comma delimited image load file in the Opticon (.OPT) format as follows:

ABC00001, VOL001, D:\IMAGES\001\REL00001.TIF, Y,,,3

Column One (ABC00001) – the page identifier

Column Two (VOL001) – volume identifier; not required, but a space is required in each line of the load file for this field as illustrated above

Column Three (D:\IMAGES\001\REL00001.TIF) – file path to the image file

Column Four (Y) – Document marker –indicates the start of a unique document.

Column Five (blank) – can be used to indicate box

Column Six (blank) – can be used to indicate folder

Column Seven (3) – often used to store page count

Data Format

13. Extracted data, including the data fields listed in Table 1 below, will be produced in a delimited data file accordance with the following technical specifications:

a. The first line of the data file must be a header row identifying the field names;

b. The data file must use the following default delimiters:

Comma	␋	ASCII character 020
Quote	þ	ASCII character 254
Newline	®	ASCII character 174
Multi-value	;	ASCII character 59

c. Date fields in the data file will be provided in mm/dd/yyyy format;

d. All attachments should sequentially follow the parent document/ email and include data fields identifying documents as "parent" documents or "attachments" with appropriate group identifiers;

e. The fields of data to be produced are listed in Table 1.

TABLE 1: Data Field List

Field Name	Description
BATESSTART	First Bates number of each document being produced
BATESSTOP	Last Bates number of each document being produced
ATTACHSTART	First Bates number of attachment range
ATTACHSTOP	Last Bates number of attachment range
CUSTODIAN	Email: User mailbox where the email resided Application File: Individual from whom the document originated
FROM	Email: Sender of an email Application File: (empty)
TO	Recipient(s) of an email
CC	Recipient(s) copied on an email
BCC	Recipients blind copied on an email
SUBJECT	Email: Subject line of the email
DATESENT	Email: Date the email was sent Application File: (empty)
TIMESENT	Email: Time the email was sent Application File: (empty)
AUTHOR	Email: (empty) Application File: Author of document
TITLE	The text in the "Title" field of an application file
DATECREATE	Email: (empty) Application File: Date the document was created
TIMECREATE	Email: (empty) Application File: Time the document was created

DATELASTMOD	Email: (empty) Application File: Date the document was last modified
TIMELASTMOD	Email: (empty) Application File: Time the document was last modified
FILESIZE	Size of application file document/email in KB
FILETYPE	Email, attachment or loose application file
FILEPATH	Email: Full file path were original email was stored Application File: Full file path were application file was stored including original file name
FILEEXT	The file extension of the native file
FILENAME	The name of the application file, including file extension
PAGECOUNT	The number of pages of each individual document
DESIGNATION	The confidentiality designation assigned to the document pursuant to any confidentiality/protective order in the case
APPLICATION	The name of the application that generated the native file
NATIVE_FILE	Link to the native email or application file
CONVERSATION ID	Email or conversation index number generated by Outlook to identify email conversations
PARENT_ID	The document number of the document identified as an attachment's parent email
GROUP_ID	The family group identifier used to group emails with their attachments
HASHVALUE	Hash value of each email or application file
TEXT	The extracted text or OCR text of the application file or email (assuming text files are not delivered separately)

f. The data file for scanned paper documents will, at a minimum, contain the BATESSTART, BATESSTOP, CUSTODIAN and TEXT fields.

Searchable Text

14. Searchable text of entire documents will be produced either as extracted text for all documents that originate in electronic format, or, for paper documents and any document from which text cannot be extracted, as text generated using OCR technology. For redacted documents, the text of the redacted version of the document will be produced.

15. Searchable text will be produced as a document-level multipage ASCII text file with the text file named the same as the BATESSTART field in the data file; text files will be placed in a separate directory for delivery.

Native Files

16. Native file documents, emails or attachments may be included in the production using the below criteria:

a. Documents produced in native file format will have the file name named the same as the BATESSTART number;

b. The full path of the native file will be provided in the data file for the NATIVE_FILE field;

c. When native files are produced because rendering the file to TIFF would not result in viewable images, a TIFF image slip sheet placeholder will be produced endorsed with the file name and the legend "Document Produced in Native Format" (or something similar);

d. The confidentiality designation applied to any document under a protective order entered in this action will be produced in the load file in the DESIGNATION field.

Deduplication

17. A producing party may deduplicate documents prior to production. Duplicate documents may be withheld from production provided deduplication is handled in the following manner:

a. As to emails that have not been printed into a paper form and remain in electronic form, these emails will be considered duplicates if (i) the hash values of two or more emails are identical, (ii) the following fields of metadata associated with the email are the same: [*list the fields to be used for deduplication*]; and (iii) the body or text of the email is exactly the same.

b. As to non-email electronic documents, these documents will be considered duplicates if (i) they have the same hash value, and (ii) the following fields of metadata are the same: [*list the fields to be used for deduplication*].

18. Should a producing party deduplicate any documents in accordance with the procedure outlined above, the parties waive any objection as to the authenticity of the version of the document produced and the fields of data associated with such copy.

19. For good cause shown, the receiving party shall have the right to request all duplicates of a produced document.

Keyword Searching

20. If keyword searching will be used to identify documents responsive to document requests, the parties agree to cooperatively develop, exchange and agree upon a list or lists of keyword search terms to be used to conduct searches for potentially responsive ESI.

Privileged Documents and Logs

21. Nothing contained herein is intended to or shall serve to limit a party's right to conduct a review of documents, ESI or information (including metadata) for relevance, responsiveness and/or segregation of privileged and/or protected information before production.

22. The parties agree to confer on the nature and scope of privilege logs, including whether categories of information may be excluded from such logs and whether alternatives to document-by-document privilege logs can be exchanged, including:

a. The parties are not required to include in their privilege logs any documents or ESI generated after the filing of the complaint.

b. Activities undertaken and information gathered in compliance with the duty to preserve discovery material are protected from disclosure and discovery under Rules 26(b)(3)(A) and (B) of the Federal Rules of Civil Procedure.

c. For email threaded conversations, the parties are required to log only the most recent, most inclusive email.

d. The parties may log documents by category rather than by individual entries for each document.

e. The parties agree that the production of such logs will occur after document production.

Inadvertent Production and Clawback

23. If a producing party inadvertently produces to a receiving party (1) any information or document without designating it as confidential as requried, or, (2) any information or document that is privileged or otherwise immune from discovery under the attorney-client or work product doctrines, the receiving party shall, at the request of the producing party, immediately return all such inadvertently produced information and documents to the producing party, including the production media, or confirm in writing that all copies have been destroyed.

24. The producing party will prepare and deliver a replacement disk containing corrected confidentiality designations of all non-privileged documents that were contained in the original production. Electronic copies of the inadvertently produced documents must be removed from the electronic system of the receiving party.

25. Pursuant to Fed. R. Evid. 502, the inadvertent production of undesignated confidential information or documents, or information or documents that are privileged or otherwise immune from discovery under the attorney-client or work product doctrines, shall not be deemed a waiver, in whole or in part, of the producing party's claim of restriction or privilege either as to specific information disclosed or information on the same or related subject matter.

26. The return or destruction of inadvertently produced privileged documents does not preclude the receiving party from disagreeing with the designation of any portion of a document as privileged and bringing a motion to compel its production pursuant to the Federal Rules of Civil Procedure. However, the substance of any such inadvertently produced privileged document shall not be referenced in the motion, except to the extent that such substance is provided in a privilege log.

27. The parties agree to meet and confer in good faith as to any discovery dispute prior to bringing any such dispute to the attention of the court.

28. This stipulation relates solely to the protocol for identifying, preserving, collecting, reviewing and producing ESI and documents

in this case. Any party may bring a motion to modify or clarify the application of this Stipulation.

29. This stipulation will be approved and adopted as an order of the court in this action.

SIGNED this ___ day of _____, 2016.

_____
United States District Judge

C.2 Sample IT Infrastructure Questionnaire

Project/Case Name:_____ Date: _____

Project Manager:_____ Attorney: _____

This form is designed to help identify, preserve and collect electronically stored information (ESI) in discovery. It is recommended that Litigation Support personnel and the client IT personnel complete this form together.

GENERAL INFORMATION

Has a formal Litigation Hold been implemented?

Yes____ No____

Is there a written records retention/destruction policy?

Yes____ No____

Have record disposition/auto-delete policies been suspended?

Yes____ No____

Date range of relevant events: _____

Sources of Potentially Relevant ESI:	[ ] Email Servers	[ ] File Servers	[ ] Workstation/Laptops
	[ ] Blackberries	[ ] Instant Messages	[ ] Text Messages
	[ ] External Media	[ ] Websites	[ ] Social Media Sites
	[ ] Databases	[ ] Smartphones	[ ] Bloomberg Msgs
	[ ] Backup Tapes	[ ] Home Computers	

NETWORK SYSTEMS

Describe the company network infrastructure and general organization of ESI, including locations of user-created files and storage areas. Are there files servers, email servers, application or Web servers? What is the operating system and version? Is this a centralized network system with a data center or separate locations or networks?

_____

_____

_____

Email System

What email application and version is currently in use?

_____

Has the current email system been in place during the relevant time period? _Yes_____ No_____

If not, describe prior system:_____

What is the retention/deletion policy? _____

Is email archived by the user or force archived?_____

Is there an email retention/archiving system in place? _Yes_____ No_____

Name and version of application: _____

Desktops/Workstations

Are PC or laptop workstations in use? _Yes_____ No_____

Type of PC/Laptop and hard drive size: _____

Can users save to local hard drive locations? _Yes_____ No_____

Is the USB, CD/DVD or floppy drive active? _Yes_____ No_____

** Client IT Staff: Please gather user PC machine names and verify locations of custodians for this project. **

Network Personal Shares (home share, user share)

Does every user have a personal network share? _Yes_____ No_____

Should the entire personal share be collected? _Yes_____ No_____

If not, specify files/folders to collect: _____

Network Group Shares (department share)

List the group or department shares to collect: _____

Should the entire group share be collected? _Yes_____ No_____

If not, specify folders/files to collect? _____

Databases (and other applications)

Are there any databases, applications or proprietary

programs that generate or contain potentially relevant ESI?

_Yes_____ No_____

Name of application, version, and format of data: _____

_____

Third Party Providers

Do any third-party providers for Internet, social media, records or data management, email routing, etc., have any relevant ESI?

*Yes*____ *No*____

If yes, who and for what and where? _____

_____

Text or Instant Messaging

Do users have a text message or instant messaging program?

*Yes*____ *No*____

Is the data stored or backed up?   *Yes*____ *No*____

Where? _____

Backup Systems

Has backup media rotation been suspended?   *Yes*____ *No*____

Is backup media available for the relevant time frame?   *Yes*____ *No*____

Name and type of backup system: _____

Describe the backup process (full, incremental, frequency): _____

_____

Policy on Former Employees

Is there a written policy on former employees?   *Yes*____ *No*____

What is the retention/destruction policy for:

Workstation/Laptop:_____

Email:_____

Personal Network Share: _____

Legacy Systems

Are there any legacy systems, old data storage or systems which may contain data within the time frame and relevant to this matter? If yes, what is the data and how and where is it stored? Please explain:

_____

_____

Paper Documents

Are there paper documents associated with this case? *Yes*____ *No*____

Approximately how many boxes of paper can be expected? _____

CUSTODIAN INFORMATION

List below the names and locations of individuals who may possess or control ESI or paper documents relevant to this litigation, including current or former employees, agents, accountants, attorneys, vendors, contractors, consulting or other persons outside the organization.

_____   _____

_____   _____

_____   _____

_____   _____

_____   _____

_____   _____

_____   _____

C.3 Sample Custodian Interview Form

Name:		Title:	
Department:		Location:	
Phone:			
Email:			
Length of employment:			
Previous positions held :			
To whom do you report?			
Who are your direct reports?			
Describe your current responsibilities:			
Who held this position prior to you?			
Where is that person now?			
Did you inherit their files (paper or ESI)?			

Location of Potentially Relevant Paper Files

Do you have any documents (paper and/or electronic) relevant to [case name, investigation]? (Yes or No)	
Where do you maintain any relevant hardcopy files and records?	

Location of Potentially Relevant ESI

Do you use a desktop, laptop computer, or both?	
Do you save documents locally on this machine? If so, where? (C:\drive, My Documents, other folder)	
What software applications do you use? (e.g., Outlook, Word, Excel, PowerPoint)	
Is any relevant data (email, text messages, photos, other files) stored on the following devices?	[ ] Smartphone/Blackberry
	[ ] Tablet device
	[ ] Cloud storage
	[ ] Home computer
	[ ] Other external device
Identify the locations or folders where you save or store elec-tronic documents (specify any drives or folders):	[ ] Network personal directory
	[ ] Network departmental directory
	[ ] Other network shares or folders
Describe how you manage your email:	
Identify any folders that may contain relevant email (Inbox, Sent, Deleted, other folders):	

If you archive email, identify the location of such files (specify folder and file name):	

Do you know of anyone else who might have documents (paper and/or electronic) or information relating to this matter/case/investigation [to be filled in by case team]?

Is there any other information you can think of that would help us locate relevant files?

_____

_____

Reminder to Custodian: You should not delete or in any other way destroy any paper or electronic files that may be relevant to this matter.

Interviewer: _____ Date: _____

Authorization for Collection of Records:

I hereby authorize [CLIENT NAME], their legal counsel, IT personnel, and/or vendors working under their supervision, to collect paper and electronic records from my office and computer systems related to this matter.

Interviewee: _____ Date: _____

C.4 Sample Collection Specification

Project Manager: _____ Attorney: _____

Project Name: _____ Client/Matter: _____

Purpose: This collection specification and any related documentation will govern the collection requirements in connection with the above project. Questions concerning this specification should be directed to the assigned project manager.

LOGISTICS / GEOGRAPHIC LOCATION

Date of Collection:	
Location of Collection/Data Center(s):	

TYPE OF COLLECTION

[ ] Full forensic acquisition (identify below assets to be collected)	[ ] Targeted collection (provide list of filtering parameters, e.g., date range, keyword, and identify target assets below)

CUSTODIAN INFORMATION AND DATA STORES

Custodian Names	Physical Location	Personal Network Share	Departmental Network Share	Workstation/ Laptop Name	Mobile/Other Device(s)

COMPANY DATA ASSETS TO ACQUIRE

Type	Operating System	Location
File Server		
Database Server		
Email Server		
Workstation/Laptops		
Web Server/Social Media		
External Drives/Devices		

TARGETED COLLECTION SPECIFICATIONS

[ ] Limit by date from _____ to _____ using:	
[ ] Date created [ ] Date modified [ ] Date accessed	
[ ] Limit collection by keyword search terms (include a list of search terms)	
[ ] Filter by file extension (attach list of file extensions)	
[ ] Exclude operating system, Windows and temporary files (De-NIST on collection)	
[ ] Collect active data only	[ ] Collect deleted data (slack/unallocated space)

[ ] Collect graphical files (PDF, TIFF, CAD)
  [ ] OCR and search
  [ ] Deliver as is
	[ ] Collect archived PST, OST, DBX, NSF files
	  [ ] Mount and search
	  [ ] Deliver as is

[ ] Collect compound files
  [ ] Mount and search
  [ ] Deliver as is	

BACKUP TAPES

[ ] Collect backup tapes	[ ] Restore and deliver file directory listing only
	[ ] Full restore of all files on tape and deliver all files

DELIVERABLE FOLLOWING COLLECTION

Output Format:	**Email Files**	[ ] Outlook PST [ ] Lotus NSF [ ] Other: _____
	Other Files	[ ] Extract all files and deliver in native file format on external media [ ] Encase LEF [ ] FTK image [ ] Other (specify): _____
Reporting:		[ ] Deliver full acquisition report [ ] Deliver collection log

Volume/ Media Label:		All media delivered should be clearly labeled, including:
		     Project name
		     Volume number (within the project)
		     Delivery Date

<u>Notes</u>

_____

_____
_____
_____

C.5 Sample Collection Log

Project Manager: _____ Attorney: _____

Project Name: _____Client/Matter: _____

Purpose: This collection log will identify each custodian and data store and memorialize the ESI collected for the above project. Questions concerning this specification should be directed to the assigned project manager or collection examiner.

Custodian	Location	Machine Name	Work-station (GB)	Network Share (GB)	Email (GB)	Mobile/ Peripheral (GB)	Total Volume (GB)
Network/ Department Shares	Location	Network Folder Path					Volume (GB)
Other Shares/ Servers/ Devices	Location	Network Location/ Folder Path/Name					Volume (GB)

C.6 Sample Chain of Custody Form

Description of Article/Device/Data			
Custodian/Company:			
Data/Device/Brand:			
Model #:			
Serial #:			

Chain of Custody			
Date/Time	Released by	Received by	Purpose of Change of Custody
	[Signature Client GC/ IT Personnel] Name/Company	[Signature Collection Examiner] Name/Company	ESI collected from client by vendor [list all ESI collected or attach collection log]
	[Signature Collection Examiner] Name/Company	[Signature Project Manager] Name/Company	Collection vendor transmits ESI to project manager at law firm
	[Signature Project Manager] Name/Company	[Signature Processing Vendor] Name/Company	Project manager transmits ESI to processing vendor
	[Signature Processing Vendor] Name/Company	[Signature Project Manager] Name/Company	Processing vendor returns original ESI to project manager at law firm
	[Signature Project Manager] Name/Company	[Signature Client GC/IT Personnel] Name/Company	Project manager returning original ESI to client

Final Disposition Notes
Original Released to: Disposition: Signature: Date:

C.7 Sample Processing Specification

Project/Case: _____ Supervising Attorney: _____

Client/Matter: _____ Project Manager: _____

Date: _____ Technical Analyst: _____

Purpose: This processing specification will govern the processing requirements in connection with the above project. Questions concerning this specification should be directed to the assigned Litigation Support Project Manager or Analyst.

MEDIA TYPE & QUANTITY

Qty	Type of Media	File Types (if known)	Approximate Size of Data (GB)

EMAIL PROCESSING (Outlook, Lotus Notes, Other)

Time Zone (Default is GMT):	[ ] GMT [ ] EST [ ] PST [ ] CST [ ] MST
Data to Process:	[ ] All Items [ ] User Mailbox (+ user created folders) [ ] Sent Items [ ] Deleted Items [ ] Drafts [ ] Calendar Items [ ] Contacts/Address Book [ ] Journal [ ] Notes [ ] Tasks/To Do List
Deduplication:	[ ] Vertical – within each custodian/source [ ] Horizontal – across all custodians/sources
Filtering	[ ] None [ ] By date: [ ] Before _____ [ ] After _____ [ ] By date range: From _____ to _____ [ ] By keyword search: _____ _____
TIFF/Native:	[ ] Deliver TIFF images all for files [ ] Deliver native only [ ] Deliver .htm

NATIVE FILE AND ATTACHMENT PROCESSING (Loose Files/Email Attachments)

Filtering/ De-NISTing:	[ ] None
	[ ] By date: [ ] Before _____ [ ] After _____
	[ ] By date range: From _____ to _____
	  [ ] Use Date Created
	  [ ] Use Date Last Modified
	  [ ] Use Date Last Accessed
	[ ] By keyword search: _____
	[ ] De-NIST and exclude system and temporary files (e.g., Windows, cookies, .exe, .dll, .ini, .cab, etc.)
	[ ] Exclude other file types: _____

Deduplication:	[ ] Vertical – within each custodian/source [ ] Horizontal – across all custodians/sources
Auto-date Feature:	[ ] Insert "Autodate" (recommended) [ ] Use document Last Modified Date [ ] Insert blank [ ] Take no action

File Processing:	MS WORD	MS POWERPOINT	MS EXCEL
	[ ] Print comments [ ] Show track changes [ ] Print color	[ ] Print notes page [ ] Print slides only [ ] Unhide slides [ ] Print comments [ ] Print color	[ ] Unhide worksheets [ ] Expand columns [ ] Display headings [ ] Remove blank pages [ ] Display headers [ ] Display footers [ ] Scaling at _____ % [ ] Print Portrait [ ] Print Landscape [ ] Print gridlines [ ] Print over then down [ ] Print down then over [ ] Print comments [ ] Print color [ ] Manual formatting
	** For other file types not listed, please contact the assigned Project Manager or Analyst for further instructions.		

TIFF/Native:	[ ] TIFF all files [ ] Native files only [ ] TIFF all files except Excel files
Exception Handling:	[ ] Skip file and deliver Exception Report [ ] Attempt manual processing, skip file and deliver slip sheet with file name, deliver Exception Report

Compound files (zip, rar):	[ ] Open, process files and deliver slip sheet with file name for container file [ ] Open, process files and do not deliver slip sheet for container file

DATABASE DELIVERABLE

Control Numbering:	BEGDOC Prefix: _____ Start number: _____ (zero-fill number to 7 digits)
Data Fields:	[ ] Deliver all standard metadata fields [ ] Custom fields (specify) _____ [ ] Deliver all fields [ ] Deliver extracted text/OCR in "Text" Field [ ] Deliver text as separate text files: [ ] Page level [ ] Document level

Special Instructions/Filtering/Search Terms/Notes

_____

_____

_____

C.8 Sample Document Review Protocol

MEMORANDUM

TO: Attorney Review Team; Junior Associates; and Project Team

FROM: Law Firm Partner

DATE: January 14, 2016

RE: Document Review Protocol

I. BACKGROUND

This document review is conducted in connection with ABC vs. 123 action. We represent the defendant 123 Corporation in the proceeding. A copy of the Complaint is attached hereto as Exhibit A. Plaintiffs are ABC International. Plaintiff's Answer and Counterclaim is attached as Exhibit B. You are referred to the pleadings (Exhibits A and B) for a full recitation of the dispute. This is a contract dispute that turns on the definition of and interpretation by the parties of the language used in the contract and an amendment to the contract. The contract and the amendment to the contract are attached to the Complaint.

II. SCOPE OF REVIEW

The parties' Requests for Production of Documents are attached as Exhibits C and D. For purposes of determining whether a document is within the scope of responsiveness, any document that discusses or mentions the contract or which contains discussion or negotiation referencing the contract or its terms and conditions are responsive.

There is no limitation on the date of a document. However, note that the Agreement was executed in January 2014 and the amendment of that Agreement was made in September 2014, and the bulk of responsive documents will fall in or around these dates.

An important part of the document review will be to identify ESI and documents that may be used as evidence of any discussion, interpretation, meaning or use, by the parties, of the terms and phrases at the heart of the controversy as set forth in the complaint. In particular, we are looking for evidence that can be used in support of our interpretation of the contract.

The 125,000 documents in the review database were collected from the files and servers of 123, including various departments and the personal files of the ten custodians listed in the review database.

III. CODING INSTRUCTIONS

A. Responsiveness Coding

You will be coding documents for responsiveness. Documents should be coded individually according to the codes below. Every document will be coded "Responsive" or "Nonresponsive." All documents in a family (e.g., an email and its attachments) will be coded consistently. If you are unsure whether a document is Responsive or Nonresponsive, code it "Question," but you must indicate in the "Attorney Comments" field the nature of your question in specific terms (do not simply indicate "unsure whether responsive").

Whether a non-privileged document is responsive or not must be determined based on whether the document responds to one of Plaintiff's non-objectionable document requests. Consult with the senior associate on any questions in this regard.

Please note that we will not be responding to Plaintiff's document request numbered 3, 6 and 9. We may also withhold documents responsive to Request No. 15, which in our view seeks privileged and/or work product information. Any documents responsive to Request 15 may be coded as "Privileged" or, if appropriate, as "Redact-Privileged" if the privileged material may be redacted from the document (see Section B, below for privilege coding).

Below are the specific responsiveness codes to be applied to documents:

CODE	DESCRIPTION/PURPOSE
Responsive	The document responds to one of Plaintiff's document requests and contains no privileged information.
Non-Responsive	The document has nothing to do with Plaintiff's document requests. However, Nonresponsive documents may receive issue coding, particularly where we may wish to use such documents in depositions or for trial preparation.

| Important | Any important document, good or bad. This code should be used for any discussions regarding the interpretation of paragraphs 17 of the Complaint and any discussion of the "approval of terms" are considered very important. |

B. Privilege Coding

You will be provided with the names of inside and outside attorneys so that you may consider communications and writings by these persons when reviewing documents for privilege. Please note that any communications with our Firm is deemed privileged unless the privilege is clearly waived. Because some emails were forwarded to other people the privilege may be waived. Likewise, any document prepared in anticipation of litigation is deemed attorney-work product.

When you code a document "Privileged" or "Work Product," that document will be withheld from production unless it is redacted. If a document contains privileged or work product information and the privileged information may be redacted while still producing the remainder of the document, you are to code the document "Redact-Privileged." If a document is coded Privileged or Work Product, and if a document contains a redaction, you will provide a description suitable for a privilege log entry in the "Privilege Description" field in the database. If you have any questions about coding privileged documents, please contact the senior associate.

CODE	DESCRIPTION/PURPOSE
Privileged	The entire document is privileged, it cannot be redacted, and it will not be produced.
Work Product	The entire document contains attorney work product, it cannot be redacted, and it will not be produced.
Redact-Privilege	The document contains privileged material, but it can be redacted, and the document will be produced in redacted form.

C. Confidentiality Coding

There is a confidentiality/protective order in place in this matter. This order requires that we designate documents as "Confidential," "Highly Confidential," and "Attorneys Eyes Only." Therefore, documents coded as responsive that will be produced and documents coded privileged but which contain redactions shielding the privileged material also need to be designated as confidential using the guidelines below.

CODE	DESCRIPTION/PURPOSE
Confidential	Standard level of confidentiality applicable to all company documents, except documents containing publicly available information (public documents do not receive any confidentiality designation).
Highly Confidential	Applicable to documents containing information related to the business operations or finances of the client.
Attorneys' Eyes Only	Highly sensitive company documents containing internal company confidences or proprietary information.

D. Issue Coding

Issue tags will assist the case team in categorizing documents in preparation for further discovery and in deposition and trial preparation, if necessary. As documents are reviewed, they will be coded with the following categories if the document falls into one of these categories:

- Accounting/Finance
- Agreements/Contracts
- Business Development/Sales
- Personnel/Human Resources
- Operations
- Negotiations
- Executive Management
- Communications w/ ABC

Any questions about this document review or the contents of this memorandum should be addressed in the first instance to the senior associate. Weekly review team meetings may be held as needed to clarify any issues that arise and to determine the progress of the review.

Our Litigation Support team is available to support you with any technical issues related to coding documents or the operation of the review database. Contact them if you need assistance.

C.9 Sample Production Specification

Project/Case Name: _____ Date: _____

Project Manager: _____ Authorizing Attorney: _____

Purpose: This production specification will govern the production requirements in connection with this project. In order to ensure accuracy and the timely completion and delivery of the production, please build as much extra time as possible into the request. Questions concerning this specification or further instructions on the production should be directed to the assigned Project Manager.

REQUEST AND DUE DATES

Date Submitted	*Time Submitted*	*Date Production is Due*	*Time Production is Due*

DOCUMENTS TO BE PRODUCED:

Database Name:	_____
Tags to Include:	[ ] Responsive [ ] Responsive-Redacted [ ] Redact-Privilege
Tags to Exclude:	[ ] Privileged [ ] Non-Responsive [ ] Question

OUTPUT FORMAT

Bates Numbering:	Bates Prefix: _____ Start Numbering From: _____ To: _____ Stamp Location: [ ] Lower right (default) [ ] Lower center [ ] Next available number (confirm with case team) [ ] Lower left

Production Format:	[ ] Single-page TIFF images (default) [ ] Multi-page TIFF images [ ] PDF image (one file per document) [ ] Produce all files in native format [ ] Produce Excel and PowerPoint files Only in native format

Image Endorse-ments:	[ ] Confidentiality Designation (as coded in Confidentiality data field)
	
	[ ] Other designation or text (specify):
	_____
	
	[ ] Redactions:
	  [ ] Black box (no text) [ ] Black (w/ "Redacted" text)
	  [ ] White box (no text) [ ] White (w/ "Redacted" text)

Image Load File:	[ ] Opticon Log File [ ] IPRO LFP [ ] Summation DII [ ] Other (specify): _____

Data Export:	[ ] Fields to Export for Production [ ] All Fields Below
	
	  [ ] Bates Start [ ] Custodian
	  [ ] Bates Stop [ ] Author
	  [ ] Attach Start [ ] Title
	  [ ] Attach Stop [ ] Date Created
	  [ ] To [ ] Date Last Modified
	  [ ] From [ ] File Name
	  [ ] CC [ ] File Extension
	  [ ] BCC [ ] File Size
	  [ ] Subject [ ] Source Path
	  [ ] Date Sent [ ] Hash Value
	  [ ] Date Received [ ] Conversation ID
	
	[ ] Do Not Export Any Data for Production

Data File Format:	[ ] Comma-delimited file (CSV) [ ] .DAT [ ] Other format (specify): _____

Extracted / OCR Text:	[ ] Include Extracted Text/OCR in Production
	
	  [ ] Individual text files (page level)
	  [ ] Individual text files (document level)
	  [ ] Include text in data file
	
	[ ] Do Not Include Extracted Text/OCR

DELIVERABLE

Media:	[ ] CD/DVD [ ] Hard Drive [ ] Flash Drive [ ] FTP
Media Label:	[ ] Standard label (Firm Name, Case Caption, Bates Range, Date) [ ] Custom label (specify): _____
Number of Copies:	_____
Deliver to:	_____

Special Instructions / Comments / Notes

_____

_____

_____

_____

GLOSSARY

This glossary focuses on the key terms and phrases related to electronic discovery, litigation support, and project management. Many terms are used in unique ways in the legal and project management fields. These words and phrases and their definitions, have been compiled by the author from multiple sources and the author's experience. Neither Stroock & Stroock & Lavan LLP, nor any related entity, endorses these definitions.

Active data

Information or files in computer systems and applications actively in use, such as email systems, database programs, or word processing applications, that are immediately accessible to users. This may include user-created files, data in a recycle bin, file histories, and other data caches. Active data is visible to an operating system and can be viewed with a computer program.

Algorithm

A sequential set of instructions written in computer code designed to perform a particular function or task. Algorithms form the basis of complex search and analytic features, such as parsing through a massive index of text.

Analytics

Generally, an advanced form of indexing, search, and analysis that converts the textual content of documents into conceptual content that identifies how words, phrases, and documents in a database relate to each other based on their similarity, syntax and the frequency of words in documents. It allows for clustering and categorization of conceptually similar documents, foreign language detection, and concept search techniques. Analytics are typically used to accelerate traditional linear document review by organizing documents into conceptually similar subsets, or may be used to "find more like this" when searching for documents. See also *technology assisted review* and *conceptual search*.

Archive

Data or information usually maintained for long-term storage, historical recordkeeping or backup purposes. Archived data may be transferred to peripheral media such as CDs, tapes, disks, or to network servers or the Internet. Offline storage of electronic records typically is used for disaster recovery copies of records. Accessibility typically requires manual intervention and is much slower than online or near-line storage. An *archive* may also refer to paper-based storage of aged records.

ARMA International

The world's largest professional organization devoted to records, information management, and information governance policy development, training, and certification.

ASCII

Pronounced *ask-ee*. The American Standards Committee II 8-bit computer coding structure for letters, numbers, and characters in which 7 bits are used to identify each individual entity (128 maximum), with 1 bit for parity. When no parity bit is used, all 8 bits can be used to represent up to 256 characters; this character set is called "extended ASCII." ASCII is a code that assigns a number to each key on a keyboard. ASCII text does not include special formatting features and, therefore, can be exchanged and read by most computer systems.

Attachment

Most commonly refers to a document that is transmitted together with an email message, e.g., the report attached to and sent with an email is an attachment. A document attached to a *parent* document may also be referred to as a *child document*. See also *parent document* and *document family*.

Backup

To create a copy of data as a precaution against the loss or damage of the original data. Data may be backed up to digital tapes, referred to as "backup tapes," to optical media, or to other secure storage. Backup typically uses compression techniques to reduce the size of the data, which saves space, but also makes restoration of the data more time consuming, especially given the lack of a uniform standard governing data compression. There are various programs and formats for backup systems.

Bates number

A number stamped or endorsed on each page of a document to enable later reference to the pages of the document. Bates numbers are usually applied to documents in the production phase of a discovery project and they commonly have a prefix that helps identify the producing party and a sequential series of numbers on each page (e.g., SMITH0000001).

Boolean search

A system of logic developed by an early computer pioneer, George Boole. In Boolean search, the "AND" operator between two words results in a search for documents containing both of the words. The "OR" operator between two words creates a search for documents containing either or both of the target words. The "NOT" operator between two words creates a search result containing the first word but excluding the second.

Chain of Custody

Documentation that identifies each person or entity who possessed or transmitted ESI. A chain of custody form is used to demonstrate that ESI has not been altered or tampered with from the time it was originally preserved or collected to the time it is used as evidence or introduced in court. Chain of custody documentation follows strict protocols to ensure authenticity and admissibility of ESI in the event that spoliation claims are made or objections are raised regarding admissibility of a document.

Claw-back Agreement

An agreement between parties in litigation or their lawyers that is designed to protect against the waiver of privilege or work product protections in circumstances where protected information is inadvertently produced. Such an agreement typically requires a party to return to the producing party any documents that are privileged or that contain work production information.

Closing

The final of the five project management process groups; the last phase of a project in which all processes come to an end, customer or stakeholder satisfaction is determined, contracts are terminated, and project records are archived. Also the phase in which a project team conducts a post-project review or "lessons learned" meeting to review what went right and what went wrong on the project.

clustering

In e-discovery, the use of analytics software to gather documents that are conceptually similar, usually by indexing and comparing the textual content of the documents, and presenting the documents in a database or document review platform in a manner that reflects their conceptual content and similarity.

coding

The process of entering document-specific information into case-specific objective and subjective database fields. Objective coding consists of entering information about a document that is judged to be non-subjective. For instance, a Bates number stamped on a document, or the author, recipient, and date appearing on the face of document. Subjective coding consists of entering data into case-specific database fields and requires the use of human judgment and subjective reasoning to decide how to code the document. Examples of subjective coding might be whether a document is responsive, non-responsive, or privileged.

collection

The phase of an e-discovery project and node of the EDRM in which the process of gathering ESI and paper documents from the client is undertaken, usually in response to a lawsuit or document request. Collection should be performed in a defensible manner that preserves any metadata and tracks the materials that are collected.

comma separated value file (CSV)

A file type typically used to store or transmit data or information about documents and records. A CSV file layout consists of rows of data with commas that separates each data field. Each row contains data about a record or document.

compound files

A container-like file that usually holds other files or one large file. ZIP files, RAR files, and TZ files are all examples of compound files. They need to be "unpacked" or "unzipped" to access the files within them.

Files within a compound file are usually compressed to reduce their size, which helps facilitate transmittal of large files.

computer forensics

The discipline that includes the physical acquisition, preservation, and analysis of ESI using methodologies that satisfy evidentiary requirements of write-protection, chain-of-custody, and authentication. This may include performing code and encryption cracking; searching for and retrieving deleted data; determining which files have been altered or deleted; recovering deleted files or file fragments; and proving user habits and navigation, which includes Internet, network access, printing, and copying.

Communication Management

One of the ten project management knowledge areas; the processes involved in managing the communication needs and expectations for the project and project stakeholders in particular. How and in what form information will be communicated, to whom, and when and where each communication will be made, and who is responsible for providing each type of communication are critical to managing a project.

Conceptual Search

Searching ESI using advanced analytic or "find more like this" features. See *analytics*.

Cost Management

One of the ten project management knowledge areas; the processes involved in estimating, budgeting, and controlling costs to complete the project within the approved budget.

culling

A form of filtering or search, usually performed in the processing phase of an e-discovery project, that uses various parameters or criteria, such as date range or file type to exclude documents that do not meet the search criteria. Culling should reduce the volume of documents, cost, and time required to process and review ESI.

custodian

An individual who is likely to create, store, or have documents and ESI relevant to a litigation or investigation in their possession, custody, or control. Often referred to as "user" by IT personnel; sometimes referred to as "source" by legal review teams.

data map/server topology

A chart or graphical representation of a computer network showing the physical or virtual location of ESI and other data on and organization's servers, PCs, and other network devices.

database

A collection of information or electronic data and documents organized and indexed to facilitate easy retrieval and manipulation. In e-discovery, this most commonly refers to a document review application in which documents and their metadata are stored. Metadata is typically stored in identified fields of a database, such as the author, recipient, date, or custodian, and users are able to perform searches or sort the data and review and code documents in the database.

deduplication ("deduping")

The process of identifying and, in most cases eliminating, exact copies of documents from a collection of electronic documents. There are generally two types of deduplication: *vertical*, which involved removing duplicate records within a single custodian's document collection; and *horizontal*, which removes duplicate records across multiple custodians' document collections. Deduplicating electronic documents reduces the cost and time associated with processing and document review. It also enhances the consistency and accuracy of attorney designations by eliminating duplicates from a review set. See also, *near deduplication*, used for identifying similar but not identical documents.

deleted data

A file that a computer user has deleted, but which still resides on the computer hard drive in a space that has been designated as available for reuse. Although a user may erase or delete a file or other ESI, that file may still exist on a hard drive or server. Most often, when deleted only the reference or link to the file name has been deleted from the File Allocation Table. Unless overwritten with new data, a deleted file can be as intact on the hard drive as any active file seen in a directory listing. *Deleted* does not necessarily mean gone forever. There are several ways to retrieve documents or parts of documents that have been deleted. For instance, when a file is deleted, it goes into the Recycle Bin. It can still be restored and collected from the Recycle Bin as long as it remains there. Once deleted from the Recycle Bin, however, a file is no longer recognized by the Windows file system. But the file itself still resides on the hard drive—either in full or in part—in the unused space of the drive. See also *slack space* and *unallocated space*.

de-NIST

The process of removing known system files from a collection of ESI, usually during processing. The National Institute of Standards in Technology (NIST) publishes a list of file extensions that form the basis of the NIST list. This list of file extensions is used to de-NIST a collection of ESI to remove file types that are unlikely to have been created by a typical user.

directed (targeted) collection

The process of collecting documents from specific locations on a workstation hard drive, a network file server, or an email server. Typically refers to files on a hard drive or server that are recognized by an operating system. Deleted data is not collected during a directed collection. A directed collection can be designed to collect particular custodians' documents, certain file types, folders, or directories that are identified in advance; or with a search using keyword terms or date ranges. The advantage of a directed collection is that only the documents identified in advance or that are responsive to broad search criteria are collected. Directed collections normally result in a significantly reduced volume of documents. System files are normally excluded by filtering out certain types of files. This is called an *exclusionary condition*. A search can also be constructed that locates specific types of files if, for instance, it is known that the client uses only MS Word and MS Excel to create documents, then a search can be designed that only searches for documents with a .docx or .xlsx file extension. This is called an *inclusionary condition*. Of the two, exclusionary conditions are preferred because they do not exclude a file of unknown origin or a file that has been renamed by an end user who may prefer the file not be located.

document family

Consists of a *parent* document and any *attachments* to the parent document. Attachments may also be referred to as *child documents*.

Electronic Discovery Reference Model (EDRM)

A standardized framework for the processes involved in the identification, preservation, collection, processing, review, and production of ESI in connection with an electronic discovery project (see www.edrm.net).

electronic discovery

The process, work-flows and tasks associated with identifying, preserving, collecting, processing, reviewing, and producing electronically stored information in connection with litigation and investigations. The process typically begins with a litigation hold within the client organization and culminates in production of documents once they have been reviewed.

electronically stored information (ESI)

As referred to in the Federal Rules of Civil Procedure, many state rules, and applicable case law; the universe of documents, images, information, or data stored in electronic format on servers, computers, peripheral devices, tablets, smart phones, in cloud computing applications, social network portals and pages that could potentially be relevant in discovery.

Email threading

The process in which software is used to identify and group together related email "conversations" for more efficient and effective review and analysis of the content. Threading can also identify the most complete or last email in a string of emails. Email threading typically relies upon message IDs found in the metadata of email message files to identify and group the documents together.

Executing

One of the five project management process groups; the phase of a project where the project manager is directing, managing, performing, and accomplishing the project work, reviewing and providing the deliverables, and providing work performance information.

extracted text

The body of an electronic document that is mined when electronic documents are processed. Extracted text is typically loaded to a field in a database and indexed for searching and other purposes. See also *OCR*.

file server

A computer hard drive or drives typically deployed in a network environment where users save their files. Several or many hard drives may be linked together in a Local Area Network (LAN) or across a Wide Area Network (WAN) configuration, and used as a storage location for files for an entire organization. File servers have larger capacity than a standard PC hard drive, and are configured to store massive amounts of data. They usually provide for redundancy and backup to ensure the data is retained pursuant to policy. File servers may be employed to store email, financial data, and word processing information, or to backup the files and data on a network.

file path

In a computer file system, the directory or network location of a file or application. In a typical directory listing, the operating system stores files in folders and/or subfolders. The file path includes the root directory (e.g., the C drive), the name of each folder and subfolder, and culminates in the file name. Example: C:\Program Files\Outlook\Data\JohnDoe.pst.

Forms of Production

The format in which ESI and paper documents may be produced in litigation. The most common formats are TIFF image, native or near-native form together with corresponding load files and a data file providing relevant metadata and searchable, extracted, or OCR text. Different document review platforms require delivery of documents in varying formats.

FTP

File transfer protocol (FTP) is a way to exchange files between computers using TCP/IP protocols. An FTP site is a location on a network to which files may be uploaded and downloaded. FTP is typically used to transmit data between locations without having to burn a CD or DVD.

forensic imaging

The process of making a bit-by-bit or copy of an entire hard drive or other media. This process copies all data, including any recoverable deleted files and captures any data in the slack space or unallocated space of a drive. This process is typically reserved for workstation or laptop hard drives in cases where there is a possibility data was either inadvertently or intentionally deleted, or when tracking user activity is an issue. It may also be used to collect an entire file server, although the volume of data on a file server mitigates against such requests. Also known as *full-disk acquisition*, forensic imaging may be used when the objective is to gather and simply preserve all the data from multiple sources. This process generally takes longer, is more expensive, and typically results in dramatically larger volumes of data. Whenever performing a forensic or full-disk acquisition, it is always best to use trained computer forensic technicians. Also referred to as *hard drive imaging*.

graphical file

A static image, photograph, or picture file, such as a TIFF image, JPEG, PDF, GIF, or bitmap (.BMP). Graphical files are generally not searchable and sometimes require special processing to convert to a searchable format.

Gigabyte

One billion bytes. Also expressed as one thousand megabytes. See also *megabyte*.

hash value

A series of numbers generated by a computer algorithm assigned to represent the properties and attributes of a document—in essence, the digital fingerprint used to identify a unique electronic document. Typically, hash values are used to compare documents and eliminate or segregate duplicate documents. Examples of hash values are the MD5 hash and the SHA1 hash. A hash value might look like this: d41c8df98d00j304j-90833776edg7284e

Human Resource Management

One of the ten project management knowledge areas; the processes involved in developing, acquiring, supporting, and managing a project team, including roles and responsibilities, assignments, staffing levels, and performance evaluations.

Identification

The phase of an electronic discovery project and the node of the EDRM that relates to identifying documents and ESI within an organization that may need to be preserved or collected in the context of litigation or an investigation.

Information Governance

A new discipline that encompasses everything from records management, compliance, data security, privacy, e-discovery, and the legal requirements of organizations related to the creation, storage, retrieval, and disposition of information. Also the first node in the EDRM.

Integration Management

The first of the ten project management knowledge areas; includes processes and activities needed to unify, consolidate, and coordinate project management activities across the five project management process groups.

image

A type of graphical file format. See also, *TIFF image*. In data recovery parlance, to *image* a hard drive is to make an identical bit-for-bit copy of a hard drive (see *forensic imaging*).

image key

The identification number assigned to the individual pages of a document in an image load file at scan time or following processing. Used for loading images of a document to a database. It is important that numbered documents have an image key that corresponds alphanumerically and links the pages of a document together.

index

In the context of electronic discovery, refers to a collection of information that may be searched, most commonly in a database. Once data and text is loaded to a database it is typically *indexed* to render it searchable.

information management

The policies and procedures an organization has in place for the creation, maintenance, and disposition of records and information, both in electronic and paper form, within an organization. See also *RIM* and *information governance*.

Initiating

One of the Five project management process groups; the phase of a project in which the business need or necessity for a project is identified, and a Project Charter and Preliminary Scope Statement are developed.

issue coding

Done in a database, usually as an enhancement to existing metadata extracted from a document. Used to categorize documents by specific topics, issues, or areas of interest, usually related to the case.

keywords

Words or phrases that are used to search documents, most commonly in a database.

legacy system or legacy data

A computer system that manages/reflects historical information or old data that is not in frequent use.

lessons learned meeting

Also known as a post-project review; a project team review after the closing of a project during which the project manager or other organization leader initiates discussion about any issues that arose during the project and how they might be addressed in future projects. This meeting presents an opportunity to improve processes and resolve issues before they occur on future projects.

litigation hold

A formal notice circulated within an organization involved in litigation that informs employees or third parties not to delete or alter and to preserve any documents or ESI that may be relevant to the claims and defenses of the litigation. Sometime referred to as a *legal hold*. See also *preservation*.

load file

A file containing data configured for loading to a database. Normally, a load file relates to a set of images and indicates where individual pages belong together as documents. More generally, refers to files containing data about documents, called *metadata*, which can also be loaded to a database.

meet and confer

In litigation, the conference between the parties involved in a lawsuit and/or their attorneys during which they agree upon which ESI will be preserved, how ESI will be produced, and other discovery plan and scheduling matters. Rule 26(f) of the Federal Rules of Civil Procedure (and many state and local rules) require parties to meet and confer.

metadata

The data elements, attributes, or properties of a document. Some metadata is simplistic and easily identified (e.g., the name of the file, its size, author, and date saved), while other metadata is hidden or embedded and cannot be viewed (e.g., some dates and times, changes to the file, location of the file, dimensions, and BCC information). The dynamic nature of computers causes metadata to change when a computer is powered on or when a document is opened. There is system metadata and application metadata. *System metadata* is usually created when using a network system or the computer system itself (e.g., name of a file or the date created), while *application metadata* is created using a specific software application or program, such as MS Word or Excel (e.g., track changes or a hidden cells or formulas).

Monitoring & Controlling

One of the project management process groups; the processes performed to measure and monitor the progress and quality of a project so that corrective action can be taken when necessary to control the project.

native file format

A file as it has been created by its associated software application, such as MS Word or Excel. It is an electronic file in its original, unaltered format. The original source document, as collected from the source computer or server, before any conversion or processing of the document.

near-native file format

A native file that has been altered from its original form, usually to render it searchable in a document review platform.

network

A group of connected computers that allow people to share information and equipment (e.g., local area network [LAN], wide area network [WAN], storage area network [SAN], peer-to-peer network, client-server network).

network operating system

Software that directs the overall activity of networked computers (Microsoft Windows, UNIX, etc.).

NIST

The National Institute of Standards in Technology; the institution that updates and publishes the list of file extensions representing system-generated files that may be removed from most ESI collections. See also *de-NISTing*.

optical character recognition (OCR)

A software process that captures alphabetical and numerical characters from a document and translates those characters into a form a computer can manipulate and search. OCR systems include an optical scanner for reading text and software for analyzing images. Most OCR systems use a combination of hardware and software to recognize characters, although some inexpensive systems operate entirely through software. Advanced OCR systems can read text in a large variety of fonts, but they have difficulty with handwritten text. OCR is not guaranteed to be 100% accurate—the degree of accuracy depends on the quality of both the image and the OCR software, as well as the quality control process. See also *extracted text*.

parent document

Most commonly refers to a document like an email message which has a document or documents attached to it. See also *attachment* and *document family*.

Planning

One of the five project management process groups; the phase of a project where the project begins to take shape, a project management plan is developed, the scope of the project is refined, specific resources are identified, cost and time estimates are prepared, and a schedule and budget are developed. A quality assurance plan is developed during the Planning phase, and the project manager will establish a clear chain of communication. Risks to the project's success will be assessed, and outsourcing decisions may be made.

Presentation

The last node of the EDRM; the process of presenting documents, ESI, video, and graphics during trial, depositions, arbitrations or hearings. Presentations are made using computers or other devices, projectors and screens.

Preservation

The phase of an electronic discovery project and the node of the EDRM involving the process of preserving documents and data relevant to an investigation or litigation, and ensuring that relevant information is not lost, altered, or destroyed. Preservation begins with the implementation of litigation or a legal hold notifying appropriate personnel to save and not delete any ESI; it culminates in the physical sequestration or collection of ESI.

process

A series of steps, actions, or operations used to achieve an objective. Process is the essence of project management. It identifies the inputs, tools and techniques, and the outputs required to produce project results. Process is a common-sense, orderly approach to the component parts of a project.

Processing

The phase of an electronic discovery project and the node of the EDRM in which ESI is ingested into software to extract the metadata and text from electronic documents and to convert ESI into a uniform format (e.g., TIFF or native) to enable consistent, efficient review, searching, and sorting in an document review platform, such as a database. Processing includes culling, filtering, de-NISTing, and deduplicating ESI. For paper documents, processing includes scanning, running an OCR program, and possibly manually coding the documents.

Procurement Management

One of the ten project management knowledge areas; the processes involved in outsourcing project work to a service provider organization, either through bids or the contract agreement process.

Production

The phase of an electronic discovery project and node of the EDRM that includes processes involved in preparing ESI and paper documents for production to other parties in litigation. Production documents are typically numbered with Bates stamps and produced either in TIFF image, native file, or paper format. See *Forms of Production*.

project

A project is a temporary, non-routine, endeavor limited by scope, time, cost, resources, and specifications to create a unique product, service, or result that meets a customer or organization need.

project charter

A formal document created by an organization that authorizes a project to move forward. The project charter typically contains the sponsor requirements; a scope statement or high-level description, purpose, or justification for the project; the key roles and responsibilities; milestones; and a summary budget.

project manager

The person assigned by an organization to achieve a project's objectives. He or she is responsible for shepherding a project through its phases from beginning to end. The project manager has experience in the industry, and brings his/her expertise, understanding of the necessary resources and work flows, and ability to interact with the different people and organizations to perform the tasks required for a project.

project management

The application of skills, knowledge, tools, and techniques to activities designed to meet a project's requirements.

Project Management Institute (PMI)

Project Management Institute is the world's leading not-for-profit professional membership association devoted to the project management profession. Founded in 1969, PMI delivers value in nearly every country in the world through advocacy, collaboration, education and research. As of the Summer of 2015, there were more than 655,000 certified project management professionals (PMP) throughout the world.

proximity search

A type of search that features the ability to find a word that is within a prescribed distance of another word (e.g., Find "glove" within 15 words of "baseball").

quality assurance (QA)

The policies and practices that lead to the implementation of quality control on a project.

quality control (QC)

Operational steps taken to ensure that a service or product is of sufficiently high standard to meet the end user's or recipients' project objectives. The operational techniques and activities that are used to fulfill requirements for quality.

Quality Management

One of the ten project management knowledge areas. Identifying the processes and activities that determine quality policies, objectives, and responsibilities so that the project will satisfy the needs for which it was undertaken.

record

Any paper or electronic document or information created in support of, on behalf of, or about an organization. Records capture and memorialize the business activities, transactions, and correspondence of a company. They include corporate documents such as financial statements, board minutes, and accounting documents; email; memoranda; instant messages; and social media posts.

Review

The phase of an electronic discovery project and a node of the EDRM that involves examining documents, typically in a document review database, and marking or categorizing the documents for relevance, privilege, and work product, or for usefulness in the context of litigation.

records and information management (RIM)

The practice of developing, implementing, and maintaining a records and information management policy within an organization that inventories all records created, stored and disposed of within the organization.

Risk Management

One of the ten project management knowledge areas; the processes involved in identifying, accepting, mitigating, avoiding or transferring risk – uncertain events that may or may not occur which positively or negatively affect a project objective. This includes planning for and responding to risk.

scanning (imaging)

The process of converting paper documents into digital images using a scanner. The scanner effectively takes a picture of the paper document and renders it as a TIFF, PDF, or JPG image.

Scope Management

One of the ten project management knowledge areas; defining and controlling what is included in and what is excluded from a project. Determinations require input from sponsors, stakeholders, and management of the project organization. A project scope statement incorporates understanding of the project deliverables, including project objectives, project boundaries, acceptance criteria, constraints, assumptions, staffing/organization, defined risks, milestones, and a cost estimate. See also *scope statement.*

scope statement

A short, concise statement identifying the purpose and goals of a project. The scope statement may evolve and change in the initiation of a project, but must be fixed before the project begins. The scope statement defines "done" or completion of the project and is the yardstick against which deliverables are measured.

single-page TIFF

A commonly used version of the tagged image file format (TIFF). Single-page TIFF images are either scanned or generated from electronic documents and saved as single-page files, making them smaller and easier to access and store. When opening a single-page TIFF file, you only access a single-page image, regardless of the established document boundaries. Once the images are loaded to a database platform, an image cross-reference file maintains the information relating the single pages to one another to form a document. See also *Tiff image.*

slack space

The space that remains on a hard drive when a file is saved that does not take up one or more complete clusters of space on the drive. If a file overlaps two and one-half clusters on a drive, that remaining half of the third cluster is slack space, and data can be saved in that location. See also *unallocated space.*

sponsor

The person or organization for whom a project is undertaken, and who typically provides financial resources for a project.

spoliation

The destruction, loss, deletion, or alteration of information—including paper, electronic documents, and email—that is relevant to the claims and defenses in a pending action or investigation.

stakeholder

Any person involved in a project whose interest may be positively or negatively affected by the outcome of the project. Stakeholders can range from a project sponsor to a customer or end user who will utilize the finished product or service. Stakeholders include the project manager, project team members, or other functional managers who contribute to or have an interest in a project.

technology assisted review (TAR)

A document review process that uses math-based algorithms and linguistics to quickly and efficiently categorize documents based on their conceptual content. Also referred to as *predictive coding* or *computer assisted review*. See also *analytics*.

TIFF image

Tagged image file format; the de facto standard for scanned, bit-mapped images: 8-bit color and gray scale. TIFF images are the most common form of document production in litigation, particularly where documents need to be redacted. The format originated in 1986 as a joint project of Microsoft and Aldus. It includes several types and groups, compressed and uncompressed.

Time Management

One of the ten project management knowledge areas; understanding the time it takes to complete a project; identifying the processes, tasks, activity sequencing, and dependencies required to accomplish the project objectives; and developing a schedule.

unitization – physical and logical

The assembly of individually scanned pages into documents. *Physical unitization* utilizes actual objects such as staples, paper clips, and folders to determine pages that belong together as documents for archival and retrieval purposes. *Logical unitization* is the process of human review of each individual page in an image collection using logical cues to determine pages that belong together as documents. Such cues can be consecutive page numbering, report titles, or similar headers and footers.

work breakdown structure (WBS)

An outline or list of the tasks involved in a project. The WBS defines the relationship between project deliverables and identifies tasks that are dependent upon the completion of other work. It can be formal in scope and involve complex network diagrams; tying together each part of a project, singular tasks, and their dependencies; or it may be less formal and involve an ordered checklist of tasks. The WBS also helps evaluate cost and time estimates.

unallocated space

That portion of a hard drive to which data may be saved, that is, empty or unused spaced on a drive. It is also the location to which files are saved when deleted, and the space to which many applications temporarily store files when they are in use. For instance, temporary Internet files are created when user visits a Web page.

ABOUT THE AUTHOR

 Michael Quartararo has worked with lawyers and at large law firms for more than 20 years. He began his career as a litigation paralegal in New York City. For ten years at Skadden Arps Slate Meagher & Flom LLP, he worked on large class action securities litigations, internal investigations, and international litigation. He managed complex legal and technology projects involving the preservation, collection, processing, review and production of ESI, and he prepared cases for trial and the presentation of digital evidence.

Since 2008, Mike has led a staff of project managers and analysts providing consulting, litigation support, and technology services to 350 attorneys and paralegals at New York-based Stroock & Stroock & Lavan LLP. As the firm-wide Director of Litigation Support Services, Mike is a member of the Firm's administrative team and is responsible for the development and implementation of Firm policy relating to electronic discovery and the use of technology in the practice of law. He is a driving force behind and a member of the Firm's eDiscovery and Information Governance Practice Group, and a principal author of the Firm's electronic discovery, document review and production guidelines. He regularly consults with attorneys and the Firm's Fortune 500 clients on the use of technology in general, and on electronic discovery in particular.

Mike also teaches electronic discovery and project management and sits on the advisory board of Tempe-based Bryan University.

At Bryan, he designed an electronic discovery project management simulation course that teaches and tests the knowledge and skills of future project managers.

Mike has a Bachelor of Science degree from the State University of New York. He studied law at the University of London for one year. He is a member of the Project Management Institute (PMI.org) and a certified Project Management Professional (PMP). He is a liaison to the advisory committee of the Electronic Discovery Reference Model (EDRM.org), a member of the national board of the Association of Certified E-Discovery Specialists (ACEDS.org), and he holds the Certified E-Discovery Specialist (CEDS) credential. Mike frequently speaks and writes on topics involving project management, litigation support and electronic discovery.

Contact Information:

Additional information, articles, other useful links, and my blog, may be found at www.ediscoverypm.com. I want people to contact me and you should feel free to do so. Your comments, suggestions, criticisms, and of course accolades, are always welcome. Feel free to email me at: mike@ediscoverypm.com.

All the best,

Michael Quartararo

Author, educator and project leader